THE BREAKING POINT

Shortly after Phil Langston broke off the affair with Virginia, he was surprised by a phone call from her dentist husband, Dr. Norman Larzelere.

"It's too painful to talk about," Doc said, almost in tears. "I know you've been sleeping with my wife."

"Don't worry, that's over. That woman you're married to is insane."

"I know. She probably asked you to have me killed, didn't she?"

Langston said it was true and started to tell him about Virginia's plan to have him killed by a man in California.

"She's got a gun out there."

Dumbfounded, Langston heard Doc describe his life with Virginia, her need for counseling, and his desperate fear of her. But as he listened, Phil realized there was no way out for Dr. Norman Larzelere. He believed that Virginia planned to have him killed, whether they stayed married or not.

Later, police found a yellow pad in Dr. Larzelere's office. On it he'd written the simple question: *How far should a man go to protect his wife?*

If he'd found the answer, it might have saved his life.

**PINNACLE BOOKS AND *TRUE DETECTIVE* MAGAZINE
TEAM UP TO BRING YOU THE
MOST HORRIFIC TRUE CRIME STORIES!**

BIZARRE MURDERERS	(486-9, $4.95/$5.95)
CELEBRITY MURDERS	(435-4, $4.95/$5.95)
COP KILLERS	(603-9, $4.99/$5.99)
THE CRIMES OF THE RICH AND FAMOUS	(630-6, $4.99/$5.99)
CULT KILLERS	(528-8, $4.95/$5.95)
MEDICAL MURDERERS	(582-2, $4.99/$5.99)
SERIAL MURDERERS	(432-X, $4.95/$5.95)
SPREE KILLERS	(461-3, $4.95/$5.95)
TORTURE KILLERS	(506-7, $4.95/$5.95)

FOR A MOTHER'S LOVE

LEE BUTCHER

PINNACLE BOOKS
WINDSOR PUBLISHING CORP.

This book is dedicated to the CID detectives in the Edgewater Police Department: Sgt. William Bennett, David Gamell, and Leo Booth.

PINNACLE BOOKS

are published by

Windsor Publishing Corp.
475 Park Avenue South
New York, NY 10016

First Printing: December, 1992

Printed in the United States of America

ACKNOWLEDGMENTS

The writing of a true crime book is a daunting task, and the author must rely on the help from scores of people. I can only mention a few. My thanks to: Edgewater Police Department, including Chief Lawrence Schumaker, Lt. Bucky McEver, Sgt. Bill Bennett, and Detectives David Gamell, Leo Booth and Cheryl Osborn; Roger Simms of *The News-Journal;* Mary Parks, correspondent for Channel 2; EVAC paramedics and dispatchers; Reba Carter; Ellen Campbell; the DeLand Police Department; the State Attorney's Office; Florida Department of Professional Regulation; Florida Department of Law Enforcement; Julie Green; and the scores of people named and anonymous who gave important insights into this story. My thanks also to my superb editor, Paul Dinas and my world class agent, Peter Miller.

AUTHOR'S NOTE

Many people who were interviewed for this true crime book wanted to remain anonymous for various reasons, but largely out of fear. Rather than attributing their comments to anonymous sources, I have italicized made-up names for real people the first time they appear. This book is based on thousands of pages of official records, including police reports, depositions, sworn statements, and official court transcripts. Many hours of interviews were conducted with people with knowledge of the case, and additional hours were spent reviewing police audio and video tapes. The dialogue is reconstructed from these records, and the best recollection of people familiar with the case.

One

Dr. Norman Larzelere was finishing lunch on Friday March 8, 1991 at his office in the small town of Edgewater, Florida, where he had a flourishing dental practice. From all outward appearances, Doc, as most people called him, was one of those lucky people who seemed to be living the very best of the American dream. He had the trappings of success: an expensive two-story Dutch Colonial house in the nearby town of DeLand, power boats, including one he used for deep-sea fishing, several ritzy foreign sports cars, a Mercedes sedan and two four-wheel drive vehicles.

Doc had married his second wife, Virginia, in 1985 and had adopted her two children, Jason and Jessica. It was Virginia's fourth marriage. Jason and Jessica were born after her first trip to the altar. Doc and Virginia had two sons together, David and Benjamin.

Although Doc was thin and of medium height, his hands were strong and his arms knotted with muscles. The dentist had dark unruly hair, with a swatch that fell down the right side of his forehead, wore dark-rimmed eyeglasses, a full mustache, and was plain rather than handsome.

But Doc's soft heart and generosity more than compensated for what he lacked in physical appearance. He had paid for Jason to attend a private high school in Ormond Beach, and at age eighteen, Jason drove a Nissan 300 ZX, an expensive sports car. Virginia's two cars were worth about $150,000, and the other vehicles brought the total value of the family automobiles to more than $300,000. In addition, Virginia had given David and Benjamin's nanny the down payment for a house, and bought a new Toyota for Kristen Palmieri, her assistant at home and at the dental practice. Virginia owned a twin engine Cessna, and flew the airplane, even though she didn't have a pilot's license.

The cars driven by Virginia, Jason and Kris were equipped with the latest electronic gadgets, including stereophonic compact disc sound systems and mobile telephones. Doc's own tastes were modest: he wheeled about in a Chevrolet Suburban that cost less than his wife's wardrobe.

In contrast to her husband, Virginia was a full-figured woman of sensual curves who radiated strength and sexuality. She had dark, loosely permed hair that fell below her shoulders, dark, smoldering eyes, and full lips. Virginia usually wore at least five gold rings, some set with precious stones, gold bracelets and necklaces. She wore expensive clothing with plenty of short skirts and blouses and dresses cut low to expose cleavage. And she knew how to make the most of what she had with the artful use of makeup. Even with the glitz of jewelry, makeup, and expensive clothes, Virginia wasn't beautiful, but she was striking, and emanated such strong sex appeal that few men could resist when she wanted to seduce them.

Doc had money, a flourishing practice that earned more than a comfortable living, and from all outward appearances, a loving family. But he was a troubled man. His marriage had been made in hell rather than heaven, and Doc felt as if things were closing in on him and he had no place to hide. Everything he had, including his practice and professional reputation, faced ruin because he had made one major mistake. He had tried to correct it, but it was too strong for him to escape.

As Doc ate lunch, he looked out at the parking lot and the splashes of color from flower beds that were brilliant under an unusually hot March sun. Kris wasn't back from lunch yet, and Emma Lombardo, his dental assistant, who usually brought a brown-bag lunch from home to save money, had gone out to eat, and had returned to the office. Virginia, who worked at the dental office in fits and starts, had finished eating, and a patient had just arrived in the waiting room for an early afternoon appointment.

The midday hiatus was suddenly interrupted by a screeching sound. Startled, Doc looked up and saw a Japanese compact car come to a halt in the parking lot. A man with a sawed off shotgun jumped from the car and ran toward the building.

He knew he was going to be killed.

Terrified, Doc jumped up and ran into the waiting room, surprising the patient, as he tried to escape the gunman. Doc hoped to get outside the building to get away from his pursuer. But the man with the shotgun was faster than the dentist. He ran down the hall and stopped near Emma, almost close enough for her to touch him. She recoiled in terror as Virginia screamed.

Doc made it into the waiting room and slammed the heavy door shut on the other side, but the gunman was right on top of him. Emma watched in horror as the man pointed the shotgun at the door and pulled the trigger. The dentist knew who wanted to murder him and screamed out the name just as the gunman fired. The door exploded in Doc's face. Buckshot and splinters slammed into his chest, tearing soft tissue and bone, ripping arteries that spouted blood. The impact lifted Doc off his feet, spun him sideways, where he dropped to the floor on his back.

Major arteries were torn and Doc lost blood fast. He knew he was dying, and tried again to call out the name of his killer. As his life ebbed away, naming his murderer was the most important thing in the world. But suddenly Virginia cradled his head in her arms and pressed her mouth on his in a long, last kiss as tears streamed from her eyes. Doc couldn't breathe or speak.

Virginia was riveted when she saw the gunman run into the office, and Emma almost went into a state of shock. Only a few minutes elapsed from the time the man entered the dentist's office, fired, and fled through a side door. There was pandemonium and confusion, but Virginia watched the gunman leave while Emma ran to Doc. He looked up at her and whispered, "Help me." But there was nothing she could do.

Chasing after the shooter, Virginia said she grabbed for him and broke a fingernail on his arm as he shrugged loose, saw him vault over a four-foot railing, and get into the passenger side of a car before it sped away. Then she ran back inside and telephoned EVAC, the emergency paramedical unit in Edgewater. She was so hysterical that the dispatcher, Carl Leninger, could hardly understand her.

"911," he said. "What's your emergency?"

"Get me an ambulance at 109 West Knapp."

"What's the problem, ma'am?"

"Somebody just came in and shot my husband!"

"Somebody what?"

"Somebody just came in and shot my husband."

"All right. Calm down, ma'am. I need your help." As Leninger spoke, Virginia screamed again. "All right. Calm down." Virginia kept screaming.

Leninger patched the call through to an EVAC ambulance and tried to talk to Virginia, but she had heard Doc crying out as he was dying. Virginia told Emma to take the telephone, ran to Doc, cradled his head in her lap and pressed her lips against his. Emma was as hysterical as Virginia had been.

"Somebody shoot Dr. Larzelere," Emma said in a soft Filipino accent.

There was more confused conversation as the dentist lay bleeding to death.

"Somebody shoot him," Emma repeated. "Came and shoot Dr. Larzelere in the office."

"Someone came in shooting?"

"Yeah. Pulled out the gun and shot him. We need an ambulance. Hurry! Please!"

"Listen to me, okay? An ambulance is on its way. How many people were shot?"

"Just one people."

"Are they awake?"

"No. Somebody please send us an ambulance."

"Ma'am. Ma'am, you have to calm down. Calm down for EVAC, okay? Is the person with the gun still there?"

"No, no."

"Find out if the person is breathing or not."

Emma shouted to Virginia, who yelled back, but Leninger couldn't understand what was happening. There was panic and hysteria on the other end of the line.

"Tell her to calm down, okay?" the EVAC operator told Emma, referring to Virginia's screams.

"Someone please, please send us an ambulance," Emma said.

EVAC immediately telephoned Edgewater police headquarters to report the shooting. Detective Sergeant Bill Bennett, head of the Criminal Investigation Division (CID), was notified. Bennett dispatched a patrol car to the scene, then sent Detective David Gamell to the dentist's office.

An EVAC team was trying to stabilize Doc when Gamell arrived, and an ambulance was standing by to take him to the hospital emergency room. Gamell knew at a glance that the dentist was not going to survive. The upper part of his chest had been blown away by buckshot and major arteries had been severed.

"He never had a chance," Gamell said later. "I think he lost all of his blood in a matter of minutes."

Officer Joe Susridge had made sure the building was safe for the EVAC team to enter, and had roped off the crime area. Virginia, weeping, stood by the paramedics working on her husband. She repeatedly screamed, "Somebody shot my husband!"

Gamell's heart went out to Virginia and he tried to comfort her. In his eyes, she was the victim of a brutal murder, too. Virginia seemed inconsolable, and it was impossible to elicit information from her because she was almost incoherent. Gamell felt so much sympathy for Virginia that he gave her his beeper number so that she could reach him any time, day or night, in case she needed support. The action showed the depth of the detective's concern for Virginia.

"I don't give my beeper number out to just anyone," he said later. "Otherwise, I'd never have a chance to get any rest or sleep."

Virginia thanked him for the beeper number, but she was frantic about her husband.

"The only thing she wanted to do was go to the hospital with her husband," Gamell said.

The ambulance took off with the paramedics and Doc, and Virginia followed as a passenger in Kris's car. Gamell had not learned many specifics from Virginia in the chaotic time he had to speak with her. The only thing he knew then was that someone had run into the office and shot Doc, then escaped. Gamell didn't press Virginia very hard at the scene, but he intended to question her later.

Kris had returned from her errands but couldn't enter the building, so she watched from behind the police barrier. When Virginia ran out of the office, she threw herself in Kris's arms and the two women clung to one another. Bennett had arrived and was looking around.

The detectives tried to interview Emma but she was still in a state of shock. But the story she told varied from what the police had heard from Virginia. The discrepancies weren't unusual in the immediate aftermath of such a traumatic experience.

By the time all of the "civilians" had left, forensic experts arrived from the Florida Department of Law Enforcement (FDLE). The Edgewater Police Department was small and didn't have the forensic resources of the FDLE. Although there is little love between the FDLE and local police departments, the Edgewater detectives wanted to act quickly because a murder trail grows cold fast.

Together, the detectives and the FDLE looked for any physical evidence the shooter might have left, and an FDLE photographer took pictures of every room in the dental building. Later on, they would build a scale model to use as a visual aid to reconstruct the murder.

Gamell was convinced the murder was not committed by a professional hit man.

"It was clear to me from the start," Gamell said. "You knew it had to be an amateur. Who else is going to run into a doctor's office with a shotgun in broad daylight? A professional would have a gun he could hide, and he would have done it in a private place. You could see that the guy didn't know what he was doing."

What wasn't so clear was who killed Doc and why. A disgruntled patient seemed unlikely, unless he or she was psychotic. There was a rumor that Doc was a gambler who couldn't pay heavy losses and had been killed as an example. Another was that he was the victim of a vengeful husband whose wife he had seduced. There were dozens of rumors, most from far out in left field, but there were no answers.

Finding the answers would be like struggling through an intricate maze filled with unexpected twists and turns, and a thick haze that obscured the truth. Gamell and the Edgewater CID found themselves matching wits with a killer who was a master of deception.

Two

Violent crimes in Edgewater were rare, and the town usually went about its peaceful commerce without the worry of robbery or murder, which plagues most of the cities in Florida. A residential town just south of Daytona Beach and north of Fort Lauderdale, Edgewater somehow escaped the bawdy and lascivious activities in both crime ridden cities. The glitzy playboy communities to the north and south spread their arms to welcome raucous visitors with money to spend, while Edgewater remained a quiet, residential community.

There were only two major shopping centers in Edgewater in 1991, and most of the town's real estate was devoted to single home residences. Condominiums, which have hidden most of Florida's beaches behind serrated concrete walls, had not yet achieved dominance in Edgewater's real estate market. Even the unimposing police department headquarters was located on waterfront property. It was a quiet town, and by 10 P.M. you could shoot a gun down A1A, the main ocean highway, and not hit anything.

There were three detectives in the Criminal Investigation Division of the Edgewater Police Department: Sgt. William Bennett, Leo Booth, and Gamell. Cheryl Osborne was temporarily assigned to the CID.

Bennett, who headed the CID, was a dedicated law enforcement professional. Well educated and intelligent, Bennett had been a voracious reader of books on criminology and law enforcement even as a teenager, and he kept at it until he earned a bachelor's degree in criminal justice in 1980 from the University of Central Florida.

After that, Bennett attended rookie school at Daytona Beach Community College to become certified as a police officer. He worked his way through the ranks with the New Smyrna Beach Police Department to the Detective Division, then went back to school and became certified as a training officer.

Bennett joined the Edgewater Police Department in 1989, and in 1990, was promoted to sergeant and became head of the detective division. A six-footer with hazel eyes, dark hair with a sprinkling of premature gray, Bennett enjoyed being on the streets, but thought being head of the CID offered him more challenges.

When Bennett became head of the CID, he tested members of the police force to find those with the highest aptitude for detective work. Gamell scored higher than any other applicant and was transferred to the CID.

Although he had been with the Edgewater Police Department less than a year, David Gamell had been a cop for more than five years on the mean streets of South Florida. A stocky man who barely met the minimum height requirement to be a Marine, Gamell had a boyish look that belied his thirty-six years, and was so self-effacing that he appeared shy. People who interpreted Gamell's good nature as a sign of weakness sometimes had rude awakenings.

Gamell had a black belt in karate, and several years before he became a policeman, Gamell had been a tough nightclub bouncer. While working at JW's Lounge in Fort Lauderdale, Gamell was a featured attraction during a "gong show," breaking a twenty-eight-inch layer of bricks with his forehead.

Four men jumped Gamell at JW's one night, but no one knew why since it was common knowledge that Gamell was an expert in martial arts. "They were afraid of his fighting ability," Fort Lauderdale Detective Sergeant James Healy told a newspaper reporter, "but they did it anyhow."

The dust cleared in minutes and there were four stunned men in various states of disrepair littering the alley while Gamell drove home unscathed. That would have been the end of it under ordinary circumstances, but the four men were enforcers for organized crime and had to protect their reputations for being tough. When Gamell arrived at his house, they were parked at the curb in two cars, and started shooting at him. Something hit Gamell hard in the chest and leg but he didn't go down. Instead, he ran to the lead car, and reached inside in a vain effort to wrest the pistol from the gunman.

As the cars sped away, Gamell noticed blood on his chest, and when he unbuttoned his shirt he saw a small hole. Thinking it was just a scratch, Gamell poked it with his finger, but decided the gunshot wounds in his leg needed medical attention. Gamell's sister drove him to a hospital emergency room.

Routine trauma procedures were followed, with Gamell being hooked to IVs, X-rayed and so forth.

"I don't know why you're making a big deal out of this," he said. "I only got shot in the leg."

"Son, you've not only been shot in the leg," the doctor said, "you've been shot in the heart. The bullet's still there."

Gamell passed out and was in critical condition while surgery was performed to remove a .25 caliber bullet from his heart and two .38 caliber slugs from his leg. Less than two weeks later, Gamell went home, but started having chest pains. When they didn't go away, he returned to the hospital.

Another .25 caliber bullet was in his heart.

Leo Booth is an undercover narcotics specialist, and Cheryl Osborne's specialty is in victim's rights, battered women and abused children. Since the department is small, the detectives often team up and work several cases at a time.

Oddly enough, Edgewater was disrupted by a series of violent crimes about the same time that Bennett and Gamell were transferred to the Criminal Investigation Division. There hadn't been an armed robbery, let alone a murder, in Edgewater for ten years. Suddenly, there were two murders within months, followed by Doc's

21

killing, which brought the total to three in rapid succession.

"I was in a state of disbelief," Bennett said. "We had gone all those years without a homicide and all of a sudden we had three in a row."

On March 8, when Doc was killed, the CID had experienced sudden shrinkage: Osborne was on maternity leave and an evidence technician was in Saudi Arabia with Operation Desert Shield/Storm. There were three murder investigations and three detectives to work the cases. Gamell was assigned case detective for Doc's murder.

A murder at a dental practice in broad daylight clued the detectives that Doc was killed by an amateur. But who had a motive? Where was the murder weapon? When, and if, they found the shotgun, proving that it was the murder weapon would be difficult. The pellets from shotguns can't be traced to a specific weapon, as can bullets from a rifle or handgun, and even the wadding used to pack shells is used by various companies.

The Edgewater police already knew something about Doc because Booth had helped the Department of Professional Regulation (DPR) investigate the dental practice for malfeasance in 1988. There had also been nuisance calls from the dentist's office, and a check with the DeLand police quickly produced an unusual number of complaints filed by the Larzeleres. The DeLand police had been called by the Larzeleres about prowlers, schoolmates attacking Jessica, neighbors throwing rocks at the dogs, and numerous other such alleged incidents.

Three

Virginia Gail Antley, one of four sisters, was born December 27, 1952, in Lake Wales, a small, pastoral town in central Florida, surrounded by lush citrus groves. On a spring day, white blossoms stretch as far as the eye can see, and the air carries a delicate fragrance. There are even a few hills, a rarity in a flatland state such as Florida.

Lake Wales had small stores where residents could buy many of the day-to-day things they needed, but most people drove to the larger cities of Lakeland and Orlando for their major shopping, including groceries from supermarkets.

Virginia, who was called Gail in her early years, and her family lived in a mobile home, a misnomer for what is now called modular housing. There is nothing mobile about the units, which are mounted on concrete blocks and have no wheels. In those days, before Walt Disney World caused an economic explosion, Lake Wales was poor, like the other towns in Polk County. Besides service jobs, people worked in the citrus processing plants, meat packing plants, cattle ranches or at phosphate mines.

Polk County alone produces more oranges than the state of California, a fact that was proudly advertised on the facade of *The Ledger* Building in Lakeland, which was headquarters for the most widely circulated newspaper in the county. The county was, and is, strongly conservative, practices segregation in fact if not officially, is against abortion and feminism, and fights against gun control. By contrast, *The Ledger* espouses a strong liberal philosophy. Because of this, the newspaper is generally hated by the people who subscribe to it.

Besides the county's citrus groves, there are large pastures where cattle graze, their tails snapping like bullwhips against mosquitoes and other tormenting insects. The cattle are hybrid, all containing Brahma blood, to make them hardy enough to withstand Florida's scorching heat and able to graze in scrub pastures. Ranching is a big business in Polk County, and although most people don't know it, Florida ranks tenth in the United States for cattle production.

The county also boasts one of the most beautiful tourist attractions in the world, Cypress Gardens, which is filled with exotic flowers, birds, and beautiful young women in antebellum gowns, looking like colorful clouds sitting on the ground. But the county is far from being purely arcadian.

Phosphate, a mineral used as fertilizer, was discovered years ago in vast quantities in Polk County, and it became one of the world's largest producers. Phosphate lies beneath the surface of the ground, and is mined by huge machines called draglines, which strip away topsoil and deposit it in slag heaps that rise like pustules all across the county. Deep pits created by mining operations make it appear as if the land is afflicted with acne. A reporter once described Polk County as "The Valley of the Moon."

A long, bitter fight has raged for years between the phosphate miners and those engaged in agriculture and ranching. Sulfuric acid and other impurities from phosphate plants poisoned the trees, grass, cattle and people. It once became so severe that the leg bones of cattle snapped because grazing land contaminated by pollution from phosphate plants made them too brittle to support their own weight. There were days when people had to stay inside or risk having chemically scorched lungs.

Living in a trailer in this isolated rural environment was not the type of life Virginia wanted for herself. She was a bright, attractive girl whose father had an unusual affection for her. Virginia was sexually molested by him from the time she was a little girl, a secret she kept to herself for more than twenty years.

In spite of the abuse, or perhaps because of it, Virginia developed a strong attraction to men early in life. Along with the attraction came a powerful sex drive, and the realization that men were drawn to her. Virginia encouraged them and learned that she could manipulate men through sex.

"She's the type of person who likes to be desirable to men," said her sister, Jeanette Atkinson. "She wants guys to look at her, and she likes to look nice and likes the attention."

Virginia wanted more than to be sexually attractive to men: she wanted nice things, a house instead of a trailer, expensive cars, and a pretty place to live outside of Polk County. She was a young woman in a hurry, and she had no intention of working years at low-paying jobs to fulfill her dreams.

Virginia met Harry J. Mathis, an electrician in Lake Wales, and married him when she was seventeen. In a town where wages were low, Mathis earned enough to set him above the middle class, but they still lived in a mobile home and maintained a simple lifestyle. It didn't take long for Virginia to become dissatisfied with her marriage. She started to look for a job. Then Edward S. O'Brien came to town.

O'Brien was a plump, cheerful man whose girth, generosity, and trusting nature made him a perfect Santa Claus at Christmas parties. O'Brien was twenty years older than Eva, his wife, and had earned a good living as an independent architect and engineer. When he reached his seventieth year, O'Brien decided that he'd put the bitter New York winters behind him and move to Lake Wales.

In spite of his age, O'Brien had no intention of retiring. He didn't want to work as hard as he did when he was younger, but he preferred to wear out rather than rust out. In 1968, O'Brien, Eva and their daughter, Ellen, moved to Lake Wales. Eva and her husband had planned the move carefully. They had set aside money to insure Ellen's college education, and there was seed money for O'Brien to establish some kind of business for himself.

It took O'Brien two years to find what he wanted: a business association with Food Industries, a company headquartered in Washington state that designed facilities associated with shipping and storing food. O'Brien sunk all of his savings into a satellite company that he operated from an office in downtown Lake Wales.

O'Brien had calculated the risks carefully because he had no pension to rely on, and at his age, starting over would be next to impossible. Shortly after he started his business, O'Brien advertised for an office manager, and that was when Virginia came into his life. O'Brien knew of her because he was acquainted with one of Virginia's in-laws. The O'Brien family knew and liked Virginia's husband, Harry. Virginia was only seventeen but she seemed capable and was exceptionally friendly. O'Brien hired her to manage the office in 1970, which included receiving and depositing all checks.

Ellen O'Brien, who was only a year younger than Virginia, was impressed by how friendly she was. The O'Briens treated Virginia like a member of the family, and frequently had her over to the house for dinner. They all thought it was strange that Mathis never accompanied his wife.

Virginia didn't strike Ellen as being especially attractive. Ellen saw her as a tall, slim, young woman with long dark hair of ordinary looks but who had a captivating personality. The two young women saw each other occasionally when Ellen visited the office, but they rarely said anything except hello and goodbye. Just before Ellen was to go to college in 1972, Virginia called to her when Ellen dropped in at the office to see her father.

"Hey, want to go for a ride in my new 'Vette?" Virginia asked.

Ellen said, "Sure."

She was startled to see that Virginia had a brand new, red Corvette convertible. Ellen was almost speechless as they drove around the small town with the top down. She wondered how Virginia could afford such an expensive car.

Suddenly Virginia said, "You know, your father's not going to be able to send you to college."

"What did you say?" Ellen asked in surprise.

"Your Dad can't send you to college."

"Why not?"

"He's not doing too well with his business. But don't tell him I'm telling you this."

Although worried, Ellen didn't mention the incident to her father. When it was almost time for her to leave O'Brien received a letter from the main office in Washington saying there was a problem with his business. Startled, O'Brien checked the financial records and discovered that his business was broke.

Virginia had been embezzling funds, draining off a little at a time so that it didn't attract attention. She wrote small payroll checks to herself for under $100 in addition to her regular check. When the company received a $2,625.65 check from Paul Schneider at the Washington office, Virginia deposited $2,300.65 to a regular account and $200 into a payroll account, and pocketed $100 in cash, then wrote herself a $200 check from the payroll account. On every transaction, Virginia skimmed a fraction, and even managed to cash checks that weren't endorsed.

O'Brien discovered that Virginia had embezzled more than $16,000 and that the business was flat broke. Virginia was charged with embezzlement but escaped going to prison by promising to pay the money back in installments of $285 a month. She was also placed on parole.

But it was catastrophic for the O'Brien family. O'Brien was in his seventies, had lost all of his savings, and his spirit was crushed. "He just went downhill from then on," Ellen said. "I was mad as hell at Gail. We just watched Daddy decline. She only paid back $11,000 and that wasn't until 1981. It doesn't sound like a lot of money, but for someone like my Dad it really was. Gail was smart. It was a real tragedy for our family."

While married to Mathis, Virginia had two children, Jason and Jessica. Virginia was employed as a bookkeeper with an engineering firm in Polk County in 1975, when she was twenty-four years old, and was accused of embezzling five thousand dollars from the company. Virginia pleaded "no contest" to forgery and larceny, was placed on probation for five years, and ordered to repay the company five thousand and thirty-four dollars. Again, Virginia escaped a prison sentence.

That same year, an event occurred that had implications far more sinister than embezzlement. Virginia was suspected of hiring someone to kill her husband, although she was never charged. On April 21, 1975,

29

Virginia told her husband that one of her relatives needed help. According to Virginia, her cousin's car had broken down on Old Chalet Suzanne Road, which was in a remote, unlit area in the middle of a large citrus grove.

It was after 11 P.M. when Mathis drove to the site Virginia had described to him. Instead of Virginia's cousin, he found a stranger with a .32 caliber handgun. The man fired four shots. One grazed Mathis's scalp and another hit his right arm, and when Mathis turned to run into an orange grove, the man fired two more shots. Mathis was able to get to the Chalet Suzanne Restaurant, where employees called an ambulance and the Polk County Sheriff's Department.

At this point, the story became bizarre.

Detective Lieutenant Ed Dice, of the Polk County Sheriff's Department, was put in charge of a four-man team to conduct an investigation into what was officially cataloged as an attempted homicide. At the hospital, however, Mathis was reluctant to talk and, to Dice, appeared frightened. Virginia had been driven to the hospital by a deputy, and Mathis knew she was in the building.

Mathis didn't tell the detective that his wife had sent him to Old Chalet Suzanne Road. According to him, he was driving on the road when he saw a man beside a stalled car.

"I stopped to help the guy," Mathis said. "I got out of the car and he asked me if I had some tools and if I would turn off my lights. He said he'd been out there a long time and the light bothered his eyes."

Deferring to the motorist's wishes, Mathis turned the lights out and was plunged into darkness. He asked the motorist what the problem was with the car so he could get the right tools. The man said he didn't know and Mathis decided to take a look at the engine.

"As I started opening up his hood he just shot me in the top of the head," Mathis said. "I started backing off from him and he shot me again. I thought maybe he was just trying to scare the daylights out of me."

Mathis turned to face the man and another shot was fired. Amazingly enough, Mathis was not just able to stand, but mounted a feeble counter attack. He hit the gunman with his fist but he was so weak that he might as well have used a powder puff.

"He grabbed me and I told him, 'Look, man, take my car, my wallet, anything, just leave me alone,' " Mathis said. "He said, 'Give me your wallet.' "

After handing the man his wallet, Mathis staggered toward the darkness of the orange groves. The man fired two more shots but Mathis didn't know whether or not he had been hit. Slowly and painfully, he made his way to the Chalet Suzanne Restaurant, where employees called an ambulance and the police.

Dice arrived at the hospital to interview Mathis, who described the man who shot him as being about twenty-five or thirty, having long, blond hair, and weighing around two hundred and ten pounds.

Mathis remembered the gunman's truck but he could only describe the gun as a black revolver.

"You were by yourself and you stopped to help him," Dice said.

"I was trying to help the dude out."

"Had you ever seen this fellow before?"

"Never."

Mathis said the man shot at him when he was running into the orange grove but he didn't realize he had been hit twice in the back. Fortunately, none of the wounds was fatal. A few weeks earlier, Mathis said, his own car had broken down on the same lonesome stretch of road and someone had stopped to help him. He said he was just returning the favor.

The interview lasted a few more minutes but Mathis had little more to add. Dice didn't buy the story and believed Mathis was withholding information. Even a good old Florida boy like Mathis wouldn't stop in an isolated area at 11 P.M. to help someone he had never seen before. The stalled car routine was often pulled by robbers and other criminals. Mathis offered no reason as to why he was on the road so late at night. It didn't lead to his trailer or to any houses that would have electrical trouble.

Virginia cast an even more suspicious cloud over the shooting. After advising her that she wasn't a suspect, investigators asked Virginia to attend a meeting at the state attorney's office in the hope that she could provide information that would lead to the man who tried to kill her husband. Dice was startled, as were other officials, when Virginia told them she would answer no questions without a lawyer present to represent her.

This unexpected wrinkle caused the meeting to be postponed until a week later. Virginia arrived, accompanied by an attorney. The state attorney only got to ask one question concerning her husband's shooting.

"I'd like to leave the room to confer with my attorney," Virginia said, and did so. When they returned, she said, "On advice of counsel I refuse to answer on the grounds that it may tend to incriminate me."

The state attorney and detectives were shocked. Virginia was not considered a suspect, but wouldn't answer questions. Mathis had stopped cooperating. Finally, Mathis told the police that Virginia sent him to Old Chalet Suzanne Road to help a cousin. That was all he would say, until he eventually told the police that he had forgotten everything before, during and after the shooting. The police had no choice but to drop the investigation.

No one was ever charged in the episode, but it was listed as suspicious. Mathis and Virginia were divorced in 1978. He went into hiding for more than twelve years, surfaced briefly after all that time, admitted that he was afraid of Virginia, and immediately went back into hiding.

By age twenty-six, Virginia had not only escaped jail twice for embezzlement, fraud, and larceny, but suspicion for conspiring to kill her husband. Divorced with two young children, she needed to find some means of support and married a second time.

Trooper James O. Matheny of the Florida Highway Patrol was a skilled investigator who had met his share of criminals and unsavory types. Matheny worked out of the Patrol's District Headquarters in Bartow, a town which was also headquarters for the Polk County Sheriff's Department. Like people in the same profession anywhere, Matheny talked shop with other troopers and deputies about crime, criminals and the latest scams. The juiciest gossip spreads through the ranks like wildfire, and cops get to know the criminal mind. They can often spot a criminal at a glance.

But even this background didn't prepare Matheny to deal with Virginia when he met her at a traffic accident she was involved in near Winter Haven in May, 1982. Virginia had perfected the art of being a victim: she had learned if men felt pity for an attractive woman, they rushed to the rescue. She mastered the role and it rarely failed her; certainly it worked with Matheny.

"She said her ex-husband abused her and their two children, Jason and Jessica, and that he was out to get her, Matheny said. "She acted like a helpless female who needed protection. She can be anything and everything you want her to be."

Two months after meeting, Virginia and Matheny were married on July 2, 1982, at his parents' home in Lakeland. Within weeks, Virginia secretly took out a large insurance policy on her husband's life. Three months after the marriage, Matheny was on the midnight shift when Virginia telephoned the Highway Patrol Headquarters. Sounding terrified, she asked to be patched through to her husband's radio, and told him someone was breaking into the house and wanted him to come home immediately.

Matheny wasn't the only one who heard Virginia's hysterical call. Polk County deputies received it, too.

Something told Matheny not to rush home immediately and the deputies, who knew about Virginia's background, raced to arrive at the house before the trooper. Virginia was caught off guard when she saw deputies instead of her husband.

She was still talking on the telephone. She held Matheny's loaded off-duty gun in her other hand.

The deputies investigated, looking for evidence or an attempted break-in and could find nothing. There was no broken glass, no footprints on the damp grass, and the police dogs couldn't find a scent. There was no evidence that burglary tools had been used in an attempt to pry open doors or windows. Virginia told Matheny's father that the man who tried to break in was Harry Mathis, her former husband.

Following this incident, Polk County deputies, who remembered the suspicious attempted murder of Harry Mathis, encouraged Matheny to read the report about the shooting. One deputy saw a connection between the shooting of Mathis and the fact that Virginia was waiting for her husband with a loaded gun. Matheny read the Mathis report, then searched his home for papers. He found documents addressed to Virginia Gail, Virginia Mathis and Virginia Antley. The documents showed that Virginia used other aliases by switching the letters in her name.

Matheny ran a computer check on the various names and found that Virginia had a long criminal history of bad checks, forged instruments and larceny. There were even outstanding warrants for her arrest in Polk County. When he moved out of the house in October, just three months after the marriage, Matheny took custody of a Datsun 280 XZ that had been bought in both names, and which had a large balance due and filed divorce papers. The trooper took the car to his parents' house and removed the ignition wires so Virginia couldn't steal it. He allowed her to use a 1977 Chevy LUV pickup truck that he purchased before their marriage.

Just days after Matheny moved out, the Highway Patrol received a call from an unidentified woman who said a yellow LUV pickup had been forced off the road. A woman hanging onto the door claimed to be the wife of a highway patrolman. Matheny went with troopers to investigate the accident and found nothing. An hour or so later, they saw Virginia in the LUV pickup, but it wasn't wrecked. A man was driving and Virginia, sitting in the passenger seat, rested her head on his shoulder. Matheny and another trooper were in an unmarked car and followed the pickup to Virginia's residence. When it stopped, Matheny, who was wearing his uniform, told Virginia, who was drunk, that he was taking the truck.

Matheny drove the pickup to his parents' home, disengaged the ignition wires, and left. A short time later Virginia arrived in an attempt to get the truck, but was ordered away by Matheny's parents. Virginia telephoned the Polk County Sheriff's office and told them Matheny had drawn his pistol and threatened to kill her, Jason and Jessica. An investigation cleared Matheny, but Virginia still wasn't through with him.

Virginia used Matheny's charge card and ran up $1,200 worth of purchases in one day. Some of the goods she bought were later found in Ohio. Matheny's estranged wife complicated the divorce proceedings by not showing up for hearings while she ran up charges in Matheny's name at stores where she opened credit accounts. Letters dunning him for payments poured in at the Highway Patrol District headquarters, putting Matheny's job in jeopardy, since he was supposed to be above reproach.

An investigation showed that Virginia had used his name, job, and credit references to get additional credit cards, and had charged each one to the limit. She instructed the stores to send the bills to a post office box she had rented. When they came in, she simply threw them away. Matheny didn't even know the charge accounts existed, but unsympathetic men from collection agencies marched to Highway Patrol headquarters and threatened to attach Matheny's wages.

Matheny's troubles continued. In January and February of 1983, he was contacted by General Motors Acceptance Corporation, the automobile financing arm of General Motors. Virginia had used his references to procure a new Chevrolet Citation with no money down, and had disappeared without making a payment.

Matheny breathed a sigh of relief when his divorce was granted on February 15, 1983, just six months after the marriage. The trooper considered himself lucky to get out of the marriage alive, if not financially solvent.

Virginia didn't wait for the divorce to be final before she married again. She met Frank Finley Ferry and they were married on February 7, 1983, in Pub 44, a biker bar, which was decorated with women's panties hanging from the ceiling. This marriage didn't last, either.

37

The month following the nuptial vows, Virginia telephoned the sheriff and claimed that Ferry had tried to kill her with a Snake Charmer .410 gauge shotgun. When deputies answered the call, Virginia was lying on the bedroom floor, seemingly unconscious, and one of her front teeth had apparently been broken.

Matheny told investigators Virginia had a broken front tooth she could remove at will, and which sometimes fell out of its own accord. Virginia merely stuck it back on by using Super Glue. The tooth fell out often and Matheny had urged her to get it fixed.

"I didn't think it was a good idea for her to be putting Super Glue into her mouth," he said.

The police charged Ferry with aggravated assault and battery, but the charge was lowered to carrying a concealed weapon without a license, which was a misdemeanor. Ferry was allowed to plead no contest and the court rendered no verdict. The marriage was annulled in August 1983 at Virginia's request.

Virginia moved on and, in no time, was in trouble again.

Four

The instability in Virginia's life had profound effects on Jason and Jessica. Jason, four years older than Jessica, was obviously Virginia's favorite; she lavished affection on him while Jessica was virtually ignored. Jeanette Atkinson, one of Virginia's sisters, said that, as Virginia bounced from man to man, "Virginia told Jason that he had to be the man of the family, that he had to protect her."

Even when he was seven years old, Jason took that responsibility to heart. During Virginia's arguments with husbands and boyfriends, the little boy stepped in with flailing fists to protect his mother. And there were always fights. Virginia was a compulsive liar who seemed unable to tolerate tranquility. She told lies and created intrigue that kept her relationships so tightly strung that they inevitably created an atmosphere of tension and endless quarrels. Jason was always there to try and defend his mother.

The bond between Jason and his mother grew closer with passing years. As an infant, he had slept with his mother, and continued to do so as he grew older. Jason was jealous of his mother's boyfriends and sometimes got into fierce arguments with them when Virginia took someone else into her bed.

Jeanette Atkinson, asked about this years later, said she didn't find it unusual, noting that she knew twenty-six-year-old daughters who slept with their mothers. But what about young men who were sleeping with mom? No, she admitted, that was different.

While Virginia and Jason became more like best friends and lovers than mother and son, Jessica was treated much like Cinderella, even though she was bright and attractive. Virginia had always found housework beneath her, and put little Jessica to work scrubbing, cleaning, ironing, washing clothes and dishes, and performing other household tasks. Jessica was such a nonentity that Virginia wouldn't even tell her who her father was. Virginia kept that a secret from Jessica until she was fourteen years old.

Being a pathological liar, and a habitual creator of intrigue, Virginia was always in some kind of trouble, and it was always Jason who gave his mother a shoulder to lean on. With each passing day, they grew more attached to one another.

"He was always raving about how wonderful his mother was," acquaintances said. "She was the greatest at everything. Virginia was Jason's best friend and he absolutely adored her. He would do anything for her."

Neither Jason nor Jessica had the slightest idea of what constituted a normal family environment. All their lives, their mother had been in some kind of trouble. She was charged with embezzlement several times, and there was the suspicious attempted murder of Virginia's first husband. The children had no contact with him after the shooting because he went into hiding for fear of Virginia, and it wasn't even certain he was Jessica's father.

"You can't blame Jason for anything he's ever done," Harry Mathis said years later. "He was manipulated by a master."

The divorce of Mathis and Virginia was the first unsettling incident in Jason's and Jessica's young lives. Matheny tried to be a good father to both Jason and Jessica during the short, tempestuous time he was married to Virginia. Virginia's rage against Matheny, her histrionics, and blaming the state police trooper for all of her problems was not lost on Jason. From his viewpoint, his mother had been wronged again . . . by a man.

The fact that Virginia always had lovers, even when she was married, didn't bother Jason or Jessica, except when Jason wanted to sleep with his mother. Both accepted their mother's promiscuity as part of her normal behavior, and usually they were only mildly curious about Virginia's boyfriends. They also became accustomed to the inevitable bitter and turbulent wreckage of their mother's relationships. Mathis had been shot. The marriage to Ferry, while Virginia was still wed to Matheny, had a turbulent end.

During the years of turmoil, Virginia and Jason

clung to one another for safety and comfort, and became even more intimate. Jessica became more of a nonperson in the dysfunctional family and was ignored except for being expected to perform work that essentially robbed the girl of her childhood.

"When you walked into the house, it was incredible," said *Tina Stiles*. "Jason would be sitting at Virginia's feet, as if worshiping her, and Jessica would look scared to death and acting like a slave."

By almost any measure, Virginia's luck took a sudden turn for the better in 1985 when she met Norman Larzelere, a dentist who had a practice in Edgewater. Virginia had escaped from Polk County to the glitzier city of Daytona Beach, the fast-track home of "Spring Break" and the famous Daytona 500 Stock Car Race, and was courting a dentist with an income far above average. Instead of orange groves and phosphate mines, Virginia had made it to the shores of the Atlantic Ocean, and had several money-making schemes in her sights, including plans to marry Dr. Norman Larzelere.

Most of the people who knew Dr. Larzelere considered him a good, kindhearted man with a wide streak of tolerance and generosity. Doc's patients acknowledged that he did good work, and sometimes gave up recreational time to handle emergencies.

"Doc loved to fish," said *Celia Lehder.* "I had a terrible toothache one Sunday and called Doc's office. He was out on the Atlantic fishing, but they got in touch with him by ship to shore radio. Doc came back, fixed my tooth, and didn't even charge me an emergency fee."

Doc was the youngest child and only son of Dr. Norman and Lucille Larzelere of Kalamazoo, Michigan. Doc would never grow into a strapping figure of a man, but he was far from being timid. "Our son wasn't a wimp," his mother, Lucy, said adamantly. "He was a strong, capable, adventurous person."

As a matter of fact, he was a northern version of Tom Sawyer in a later century. Norman not only sailed small boats with his dog Sammy on board, he rode his bicycle in Michigan's more temperate months with a pet crow on the handlebars. He was the apple of his parents' eyes.

"Norman was our only son," Lucy Larzelere said. "We were so happy when he was born."

When he was a teenager, Norman decided to build a seventeen-foot sailboat. But prefabricated boats were not for him; he wanted to build it from scratch, cutting all of the pieces of wood, fitting them, putting in the hardware, and attending to all of the arcane details of creating a capable vessel that was seaworthy.

The project took two years and occupied the family's two-car garage the entire time. Norman's mother, Lucy, remembered it well. "I used to get so tired of that thing taking all the space in our garage," she said. It was a gentle complaint because, in truth, Lucy was proud of her son.

"Normie was always gifted with his hands," she said. "He was always working on things, models, boats, and wood. I remember the day the boat was launched. Everybody was there."

Norman loved animals, played the guitar and sang in

the church choir, liked the outdoors, and was active in Cub Scouts. At the tender age of six, Norman, aided by a mischievous sister, decided to become a hobo and run away from home. He had his favorite things tied in a handkerchief on the end of a stick and was ready to hit the road, but like little boys everywhere, he realized being a hobo was just an adventurous, whimsical dream. Certainly he had nothing to run away from.

Norman was an average student in high school, but his grades were good enough for him to be accepted by Michigan State University. Although his father was a successful dentist, Norman had other interests, and graduated in 1976 with a degree in geography and anthropology. Becoming a dentist, like his father, wasn't something he contemplated until he encountered a young dentist in his father's practice who was filled with fire for his profession. Norman was captivated by the dentist's enthusiasm, spent a semester fulfilling pre-dental school requirements, then enrolled at the University of Michigan dental school in Ann Arbor.

An outstanding dental student, with a strong desire to help the handicapped and those in poverty, Norman spent his free time reading to the blind and repairing the teeth of migrant workers. Besides these humanitarian endeavors, he earned membership in both the student and honor councils, and was highly intelligent and well regarded by the other students.

Norman's adventuresome spirit was not quelled by the demands of college, nor was his love of open water. While still in college, he and three friends went to England and bought a creaky, fifty-three foot sail boat that was far from being seaworthy. The four youths restored the boat, at least partially, and sailed it out of England, through the Bay of Biscat off Spain, then into the open Atlantic until they reached Portugal. The trip was not without its risks, and Norman's parents worried until they heard that the boat had reached its destination with all hands sound of body and mind.

If Norman had a fault, it was that he was a pigeon for people with hard luck stories. Having been a hitchhiker in his youth, he often gave rides to total strangers, never giving a thought to his own safety. He gave money to almost anyone who had a tale of woe. "Sometimes his compassion was mixed with a little bit of poor judgment," his mother said. "He just couldn't say no. He never refused to help people in trouble."

Norman Larzelere graduated from the University of Michigan School of Dentistry in 1980 and moved to Edgewater, where he began a practice. He married, bought a house, and then joined the ranks of the divorced. That was when Doc, the softhearted man who couldn't say no to a person in need, met Virginia.

To Doc, Virginia was a vision of loveliness. She was pretty, sophisticated, and exciting, but she was down on her luck . . . or so she told Doc. Virginia had become a master of weaving spells, and she convinced Doc that she and her two children had been abused by her previous husband, who had then thrown them out of the house. Although Virginia had told the same lie before, it had a deep appeal to Doc's softhearted, if sometimes naive, approach to life. Virginia needed a White Knight, and although Doc was neither handsome or dashing, Virginia made him feel that he was both.

"I think Doc considered himself lucky that Virginia was interested in him," Gamell said. "He probably didn't know anything about her background, but if he did, I think he blinded himself to it."

Virginia really *was* down on her luck when she met Doc, but as usual, it was trouble of her own making. While working as a bookkeeper for the R.U. Construction Company in Daytona Beach, owned and operated by Randy Upson, Virginia had embezzled about $50,000, using the methods that had been successful in the past. Only this time, she had plucked the feathers from the wrong pigeon. Upson not only fired her, he called in his lawyer, Theodore Doran, to file suit and press for criminal charges.

This was the dark cloud hovering over Virginia's head when she, Jason and Jessica moved in with Doc, who was the answer to her prayers. Whether or not Doc knew about Virginia's past at that time is a matter of conjecture. The only obvious thing about Doc is that he was deeply in love with Virginia.

But there was trouble in the relationship from the beginning. Virginia continued to lie and spin webs of intrigue that kept Doc in a state of uncertainty. They had fierce arguments even before they were married, which didn't go unnoticed by Jason, who was sworn to be his mother's protector.

Judith Larzelere, Doc's sister, said Doc told her about a frightening incident that occurred not long after Doc and Virginia began living together. "He (Doc) confided in me that they were both drinking a lot and fighting a lot," Judith said. "And that at one point the fighting was so violent that Jason took a ceremonial sword off the wall and rushed into the bedroom where they were fighting, and threatened to kill my brother if he didn't stop fighting with his mother."

This type of behavior was startling to Judith. "That's a lot of violence," she said. "That was way back when Jason was eleven years old. I guess that would also show the bond he had with his mother . . ."

The incident shocked Doc so much that he and Virginia agreed to stop drinking alcohol, because it made their fights worse, and more frequent. Doc had no way of knowing that fighting with her husbands and lovers was normal behavior for Virginia. And alcohol wasn't the sole cause of it. Virginia took amphetamines, tranquilizers, and used cocaine, all of which kept her on a roller coaster of mood swings. By all accounts Doc knew nothing about Virginia's drug use in the beginning.

In spite of their frequent arguments, Doc and Virginia were married June 14, 1985, in DeLand. Virginia, who had a noose closing around her neck from R.U. Construction, saw a way out of her trouble. As a dentist, Doc earned an income far above average, and his parents were well-to-do. This last fact saved her neck, although Doc was not aware of it at the time.

Doc's parents, Norman and Lucy, had bought a home on Anna Maria Island, one of the small keys off Florida's Gulf Coast, just west of Bradenton. They intended to spend their retirement years between Michigan and Florida, leaving the snow of winter behind in Michigan, and going back during the hot, humid Florida summers. On a visit to Doc's parents' home in Anna Maria, shortly after the marriage, Norman and Lucy met Virginia.

At first, Doc's parents liked Virginia and thought she would be a good daughter-in-law. Virginia seemed to have a very nice personality. They became aware of inconsistencies in Virginia's various stories but it was too late: their son had married Virginia. Doc's parents knew they had a daughter-in-law who constantly contradicted herself, and they knew Virginia lied to them.

After Doc and Virginia returned home, Theodore Doran, the lawyer for R.U. Construction, was building a case for embezzlement proceedings against Virginia. Undaunted, Virginia used the embezzled funds to create a home construction company that she called V-LAR, short for Virginia Larzelere, and started to build houses. Before V-LAR sold its first house, Doran filed suit against Virginia for civil theft, racketeering, and other charges associated with the embezzled funds from R.U. Construction.

Doran was a tougher opponent than Virginia had faced before. He wanted criminal charges filed against Virginia, rather than restitution and a slap on the wrist. However, an unusual political situation was involved. It was an election year and Doran was running for the office of state attorney, as was John Tanner, the lawyer representing Virginia. After a lot of wrangling, Doran pressed the incumbent state attorney to file a criminal charge, even though he resisted because Virginia's activities were "white collar" crime.

Doran still wasn't satisfied. He researched courthouse records to get the legal descriptions of the homes V-LAR was constructing, then slapped a lien against them on behalf of R.U. Construction. This caught Virginia by surprise and frightened her: for the first time, there was a strong possibility that she might go to prison.

Virginia was desperate. Without telling Doc, she called his parents.

"We're in dire need of forty thousand dollars," Virginia said. "The Internal Revenue Service is going to close down the dental practice within five days if we don't come up with forty thousand dollars."

Virginia told them that Doc's first wife had filed inaccurate income tax returns, and that was what had caused the trouble.

Doc's parents were worried for their son. "We'll do what we can to help, but we'd like you to send us copies of the IRS letter," Lucy said.

"I will."

Lucy, fearful for her son's practice, wired forty thousand dollars directly into the bank account that Virginia gave her. At Lucy's insistence, Virginia promised to send her a copy of the IRS letter. But she never did. Later, Lucy and Norman, Sr. discovered that checks from the account they wired money to had been written by Virginia, paying thirty thousand dollars to R.U. Construction and ten thousand dollars to Doran in exchange for their dropping of all criminal charges. The checks were written the same day they transferred money into Virginia's account.

Doc's parents contacted Doran and he told them that Virginia had used the money to settle her case with R.U. Construction. Virginia told Doc about the loan she had secured from his parents, but convinced him it was to save his practice from seizure by the IRS.

"He knew that it had been loaned," Lucy said later, "but he thought it was for the purpose that she had stated. She had him buffaloed all the way."

Doc's parents had a document drawn, specifying the sum and number of monthly payments to repay the loan. Payments were made for four months, and then a check bounced. When Lucy telephoned about it, Doc and Virginia said the payments represented a major hardship for them.

The original agreement was that the loan would be repaid in two years, which Doc's parents realized was next to impossible. The contract was changed to stretch smaller payments over a longer length of time. Virginia wrote a letter of thanks for their consideration, and the new payment schedule began with no problems.

Notwithstanding the rocky start to their marriage, Doc adopted Jason and Jessica, and Virginia went on a spending binge. She convinced Doc to buy a larger house in DeLand, a small town twenty miles inland, which was the county seat for Volusia County. The house they bought was a two-story Dutch colonial with one-floor extensions on both sides. A green steel mesh fence, called a hurricane fence in Florida, surrounded the lot. The house had the usual rooms for normal living, and it contained five bedrooms and a tanning room.

The house itself was attractive, painted white with neat, green, imitation shutters and a green roof. There were columns beside the front entrance. No great care was given to landscaping, there were no flowers, and the few decorative plants were leggy and thin from lack of care. Several live oaks were dying because they were being deprived of sunlight by masses of gray Spanish moss that hung like rags from every branch.

Directly across the street was a bleak lot with a dirt road that sliced through it and, beyond that, an off-brown stucco building used for light manufacturing. Next to the vacant lot was a small, unattractive park with two covered cabanas and permanently affixed picnic tables with rusty grills. There were additional light manufacturing facilities behind that.

Being a dentist's wife, Virginia found it easy to get credit cards, and she had dozens of them that Doc never signed for — and never used — although Jason did. Virginia also began a campaign to take over every aspect of Doc's life. At first, he appreciated many of the things she did, only to discover that he had been effectively cut off from his family and friends. Worse, the arguments with Virginia continued and intensified. Virginia had firmly ensconced herself as the business manager at the office. Doc found no peace either at home or at work.

Five

Jason and Jessica had their first real chance to live a normal home life, with above average opportunities, after their mother married Norman Larzelere. Doc wanted nothing but the best for the children; he was uncommonly loving and tolerant to a fault, a trait that ultimately proved to be his undoing. It was hard to find anyone who disliked him, and he lavished affection on Virginia and his adopted children. When Jason was old enough to get a license, he was given a BMW to drive. Doc paid for Jason to attend private schools, where he usually got into trouble, often requiring the services of an attorney to smooth his way and to allow him to continue.

Jessica was often in trouble, too, and had one fight with a classmate that resulted in her braces being broken. Another time she and a friend who had no driver's license drove off in one of Doc's cars. In spite of Doc's efforts, the Larzelere household was in constant turmoil.

A family friend, when asked to describe Jessica, said

she was a "miniature Virginia." Another person who knew Jessica well said, "I think her life is a tragedy. Her childhood was stolen from her."

Turmoil was Virginia's stock in trade, and Jason and Jessica were used to it. Doc wasn't, but Virginia stirred the pot more vigorously after she married Doc, and kept him in a state of confusion. Instead of diminishing, the arguments they had before they were married became more frequent and intense. Doc had no way of knowing that Virginia was a pathological liar and a compulsive crook. Listening to Virginia, it was impossible to tell where the truth ended and the lies began.

Jessica and Doc's parents were aware of an unnatural closeness between Virginia and Jason. Doc's mother believed that Jason was jealous of Doc and considered him a rival for Virginia's attentions. Doc once had to throw the youngster out of the bedroom. Jessica said the relationship Jason had with his mother was "like man and wife."

Jessica recalled that Jason was so intent on sleeping with Virginia that he often got into fights with Doc about it. Doc defended himself against Jason, but never hit back. After one such conflict, he told Jessica, "I think your mother needs psychiatric counseling. She needs help, and so does Jason."

Virginia gave birth to a son, Benjamin, on May 6, 1986, about a year after she and Doc were married. People close to the situation, including Jessica and Doc's parents, wondered if Doc was the father. Doc's feelings on the subject are still unknown, but others thought Jason was Benjamin's father.

"When Norm's first child was born," Doc's mother noticed, "Jason took over the care of that child. He was very caring, but his relationship with Ben was like he was his father."

Lucy Larzelere wasn't influenced by rumors, but by her own observations. "And we have photographs taken of the children and a lot of the family," she said, "and Jason was always the one holding Ben on his lap. And he physically cared for Ben from the time he was little; feeding him, changing him. I thought he was acting like a father but maybe he was acting like a mother."

Jessica had even stronger feelings. She said outright that Jason was Benjamin's father, and that as Benjamin grew older, Doc became upset because Benjamin complained about how Jason treated him.

"Ben said that Jason was playing with his tummy whacker," Jessica said in a sworn statement, "and asked if it was all right."

According to his grandparents, Jason not only had trouble at school, getting along with teachers and other students, but also had homosexual tendencies. His grades were poor. On more than one occasion, Doc told principals that Jason needed psychiatric help, and urged them to keep him informed if there were other additional problems.

Like his mother, Jason seemed to court trouble, and was expelled from five different schools because of behavioral problems. Once Jason was booted out because he took a .22 caliber air pistol to school and threatened to kill a student who had chided him for being a "faggot."

A tall, skinny youth at age fourteen, Jason threw himself into a vigorous bodybuilding program and beefed up to over 190 pounds of muscle. But psychologically, he was a confused young man.

"He was having a hard time coming to terms with being gay," according to Steve Heidle, a gay friend who had a one-time sexual encounter with Jason. "He used to talk to me about it. It was something that really bothered him."

Doc was squeezed at home and at work. Instead of tapering off, the arguments became even more frequent. Usually they centered around Virginia's numerous sexual affairs, which she made no effort to hide, even from her children. Sometimes she took Jason and Jessica on dates. Virginia practiced equal opportunity when it came to distributing her sexual favors; she had affairs with waiters, pool maintenance workers, salesmen and doctors.

Once Jessica caught her mother outside, having sex with a young man who serviced the pool. They were hiding under a blanket but it had slipped away. "He came around to check the pool every day after that," Jessica said, laughing. Virginia didn't always know when she would find a man to sleep with and always prepared, never going anywhere without a douching kit in her purse.

According to the manager of a restaurant called Mr. Dunderbox in Daytona Beach, Virginia arrived one night for dinner, accompanied by Jessica. Virginia flirted outrageously with the male waiters, and tried to draw Jessica into it.

"Which one do you want?" she reportedly asked Jessica, who was embarrassed.

The young waiters, unaccustomed to such blatant overtures as Virginia made, were more than curious, but they aroused Virginia's ire by giving Jessica most of their attention. Virginia got up from the table and said, "I'll be back." Some thirty minutes later, Virginia arrived wearing a see-through black dress and little underneath.

It seemed that Virginia could not resist any type of scam. When she wanted plastic surgery on her body, she filed insurance papers claiming she had a mastectomy and needed reconstructive breast surgery. "She just wanted them bigger," Jessica said. Virginia also had a tummy tuck and liposuction.

As the business manager at Doc's dental practice, she quickly took over complete control, even to the point of writing prescriptions and forging Doc's name. The prescriptions were for patients, but she also ordered large quantities of amphetamines, barbiturates, vaginal creams and other drugs that she used and sold. According to acquaintances, "Virginia took Valium like aspirin, and gave them to Jason, too."

All of the mail to the DeLand residence was routed to a Post Office Box that was under Virginia's control. Additionally, she screened the mail at the dental practice, which went directly to her. Virginia pocketed all of the cash payments, never telling Doc or reporting it to the Internal Revenue Service. By screening all incoming and outgoing mail at the dental office and in DeLand, Virginia squeezed off Doc's pipeline to his family and friends.

Doc's parents knew Virginia was doing everything she could to isolate their son. "By . . . having it (mail) delivered to a post office box that she could control . . . a lot of mail he never got," Lucy Larzelere said. "We did send some registered letters to him to make sure he would get them, but even then she could sign for them in the office. For a long time he could call us only from the office when she wasn't there or go to a telephone booth . . . and we never felt we could call him."

Besides pocketing cash and forging Doc's name on prescriptions, Virginia billed patients for dental work that wasn't done. Since she handled the bookkeeping and bank accounts, Virginia deposited the amount paid for actual work, and deposited the remainder in other accounts she opened in her name only. There was never a time when Virginia didn't have thousands of dollars in her purse.

Less than two years after they were married, Virginia had almost completely taken over all aspects of Doc's life. His contact with his parents and friends had been effectively shut down, and Virginia bombarded him with lies, always spinning her webs of intrigue. She flaunted her affairs in front of him, but argued vociferously that *he* was the one who was unfaithful.

Their arguments were constant now, and even spilled over into the dental office. Patients didn't hear them, but the employees were well aware of the rancor between Doc and Virginia.

At home, Jason continued to cause trouble, and interjected himself into the arguments between Doc and his mother. Having abandoned his weight training, Jason had lost his bulk, but at six feet tall and weighing one hundred thirty-five pounds, he remained strong.

Virginia taunted Doc. "You're ugly," she spat at him. "I can't stand you. I wish that you were dead."

When Doc confronted his wife about her affairs, Virginia told him that they were lies. She called on Jason and Jessica to support her, even though they had been on dates with their mother and her lovers.

After one particularly violent argument at home, Doc sat with Jessica, who had learned to love him. "Your mother needs psychiatric counseling," he said. "She's just sick, that's all. And Jason has to learn how to control his temper or he's going to kill somebody. Right now, I think it might be me."

Later, Virginia told Jessica, "Your father's so ugly, I can't stand him anymore. I wish he would die."

"Doc was psychologically battered by Virginia," Detective Gamell said later. "He was a battered parent and a battered husband." Lucy Larzelere agreed. "Virginia told so many lies and cut him off so effectively that he was confused," she said. "He was brainwashed."

Several patients who had been overbilled by Virginia filed complaints with the Florida Department of Professional Regulation, and the DPR's dental specialists initiated an investigation into Doc's practice. A bad report could mean that Doc would lose his license to practice, and that would deprive Virginia of the huge sums of money she was embezzling. That would be catastrophic to Virginia, who had grown accustomed to having the best that money could buy. It began to seem logical that she would be better off with Doc dead, especially since he was insured for millions of dollars.

Six

Norman Karn's own words were: "I thought I had bitten the golden goose in the ass and I didn't want all of those beautiful golden eggs to get away."

The "golden goose" was Virginia Larzelere.

Karn, a loquacious, easygoing man, had never thought of himself as being greedy. He earned a comfortable living in California by operating his own contracting firm and was content, except for having to pay his ex-wife a bundle in alimony. The comfortable, contented life Karn led was to change drastically in late December, 1988. That was when he met Virginia Larzelere.

Karn flew from California to Florida to visit his parents in Edgewater over the holidays. Karn's father, who was one of Doc's patients, got his son a blind date for lunch with Arlouine (A.J.) Ellis, a clerk and secretary at Doc's office.

The Californian, at 6 ft. 5 inches tall (in his cowboy boots) and 235 pounds, was an impressive figure of a man. "This was back in my slim, wide-shouldered, narrow hips days and I wouldn't have been afraid to take on

60

Mike Tyson," Karn said. "I went in there (Doc's office) looking kind of good."

Virginia gave Karn a seductive look, turned away briefly, and when she looked back, she had opened two buttons on her blouse. Karn's eyes were riveted to Virginia's full bust, and when he was able to look away, he noticed that she was pretty. And she couldn't have been friendlier. She was delighted to let A.J. take an early lunch. When Karn returned with A.J., it seemed to him that Virginia was being seductive.

It was possible that he was misreading Virginia's signals, Karn knew, since Virginia was married to a successful dentist. On the other hand, his tall, slim figure had caught the eye of dozens of women. Even after Virginia told him to turn in his rental car and borrow one of hers during his visit, Karn wasn't certain of her interest in him.

"I saw A.J. at the office for about eight days and Virginia just kept getting friendlier and friendlier," Karn said. "Finally she ended up having me, A.J., my Grandmother Stevens and my Grandmother Halker over to her house in DeLand."

Karn had been driving Virginia's Suburban for about ten days when, on December 28, she drove him to a private airfield in DeLand to see her airplane, a twin engine Cessna. The tall Californian was already impressed, but he had never known anyone personally who owned an airplane. Virginia told him she was a licensed pilot, which was a lie, even though she often flew the plane across the country. Karn couldn't believe his luck: Virginia seemed too good to be true.

* * *

In the few days he knew her, Virginia had Karn completely bamboozled. He believed that Virginia was the daughter of a Cherokee Indian Chief, and that she received monthly royalties from oil wells on the reservation. Virginia told him that she was worth $39.6 million, a figure that blew Karn's mind.

"She told me that she and her husband didn't have any kind of sexual relationship," Karn said. "She was almost making out like he was homosexual and it was her money that was keeping him in business."

That was when Karn began to think about all those beautiful golden eggs that could be his. Thirty-nine million dollars' worth. All Virginia had to do was divorce her husband.

"I can't do that," Virginia told him. "If I divorce him, he would get half of my fortune and I don't want that to happen."

It seemed to Karn that Virginia was fishing for a way to get rid of Doc that would prevent him from sharing in any portion of her millions. Karn didn't think of foul play then; there just wasn't time for him to dwell on everything Virginia said. His head was spinning with heady thoughts of becoming a millionaire without having to work for the money. All he had to do was marry Virginia.

The holiday trip was coming to an end when Karn told Virginia he'd like to visit his sister Norma, who lived in Jacksonville, North Carolina. He hadn't seen her for about thirteen years.

"I'll drive you up in my Suburban," Virginia replied.

"No, thanks."

"I'll fly you up and back," Virginia said.

That sounded just dandy and on New Year's Day, 1989, Virginia and a man she said was her copilot, flew off in her Cessna to North Carolina. Among the things Virginia had Karn believing was that she was a contractor, investor, dentist, and a certified accountant. At the time, Karn believed she was all of those things.

When they landed in North Carolina, Norma met them at the airport. Karn and his sister hugged and kissed at the happy reunion, while Virginia sat silently on a wing, a petulant look on her face. Norma drove Karn and Virginia from the airport while the copilot remained to oversee refueling and to file a return flight plan.

Virginia remained silent, except for a few terse comments, after they arrived at Norma's house. Her petulant expression seemed frozen on her face, and occasionally she glared at Karn.

"How are you doing?" Virginia asked Karn in a mocking voice.

"I'm finer than hell," Karn replied. He was ticked off by her attitude.

Virginia slowly looked him over. "I'm beginning to wonder about that," she said.

That did it. Karn snapped, taking Virginia's comment as a challenge to his manhood. He decided to embarrass Virginia in front of his sister.

"Norma, do you mind if I borrow your car?" he asked.

"No, you can borrow it."

"Where's the closest motel?"

"Why?"

"It seems as if this woman wants me to put it to her."

Instead of being embarrassed, Virginia sat unruffled, calmly smoking a cigarette, as if they were discussing the weather. The statement backfired, embarrassing Karn so much that he wanted to disappear into the floor, as Virginia sat studying her fingernails.

"Hell, why go to a motel?" Norma asked. "I've got five bedrooms. Just grab one."

"Do you mind?" he asked Virginia.

"No."

Karn gave his sister a sheepish look as Virginia took his hand and led him to the bedroom Norma had indicated. A short time later, Karn learned the secret of Virginia's magnificent breasts. He pressed down on them and, instead of springing back, the indentations of his fingers remained. It was a phenomenon Karn had seen before, "those phony, blown-up titties," as he called them.

After they made love, Karn said, "You've got a beautiful body. What'd them tits cost?"

"Those are mine."

"Yeah," Karn said. "Everything is yours when you pay for it."

"How did you know they're phony?"

"I've seen them little slits on the bottom before," Karn said. "They crush when they're touched. I mean—"

"That's enough," Virginia said.

This was the beginning of what would become a brief, but whirlwind, transcontinental affair that left Karn with his head spinning. Karn had picked up a

64

habit that he never mentioned to Virginia. After he had to pay his ex-wife a large settlement when they were divorced, Karn was suspicious of women and kept a daily log of his activities, hoping that it would chronicle his life so that a woman could never again take financial advantage of him.

In the few days Karn had left before returning to California, Virginia told him Doc was not only a homosexual, he had a violent temper and frequently beat her, Jason, Jessica and Benjamin. Karn, who was blinded by the thought of marrying a woman with $39.6 million, didn't know what to think. He was inclined to believe the golden goose.

"I don't like to admit it," he said, "but I'm a working guy, and I was thinking, 'Hey, there's a way to get rich without having to bust your ass.' It really fucked me up with my work ethic."

Just a day after he had bedded Virginia, Karn was invited to the Larzelere home for dinner. Karn went outside to sit in the backyard with Doc. They looked at the bright stars, petted the dentist's two German shepherds, and chatted about Doc's boats and other things. Doc asked perceptive questions about Karn's masonry business and seemed to really like him.

Karn thought, *Here I am having an affair with Virginia and I'm sitting out here talking with her husband who seems to be a really decent guy.* His conscience bothered him, but the $39.6 million blinders clicked on and Karn rationalized that Virginia wanted him. At the least, her husband would end up with a few million dollars in a divorce, and that wasn't too shabby. Something else niggled at Karn's mind as he and Doc talked; it seemed as if the dentist was auditioning him to determine if he was good enough for Virginia.

Doc made Karn feel even more low-down when he mentioned that Virginia might have had an affair with their swimming pool contractor. Although he knew nothing of Virginia's affair with the pool man or anyone else, Karn wanted to hide under a rock.

"We've had a lot of work done around here on the pool," Doc said.

"Yeah?"

"There was a man, Buzz Davis, who rides a motorcycle," Doc said. "Some people started rumors about Virginia and Buzz having an affair. I don't believe it. Do you?"

Doc looked at Karn, who tried hard not to fidget, and just shook his head, no. It made Karn uncomfortable for Doc to mention this to him since he was currently bedding the dentist's wife.

Before Karn returned to California, Virginia wined and dined him, always picking up the tab. Sometimes Jason and Jessica joined them for dinner. Money flowed from Virginia's purse: she took Karn to Counts Western Wear and bought him a pair of cowboy boots that cost $160, and that was just the beginning of thousands of dollars she spent on him. On January 4, the day Karn returned to California, Virginia rented a room at a Marriott Hotel near the airport so they could spend the last few hours together before his plane left.

* * *

Rather than ending the affair, Karn's return to California seemed to intensify it, and Virginia presented an urgent need over the next few weeks to be rid of her husband. Virginia telephoned Karn the day after he returned home, then flew out to see him January 20 in the Cessna. On this visit, Virginia increased her complaints about how Doc treated her and revealed her version of his abuse in more graphic detail.

Sometimes, Virginia said, her husband became violent and threatened to have her killed so he could inherit her fortune. Karn couldn't visualize the man he had chatted with in DeLand about dogs, boats, masonry and fishing becoming violent. Certainly he didn't think Doc was capable of murder or hiring someone else to commit murder.

During the courtship, Karn made three first class round-trip flights to Daytona Beach, courtesy of Virginia, and stayed at upper echelon motels at Virginia's expense. On one visit, Virginia met Karn at the airport with a stretch limousine and a driver named Roger, who stood about six feet tall, wore eyeglasses and had sandy hair.

The two men stood outside of a Holiday Inn on the Daytona Beach boardwalk waiting for Virginia to return from Counts Western Wear, where she had driven to in her Mercedes to buy clothes for Karn. To pass the time, Karn tried to strike up a conversation with Roger, whom Virginia had presented as her bodyguard, in addition to being her chauffeur.

"How long have you known Virginia?" Karn asked.

"Hell, I don't know," Roger said. "She just called me

the other day. This is the last time I'm driving her around."

"Oh really?" Karn asked, surprised.

"I don't mean to be disrespectful, but that woman is a little bit weird."

Virginia had lied again but Karn was sucked so far into the maelstrom Virginia created that he ignored the warning. It was no wonder his head was turned: From January 20 until the end of February, Virginia spent more than $20,000 on Karn, including airfare, hotels, jewelry and clothes. She spent hundreds of dollars on their meals and bar tabs. And on her trips to California, she and Karn zoomed around looking at multi-million dollar mansions.

"I want to live out here with you once Doc's out of the way," she said.

Karn didn't immediately realize the sinister implication of her words. She didn't say, when they were divorced. She said *when Doc is out of the way*. This choice of words would make sense to Karn before long.

Virginia did everything with dizzying speed, and on a scale that overwhelmed Karn. She telephoned real estate brokers to have brochures describing multi-million dollar mansions mailed to Karn's address. Virginia reviewed them, and then took Karn along to look at the ones she liked, after having already siphoned off the undesirables.

As a contractor, Karn had done masonry work on some of the mansions and he knew how expensive they were. He couldn't afford to pay for one of the driveways, but Virginia decided that a huge estate called Dover Manor would suit her just fine.

"I want to live here with you and my children when Doc is out of the way," she told Karn. "I hate the humidity in Florida."

Again, there was no talk of divorce, just *when Doc is out of the way.*

Karn called his lawyer to put things in motion for Virginia to buy Dover Manor. Virginia wrote a check for $2.5 million to be put in escrow and held as a down payment on the estate. Since it was to be held in escrow, the check was never presented to a bank to be cashed. No one, least of all Karn, who had experienced Virginia's free spending ways, and who thought she had a $39.6 million fortune, had any reason to think the check might not be good.

But as extravagant as that was, Virginia wasn't through tossing checks around: Karn's eyes bugged out when she gave him two blank checks with her signature. He could write in any amount of money he desired to be received by anyone he chose — including himself. But why take that risk and lose the golden goose? Virginia instructed Karn to buy a Ferrari, plus another expensive automobile, and fill in the total purchase price. Karn was never able to remember the make of the second car, but he recalled how it looked: "It was a beautiful convertible. It had a gold plate in the damn door that had the names of the guys that made it. It was really awesome."

Bedazzled by multi-million dollar mansions, expensive sports cars, clothing, jewelry and airplanes, Karn convinced himself that Virginia was not a liar, just eccentric. Some of the things she did, however, were decidedly strange.

* * *

Once she placed a frantic telephone call to Karn's California home from Florida.

"Oh, Norm!" she said. "I've been kidnapped and I don't know where I am."

"Jesus, you live in Florida. What do you mean you don't know where you are?"

"I'm in New Smyrna Beach someplace, but I don't know where I'm at."

"Well, Christ, why don't you call the cops? You're calling long distance to me, you know."

"Well, A.J. abducted me and took my purse and nobody believes who I am."

Karn knew that A.J. was about as likely to commit kidnapping as Tinker Bell. The whole thing was crazy, Karn thought. If Virginia had access to a telephone, why call him in California, where he could do nothing, when she could call the local police? Or Doc, for that matter.

"Where are you calling from?" Karn asked.

"A policeman's house."

"A *what?*"

"A policeman's house."

"Jesus Christ!"

"He picked me up and felt sorry for me and dropped me off here at his house and left."

"What's the address?"

"I don't know."

Karn finally got off the telephone, amazed at the conversation. He was trying to sort it out when, minutes later, Jason called.

"Where's my mom?" he asked.

70

"She's somewhere in New Smyrna."

"I'd better go get her," he replied and hung up.

How could he go get her if he didn't know where she was? Karn wondered.

Thirty minutes later, Jason called back and said he had driven from DeLand to New Smyrna and back but couldn't find his mother. Who did he think he was kidding? Karn thought. No one can drive over seventy miles in thirty minutes. As strange as it was, it got even stranger. Twenty minutes after Jason's call, Virginia telephoned and said she was home and that everything was all right.

But there was this problem: Doc was trying to have her killed.

Karn was exasperated and bewildered by Virginia's strange behavior and her contention that Doc was trying to murder her. By this time, he realized Virginia was eccentric, but the promise of so much money kept him on the hook. "Well, Jesus Christ, man, did I fall into a rich thing?" he asked himself. If Virginia was merely odd, he could tolerate it because he was becoming accustomed to the high life that her money could provide. Ironically, he started to think of *himself* as a millionaire.

Virginia frequently asked if he knew anyone who would kill Doc. He told her no, and that he wouldn't do such a thing himself.

When Virginia was in California to write the $2.5 million check for Dover Manor and sign her name on blank checks for Karn, she brought Jason and Jessica along. Along with Karn's daughter, Stacy, they went to a night spot in Downey called The Dixie Belle for dinner and drinks.

Stacy wanted bigger breasts and, somewhere between salad and dessert, Virginia said she would pay to have them enlarged by plastic surgery when she and her kids moved into Dover Manor. Karn was pleased that Virginia was willing to spend money on his daughter.

The featured country singer at The Dixie Belle was Ron Hayden, a man entering middle age who Karn thought had money problems. Maybe he did and maybe he didn't, depending on who you believe, but the intrigue was far more complicated than just money.

Karn didn't know Hayden until he discovered that the singer was having an affair with his wife, Karen. Instead of confronting his wife or Hayden directly, Karn decided to befriend the musician, thereby shaming him into dropping the affair and simultaneously depriving his wife of her lover. Karn's ploy worked and, after he and Hayden became friends, he surreptitiously seduced the singer's wife. The two women discovered the devious plot, divorced their husbands, leaving their respective mates bewildered, possessing less money, but with an odd kind of friendship.

Karn thought of Hayden as a man who had let life pass him by, whose music had left him broke and struggling. Hayden's opinion of Karn was essentially the same, excluding music. Each viewed the other as a loser, and although they were friendly, it was a decidedly fragile friendship.

On the night Virginia, Karn and their respective children were at The Dixie Belle, the plots and subplots underlying the conversation were thick and complex when Hayden joined their table.

"His van was broken down and he didn't have money to get it fixed," Karn said. "He complained about his whole financial situation."

According to Karn, Hayden said, "Jesus Christ, I'd do anything for two thousand dollars."

"You would?" Virginia asked.

"Yeah."

Virginia moved away from the table and motioned for Hayden to follow. Jason and Jessica stayed at the table, and Stacy went to the rest room. Karn wasn't about to leave Hayden alone with his golden goose, given their past histories, and tagged along with them. He listened to the conversation and suddenly it was as if someone had switched a light on in his head, illuminating things he had been unwilling to see. While Virginia and Hayden were talking, Stacy emerged from the rest room and started to come close to the three adults, but Karn shooed her away. He didn't want her to hear what Virginia and Hayden were discussing.

It became clear to Karn that Virginia was serious about wanting to have her husband killed. Several days passed and Karn lost contact with Virginia, even though he wrote and telephoned several times. On March 8, 1989, he received a letter from Virginia telling him the affair was over. Karn's golden goose had flown the coop.

Seven

Doc was inundated by trouble. He suspected that Virginia was having an affair with Karn, but he couldn't be certain. She left home for days at a time and never explained her absences, even when she took Jason and Jessica with her. By this time Doc was almost afraid to question Virginia about her activities, because of the scenes she created.

One good thing came of Virginia's absences: Doc was able to talk with his parents. There was a single compelling thought on his mind.

"I have to do everything I can to keep this family together," he said. "They need my help."

Doc expressed his fear that Virginia was having an affair with Karn, after she had been gone for a week. Supposedly she was in Oklahoma to finish testing to get her pilot's license, but she didn't show up for the examinations.

Doc was astounded when he learned, during the time Virginia was having her fling with Karn, he was being investigated by the dental examiners with the Florida Department of Professional Regulation. The charges being investigated by the DPR stemmed from things Virginia had done, but Doc was responsible. Virginia could not be punished by the DPR because she wasn't a licensed dentist, but Doc could lose everything, including his reputation.

Since Virginia started to work at Doc's dental practice, complaints had trickled into the DPR, which is charged with maintaining minimum standards for various professions. The organization allows a great deal of latitude to fellow professionals, but so many improprieties had been reported about Doc's practice that they were prompted to take action.

It also prompted Doc to act. He saw all of the years of school, hard work, and struggle to earn the respect of the community, as well as the ability to provide a good living for his family, facing destruction. At the very least he could be placed on probation and fined; at the worst he could lose his license to practice in Florida, an indelible black mark on his record that would probably prevent him getting a license to practice anywhere in the United States. His career was threatened with total ruin.

The complaints the DPR received came from patients of Norm's who had been stung once too often for overbilling or being charged for work that wasn't even done. The bills were made out by Virginia. Other complaints came from dentists who saw Norm's patients when they sought second opinions concerning dental work Virginia had entered on their records. The dentists reviewed the records and discovered the patients were charged for nonexistent bridgework, fillings, and had been scheduled for dental work that wasn't necessary.

Doc remembered Ted Doran, the lawyer who had represented R.U. Construction in the case against his wife. He made an appointment with Doran late in 1988 to file for a divorce.

"You really nailed her on that embezzlement case," Doc told Doran. "Maybe you could do the same on a divorce." He told Doran that Virginia was intimidated by him because of the R.U. Construction and V-LAR legal proceedings.

"He used stronger language than that," Doran said later. "He described a lot of aberrant behavior and he wanted me to proceed forcefully with the dissolution of marriage."

Doc's primary concern was to get custody of Benjamin, his youngest son. "I want you to focus very heavily on that as the primary issue of the dissolution proceeding."

The meeting was on a Friday and Doran worked through the weekend to prepare the legal papers. Both he and Doc were certain Virginia knew enough about the legal system to delay having papers served on her. Doc was afraid Virginia would take Benjamin and leave the state and tried to get temporary custody. Doran intended to secure permanent custody for Doc but, failing that, he wanted a restraining order to keep Virginia from leaving Florida's jurisdiction with Benjamin.

After Doc told Doran to start divorce procedures, he took Benjamin to Anna Maria to stay with his parents. Then he studied the complaints from the DPR and discovered just how far Virginia had led his practice down a crooked road. Doc discovered frequent overbilling, and bills sent to patients who hadn't even had appointments. The billings were wildly exaggerated. Virginia was clearly the culprit, but that made no difference to the DPR, whose investigators said Doc should have been aware of the scams and nipped them in the bud. If Doc wasn't aware of the improprieties, the DPR said, he should have been.

The DPR investigation allowed no wiggle room for the dentist.

It was devastating for Doc to learn that patients were being bilked, but there was more bad news: the DPR said Virginia, who was not a doctor, wrote prescriptions and forged Doc's signature. According to the DPR, the prescriptions were not always for patients: "She dispensed or utilized (prescriptions) for her own purposes." The DPR said Virginia ordered large quantities of drugs that "have nothing to do with the practice of dentistry." Virginia also represented herself to patients as a doctor.

The DPR claimed Doc was "operating . . . a dental office in such a manner as to result in dental treatment that is below minimum acceptable standards of performance. . . ." The investigators recommended that Doc's license be revoked or suspended, or that he be fined, reprimanded and placed on probation.

Doc was in deep trouble. Virginia had placed him in a perilous position, and she had put him thousands of dollars in debt. Benjamin was safely out of the house when Virginia returned, and a furious argument erupted that went on all night.

Doc and Virginia screamed and yelled at each other while Jessica tried to stay calm. She was accustomed to the stormy relationship between her mother and father, but they usually centered around Virginia's extramarital affairs. This argument was different because Doc took a firm stand, blaming his wife for his trouble with the DPR, and sacrificing the family in her pursuit of extramarital affairs.

"I'm not having any affairs!" Virginia yelled. "You're a liar."

Jason stepped in and screamed at Doc to leave his mother alone. He was wild, and his fists flew at Doc, who retreated without trying to hit Jason. Doc was far too upset to be cowed this time; Virginia had gone too far.

"I'm going to file for divorce," he said, and walked away.

Virginia was shocked at Doc's uncharacteristic show of strength, and saw the source of her wealth and drugs threatened. But she was taken aback only momentarily and, as she had in the past when in trouble, reacted with a vigorous counteroffensive. The smoke of battle had not yet cleared before Virginia hurried to the Volusia County Courthouse and filed several petitions for injunctions against her husband.

One accused Doc of physically and psychologically abusing her. Another asked that he be kicked out of the house, enjoined from being near her, that she be given a living allowance, and custody of Jason, Jessica, and Benjamin.

Such petitions are so common in Florida that courts have complaint forms printed with boxes to be checked and dotted lines to be filled in. There is also space for additional information not covered by the form. As always, Virginia lied outrageously. She filled in the blank spaces by hand, alternating between block printing and cursive. The penmanship appeared to be written by someone in a hurry.

Virginia wrote that Doc had "mentally abused" her "to the point of being admitted to Intensive Care Fish Memorial New Smyrna." In reality she had gone to the hospital for a minor heart attack brought on by drugs and alcohol.

Claiming she was the custodian of Jason, Jessica, and Benjamin, Virginia asked that Doc be booted from the house, a moot point since Doc had already left. Virginia claimed she had no means of support because "husband has all savings/checking accounts." The reality was exactly the opposite; Virginia had been squirreling money away in private accounts since their marriage. She said she "genuinely fears that the respondent (Doc) will abuse, remove, or hide the minor children . . . because he already had his parents remove the three-year-old (Benjamin) and taken him to Anna Marie Island."

Virginia checked boxes on the printed form to enjoin Doc from committing any acts of violence, to get immediate custody of the house, custody of the children, financial support for herself and the children, and asked that Doc be ordered to get "treatment or counseling."

The form required Virginia to describe the last time she was abused, time, date, where it occurred, and the nature of her injuries. She wrote:

"Abuse started Sunday again 2/10/89 accusations and physical/mental abuse about me having an affair. We argued all night, pushing, shoving, and throwing objects. I went to Dr. Crewe on 2/13/89 explained in confidence all the abuse for several months. He did an examination, electrocardiogram and admitted me to Intensive Care Unit Fish Memorial New Smyrna. Due to bruising/stress, he said I had a heart attack. He suggested to nurses not to admit husband to room. Last night we argued all night after I got out of the hospital Ormond Memorial. He was very violent, kicking throwing and screaming things — He close (sic) all bank accounts today. My three year old was taken yesterday by Norman to 911 North Shore Drive Anna Maria. I was advised to be admitted to Shands Hospital today 2/16/89 because of all the stress and actions."

Included in Virginia's barrage of complaints was a Financial Affidavit, another printed form with accusations to be checked and blanks to be filled in. On this form Virginia claimed she received no salary or benefits from working at the dental practice, and had no money to maintain the house, buy food and groceries, or pay for anything else. From the affidavit, it seemed Virginia and her children would live in wretched poverty, even though the dental practice grossed more than half a million dollars a year. The practice actually grossed far more, but because of Virginia's embezzling, what actually went into the business bank account was far less than Virginia claimed.

Virginia filled out a form that asked her to list Doc's income and expenses. She listed Doc's gross income at $45,000 a month, adding that she worked at the dental office with no compensation whatsoever. She said Doc's take home pay was $25,000 monthly.

Virginia had a long list of expenses to maintain her family: a monthly mortgage of $1,208; $900 for food; $300 for clothing; $200 for transportation; $1,377 for medical, life, and automobile insurance; $650 for utilities; installment payments of $1,875; which included $400 for private schools, $175 a week for a nanny, and loan payments of $900. She listed personal expenses of $100 and unspecified expenses totaling another $400. The largest expenditure was $10,000 a month for medical expenses.

The $10,000 a month in medical expenses didn't cause any raised eyebrows because Virginia explained that she had suffered from cancer, undergone a radical double mastectomy, and needed follow-up treatment. That was a lie, of course, since Virginia had never had cancer: the bill was for cosmetic plastic surgery.

Virginia's request for an injunction claimed that monthly family living expenses were $20,409, not including Doc's business expenses, which were close to half his gross. At least, they would have been, if Virginia had withheld Social Security and income taxes for Doc's employees, instead of keeping the money for herself.

That justice is indeed blind was proven when the court approved the injunction against Doc. It ordered him not to harm, harass, abuse or molest Virginia anywhere, at any time, but said he could remain in the house and pay for family expenses, but he didn't have to pay support to Virginia.

Doc's mind seemed to have been muddled at the time. Whether he still loved her, or was brainwashed into thinking he did, Doc wanted to hold the family together. Virginia added to his guilt by telling him he was destroying her and the children. During this time, Virginia was talking with Doc while they were driving, and became so distraught that she attempted to throw herself out of the car. At least that's how it looked to Doc.

In spite of everything, Doc was torn between saving his marriage or his career. He met with Doran to enter a divorce suit but, just days later, he personally filed a motion to dissolve Virginia's injunctions against him so they could resume their marriage ties.

In his petition to dissolve the injunctions, Doc answered all of Virginia's charges against him and leveled his own accusations against her. Not once had he harmed Virginia, he said, and explained that her admission to Fish Memorial Hospital in New Smyrna Beach was "false and without factual foundation whatsoever."

The third item in Doc's petition was more eloquent for what it didn't say than what he wrote. Although he had not been ordered to leave the house, Doc wrote, he moved out because he was afraid to stay there. He didn't elaborate on the reasons for his fear, but told the court he wanted to return home now, provide for the children, and try to reconcile the differences between himself and Virginia. Doc told the court it should order Virginia to seek counseling, and volunteered to do the same.

Since Doc had trouble with Virginia even before they were married, was aware of her affairs and of her unnatural closeness with Jason, why would he want to reconcile? For whatever reasons, Doc still loved his wife, Jason, Jessica, and Benjamin. Furthermore, Virginia informed him she wanted to have another baby. Perhaps he thought that would change things. In his petition, Doc noted that he was concerned about Virginia's mental and physical health, and her activities convinced him she needed physical and mental evaluation and care. By this point, Doc seemed so psychologically dominated that he needed help to save his own sanity, if not his life.

The court dismissed Virginia's injunctions against Doc without prejudice, following Doc's petition, and Virginia consented after the court acquiesced to her demand that she didn't need psychiatric counseling.

Virginia stopped Doc's attempt to get a divorce without even consulting a lawyer.

Doc contacted Doran and told him to withdraw the

petition for dissolution of the marriage because they had reconciled. Doran had experience with divorces, and knew that reconciliations were sometimes temporary. More often than not, the person who filed for the divorce would return in a few months to pursue it once again.

"When . . . somebody comes in and says, 'I've reconciled,' what you don't do is immediately file a voluntary dismissal," Doran said, "because what you end up doing six months later is repaying the filing fee . . . because the reconciliation doesn't work . . . and if you've dumped it, then you have to start over from scratch."

For this reason, Doran filed the petition for dissolution of marriage, which was pre-dated March 8, 1989. If Doc changed his mind later, the work would already be done; and if not, the petition would simply die. Ironically, the same date Doran filed for Doc's divorce was the same day Karn received a letter from Virginia, telling him their affair was over.

In view of Virginia's monumental personality flaws, it's almost inconceivable that Doc would try to keep his marriage intact. But Doran said "it was definitely his idea" to reconcile with Virginia. The petition for divorce, filed by Doran, shows that Doc knew Virginia was a habitual liar, and was aware of her past criminal activities, by the time he filed for divorce. Doran's petition depicted Virginia as an unfit mother, drug user, and habitual criminal.

Doc asked for sole custody of the children because

Virginia was a bad influence whose criminal activities could lead to her imprisonment. Virginia was addicted to mind-altering drugs and had established a "pattern of immoral and illegal conduct," the petition said. What's more, she had shown herself to be suicidal by trying to jump out of a moving automobile.

The trouble Virginia had caused Doc with the DPR was mentioned, including Virginia's "extreme and aberrant drug use," and her forging his signature on prescriptions for mind-altering drugs and narcotics that she hid before Doc could find them. Doc said Virginia lied constantly, told patients she was "a doctor, model, licensed contractor, multimillionaire and a financier."

In the petition, Doc stated he had just recently discovered Virginia had engaged in "a continuing pattern of criminal conduct, including theft, larceny, embezzlement, forgery and other white-collar crimes." She had used a number of aliases including Virginia Gail Matheny, Virginia Gail Mathis, Virginia Gail Antley, Virginia Gail Serry, Virginia Gail Ferry and Virginia Gail Surrey.

If Doc had followed through and received a divorce, it would have saved his life. People wondered why he reconciled with Virginia when he knew about her past, and her present behavior. Ironically, Doc's petition to end the injunctions Virginia had against him was approved on March 8, just one day after the divorce papers were filed. The divorce petition died of neglect, and the marriage stumbled fitfully along with screaming fights and arguments that grew worse instead of better. Doc still faced the disgrace of losing his license and livelihood, and Virginia had come perilously close to losing her source of money and drugs. Lying as usual, Virginia made light of the divorce papers Doc had filed.

"We were separated for a little while," she told *Pauline Beecher,* "but we never intended to get a divorce."

Doc wasn't happy with his life. His marriage was a sham, he wasn't thinking clearly, and the few contacts he had with his parents ended in arguments, all of which had been initiated by Virginia's clandestine maneuvers.

Virginia had saved the marriage, and more importantly, the things it represented, by the skin of her teeth. It had been a major scare. Badly jolted, Virginia engaged in a frenzy of activity to become independently wealthy, while she awaited the birth of her fourth child.

Eight

David Larzelere was born on November 18, 1989, and left the hospital to live in the turbulent home of his parents. The arguments between Doc and Virginia continued to erupt with the fierceness of a Florida thunderstorm.

Never one to pay much attention to her family, except for Jason, Virginia hired a new nanny to care for Benjamin and David. The nanny was Juanita Washington, who was amazed when Virginia gave her money to make a down payment on a house.

Life continued in fits and starts and, in the late spring of 1990, Virginia was looking for a part-time replacement for a clerk at the dental office. At this time Kristen Palmieri, the only daughter of a fiercely devoted Italian family, was attending college and working for Kelly Temporary Services. Kris had been a student at Embry Riddle Aeronautical Institute in Daytona Beach, studying to be an aeronautical engineer or, as her mother put it, a "space monkey." Attending Embry Riddle was not without its problems. It was time consuming in addition to being expensive. Kris lived with her parents in Kissimmee, making a round-trip commute of more than one hundred miles on days she attended classes.

Deciding not to carry the workload, Kris put her slide rule away after a year and transferred to Daytona Beach Community College to enroll in the liberal arts program as a part-time student. She rented an apartment in Daytona Beach and, without the long commute, she found time to work with Kelly Temporary Services as a clerk/secretary. The arrangement allowed Kris to juggle her time between school and work.

When Virginia telephoned Kelly for help, Kris reported for duty at Doc's office. "It was a mess," Kris said. "There were boxes stacked all over the place."

"It's just too crazy and mixed-up, isn't it?" Virginia said. "The other girl just got up and left." She neglected to add that she had fired A.J. because she refused to forge Doc's signature on inflated patient billings and drug prescriptions.

On her first day at work, Kris overheard Virginia tell another temporary worker that Kris wouldn't work out because she knew nothing about dentistry or medical office management.

"I can do it," Kris told Virginia. "I can learn about teeth."

"If you think you can do it," Virginia said, "you can stay."

Soon afterward, Kris performed her job so well

that Virginia asked her to leave Kelly and work only for her. Kris agreed after being assured her hours would be flexible enough so she could still attend school.

Everything about Virginia initially shocked Kris, even though she was twenty-two and was somewhat worldly wise. Virginia flirted with men in Doc's presence, causing Kris to think of her as something of a sleaze.

The clothing Virginia wore at the office, consisting of dresses and blouses that revealed a great deal of leg and bosom, seemed scandalous to Kris. It was obvious to Kris that Virginia liked to show off her body and draw the admiration of men.

"Her clothing would have been suitable for a nightclub," Kris said, "but not for a place of business. Maybe she thought those kinds of clothes helped sell teeth."

Clearly, Virginia's flirting upset Doc, which seemed to please Virginia. But when Doc lost his composure, Virginia would act surprised that he thought she had done anything wrong.

Doc impressed Kris as a calm, peaceable person, and that Virginia knew exactly which buttons to push to make him angry and suspicious. Certainly, he had good reason not to trust his wife, and was constantly trying to figure out what schemes she was involved in, and which men she was having affairs with.

The incessant arguing and intrigue grated on Kris's nerves. At first, she thought it was all Doc's fault, since he was the one who did most of the screaming and yelling, but then she noticed it was always Virginia who planted the seeds of discontent. Nevertheless, Virginia portrayed herself as an innocent victim who didn't understand why her husband was so touchy.

The usual scenario was for Virginia to do something that made Doc blow up, then she retaliated by yelling and screaming at him. It went on day after day. They argued because Virginia was hardly ever at home, frequently didn't show up at the office without notice, and because Doc thought she was neglecting the children. The investigation by the DPR caused strife, as did the fact that Virginia would disappear for a week at a time without telling Doc where she was.

It was no secret to Doc, the children, or Kris that Virginia had regular affairs. She flirted with almost every man she met, and she couldn't seem to have enough men. Kris understood why Doc lost his temper.

"If normal people love someone and you know something aggravates them, you're going to try and not do it," Kris said. "You're going to try and eliminate everything that's going to agitate the marriage. Virginia would just do it more and more and more. I mean if you marry someone, and you love someone, you're not going to be worried about what they're doing behind your back for twenty-four hours."

Kris was introduced to Jason, who came into the dental office regularly to deliver supplies, or say hello to his mother.

When Kris first met Jason, she thought he was "a young, naive pain in the ass." He stopped by her apartment without being invited, asked her to go out, and generally disrupted her life. She didn't want to be bothered by him, but she was reluctant to ruffle the feathers of her boss's son. Jason started asking Kris for dates in the summer of 1990, and she finally accepted, thinking, "It won't kill me to be nice to him."

As the months passed, Kris became more deeply involved in family affairs. Virginia, Jason, and Doc all confided in her, and the arguments at the office seemed only to touch the surface of the trouble in the Larzelere family. Doc told Kris he loved Virginia, but didn't trust her.

According to Kris's sworn statement, Jason confided that he was a drug dealer, and told Kris he made trips to Indiana, Texas, New York and Miami to buy and sell. One day, Virginia asked Kris to receive a Federal Express package that Jason was sending to Edgewater.

"I don't want anybody else to receive it," Virginia said. "Don't open it and don't let anyone else open it."

Later Kris asked Jason what was in the package. "Drugs," he said. "I had to mail them because I had no other way of getting them home. I didn't want to have them in my car."

Kris didn't know what kinds of drugs were in the package, if any. But she suspected they were illegal because she knew he was a user. Kris told the police on various occasions that she saw Jason use cocaine and other drugs, including Quaaludes, Valium, and various amphetamines and barbiturates.

As for Virginia, Kris found herself both fascinated and terrified by the older woman. Even today, there is confusion as to how Kris felt about Virginia in the beginning, with some contradictions coming from Kris's own lips. One version is that she considered Virginia a generous friend, but months later, she couldn't stand the woman because of her flirtations and lies.

Whatever the situation was, within a few months after going to work at the dental practice, Kris helped Virginia delude Doc about Virginia's lovers by lying for her. She was also involved in some of Virginia's unending intrigue, and at least part of the time, she was a willing participant. Before she knew it, Kris felt like a puppet, with Virginia pulling her strings.

Doc and Virginia not only argued about Virginia's love affairs, he complained also about the illegal billings and the prescription drugs Virginia ordered by forging his name. But despite Doc's objections and the ongoing DPR investigation, Virginia continued her illegal activities.

When cash came into the office, Virginia told Kris, "Don't give the cash to Doc. Make sure it comes to me." Virginia put the cash in her purse and never recorded it in the financial ledger. Kris sometimes sat beside Virginia when she completed the bank deposit slips. Virginia not only kept all of the cash, but she diverted thousands of dollars in checks away from Doc's business account.

In November 1990, either Doc or Virginia approached Kris with an unusual proposition. Kris said it was Doc who suggested a new arrangement, even though it gave Virginia more control over Kris's life.

According to Kris, Doc said, "Virginia needs help at home. We've got a lot of room. Why don't you come and live with us? You wouldn't have to drive so far and you could work for your room and board."

Kris was interested, but said, "I'll have to clear it with my dad first."

Although Kris was twenty-two, her father wielded considerable influence over her, and she needed his consent. He didn't know either Virginia or Doc. Virginia arranged a dinner at her house where Kris's parents met Doc, Virginia, David and Benjamin.

The gathering was a success and Kris's father gave her permission to move into the Larzelere home.

Kris spent Christmas with her parents, then moved into a private room at the Larzelere home just before the end of 1990. She found a terribly dysfunctional family. The house was a mess, and Kris considered Virginia "a major slob" who paid little attention to David, Benjamin, or Jessica. The arguments between Doc and Virginia were even more intense at home than at the office. Often, Kris found herself in the middle of these arguments and, because she was manipulated by Virginia, took her side. Doc fired her three times from the dental office and told her to pack up her things and leave the house, but Virginia countermanded him each time, and she was clearly the boss.

Kris was paid $300 a week for part-time work, but neither Virginia or Doc explained what her duties were. She ran errands for Virginia, both at Edgewater and DeLand, but Doc never gave her instructions. Kris lived at the house free, earned $300 a week, and continued to attend college.

Shortly after Kris moved into the Larzelere home, Virginia made the down payment on a 1987 Toyota for Kris after her blue 1980 Chevrolet Malibu conked out. Doc took the Toyota for a test drive and didn't like the way the brakes squealed.

"Take it back and have them make repairs," he said. I don't want you driving anything that's not safe."

Even after repairs, Doc wasn't satisfied.

"Take it back and get a new one," he told Virginia.

The car Kris ended up owning was a brand new white 1990 Toyota Celica. Virginia equipped it with a mobile telephone and paid the monthly bill, explaining that "we should always be in touch."

By the time Kris started to live at the Larzelere home, Jason had a house in Orlando that Virginia was renting. Jason showed up frequently in DeLand, or at the dental office in Edgewater to deliver medical supplies he picked up in Orlando. Jason didn't see much of Doc, but during the times he did, Kris said, the softhearted dentist talked to his son about going fishing. "Doc always talked about going fishing," Kris said, "but he never did get to go."

Moving into the Larzelere home marked the beginning of a strange boss-employee relationship. Kris contributed to confusion that still exists as to whether or not she continued to be paid after the move. On different occasions Kris said she continued to earn a $300 weekly salary, but also said the salary was stopped, even though she ran errands at the house and worked two or three times a week at the dental office.

Instead of a salary, Kris said, Virginia paid all of

her expenses, including clothes and college tuition. "Virginia paid me under the table to do errands for her. Virginia was paying me to make phone calls for her. Virginia was paying me to go and pick up prescriptions for her, to go to the office and do paperwork for her." Sometimes Virginia withheld money, forcing Kris to ask for cash.

Kris hated to ask Virginia for money. "She would make me feel like I owed her a favor."

Usually that meant doing something behind Doc's back. On several occasions, Virginia sent Kris to a pawn shop to get cash for gold coins Doc didn't know she had. The coins were Walking Liberty commemorative pieces worth about $400 each, depending on the fluctuating value of gold. When Kris needed money and borrowed from Virginia, her favors included signing fraudulent papers, lying to Doc about something, and "being nice" to certain male patients.

One patient Virginia wanted Kris to be nice to was Ted Goodman, a man who was old enough to be her father . . . and then some. Goodman, who lived on the shady side of the law, not only had bad teeth; he had terminal cancer. When Kris met him in 1990, he told her he had only a few months to live.

"I want you to be nice to him," Virginia told Kris.

"The guy's a pain in the ass, excuse my French," Kris had said.

Goodman, a sometime dental patient, had been

bowled over by Kris when he arrived at the office to have a tooth filled. The thin, frenetic man, who had been diagnosed as a manic-depressive, had already been bedded by Virginia, who deftly guided his attentions toward Kris. Before long, Goodman was bringing dozens of flowers to the dental office and doing his best to win Kris's favor.

Jason teased Kris about the deluge of roses and other flowers that Goodman sent. Besides flowers, Goodman flattered Kris where patients in the waiting room could hear, telling her how lovely she was. Kris gritted her teeth, but Virginia encouraged Goodman to continue wooing his lady love, and told Kris she should give in to him.

Kris didn't like it. She clamped her jaw when Goodman told her she was gorgeous.

"You're young and you're beautiful," Goodman said.

Kris thought, *Yeah, and you're a deadbeat who's old enough to be my father.*

Doc didn't like Goodman turning his office into a courting room or his amorous overtures to Kris because it disrupted business. He mentioned it to Virginia once after Goodman left the office and there were no other patients within earshot. Virginia's response to him was, "Get off your lazy ass and go to work."

Kris's would-be lover showered her with expensive jewelry, which Kris said she threw away. But even though she claimed to reject Goodman's gifts, she accompanied him to expensive restaurants for lunch and dinner, where he invariably flashed big rolls of one-hundred dollar bills.

"I can make you happy for the rest of your life," he told Kris. "You don't know what I can offer you."

Kris was noncommittal and Goodman sensed her resistance.

Undeterred, Goodman asked Kris to accompany him on a weekend trip to West Palm Beach just before Christmas of 1990.

"Once you see the real me and what my friends are like, you'll like me," Goodman said. "You haven't seen the real me."

Kris procrastinated, but Virginia wanted Kris to go with Goodman. By this time, her influence was stronger than any other consideration. Her resistance overcome, Kris capitulated.

"I'll go with you and be with you this weekend," Kris told Goodman, "if you promise that if I don't like the 'real you,' you'll never bug me again."

"Agreed."

Kris gave several accounts of her involvement with Goodman and her weekend with him in West Palm Beach. The incidents she related are true but there was much more involved than she was initially willing to divulge.

Kris didn't like the world Goodman showed her in Palm Beach. It was filled with sleazy characters and the stench of marijuana smoke, which made her sick, because she was allergic to it. There were visits to sleazy bars, cheap motels, and encounters with weird characters. Goodman was about the weirdest of all.

All day Saturday, Goodman continued to hustle Kris from one place to another. He made constant telephone calls and took her from one bar or restaurant to another. Kris fought nausea brought on from the marijuana that surrounded Goodman and his friends like a gray, fuzzy aura.

Kris was sick when she returned to her hotel room, and still sick when she got out of bed the next morning. She telephoned Virginia.

"Virginia, I can't take this. Get me home. If my parents find out about this, I'm dead, and if I go home with this guy on the road he's gonna kill both of us because he keeps smoking."

"I didn't know he did that. Let me see if I can get you home."

In the meantime, Goodman was yelling at the desk clerk about something. Embarrassed, Kris put the phone down, picked up a glass of complimentary orange juice, and walked a few paces to distance herself from Goodman.

Later in the day, Goodman took her to a bar and Kris telephoned Virginia several times. Virginia informed Kris that she had reserved an airplane seat for her to fly home.

"Something's wrong with my parents," Kris told Goodman. "They got in touch with Virginia and now I have to go home."

"I'll get you home. We'll be home in two hours."

Kris said, "I'm not going anywhere with you stoned out of your mind in a car, trying to get to Kissimmee in two hours."

Goodman continued to argue with her when they left the bar to visit one of his friends. There was still time to kill before Kris's flight departed. But when it was time to leave for the airport, Goodman insisted he would drive her home.

"No," Kris said. "You either take me to the airport or I'm walking."

At the last minute, Goodman drove her to the airport and Kris caught her flight with only two minutes to spare. Everyone had already boarded when she got on the passenger ramp.

"You'll give me your answer Monday!" Goodman shouted.

"About wanting to go out with you? I think you know the answer now."

Kris's involvement didn't end there, according to her initial story, but the entire household seemed to be involved with Goodman in one way or another. Goodman continued to telephone Kris and ask for dates, which she refused. He asked, "Why don't you go out with me? What's wrong with me?" Kris's ardent pursuer wanted to talk to Virginia and Doc about dating Kris.

Once Goodman was arrested and Doc bailed him out of jail on an unspecified charge, then Goodman failed to appear in court.

"What happened to the bail money?" Kris asked Doc.

"He paid me back. As far as I'm concerned, I don't care what happens to him. They can lock him up."

The terminal disease that had afflicted Goodman claimed his life just a short time after Kris's trip with him to Palm Beach.

Nine

Although Doc and Virginia had agreed not to drink alcohol because it made their fights worse, alcohol had little part in the ongoing conflict. Virginia did stop drinking at home, and she rarely drank when she went out, even though she was usually on drugs. But when she did drink, it was as if there were no tomorrow. She drank VO whiskey and Coca-Cola, and it wasn't unusual for her to polish off half of a fifth of VO in one sitting.

Virginia always carried thousands of dollars in cash, with a stack of hundred dollar bills the size of a brick in her purse. She used the money to impress people. Jason carried thousands of dollars, too, which his mother gave him. Kris once saw Jason with twenty-thousand dollars in cash as walking around money. On the other hand, Doc was virtually penniless. He often borrowed five dollars from an employee to buy enough gasoline to drive home.

Doc's parents, and others, had noticed that Jason treated Benjamin more like a son than a brother. In a sworn statement to police, Kris said that Jessica and Jason had told her that Benjamin was not Doc's son, and Virginia hinted at it. Jessica was more direct, according to Kris's sworn statement, in which she recalled the following conversation:

"Do you think he looks like Doc?" she asked.

"He definitely doesn't look like your father," Kris said.

"Does he look like anybody familiar?"

"No."

"Benjamin isn't Daddy's son," Jessica said. "He is Jason's."

Kris was surprised, even though she knew the relationship between Jason and Virginia was unnaturally close. She didn't go behind Virginia's closed bedroom door when Jason and Virginia were in there together and wasn't sure what went on.

Jason doted on David as well and remarked on how different the little boys were from Jessica. When David did anything unusual, Jason glowed. He was particularly proud of David's strength.

"He's strong for his age," Jason said. "He's a brute."

"That's not from Virginia," Kris said.

"No, it's not from my mother and it's not from Norm, either."

Kris stared questioningly, and Jason said, "The

103

way my mother goes, you never know whose he is."

However, Jessica didn't seem particularly close to her little brothers, even though Jessica had to accept a great deal of responsibility for taking care of them. But by all accounts she gave them far more attention than Virginia did.

The relationship between Jason and Virginia was another matter, since they were more like friends than mother and son. Once Kris accompanied them to Victoria's Secret, a store that specializes in sexy bedroom apparel for women. Virginia wanted to buy something sexy to wear when she met her new lover.

"Who is he?" Kris asked.

"Never mind."

The outfit Virginia looked at consisted of a black bra and garter belt. She offered to buy a similar outfit for Kris, who refused. Kris was embarrassed, especially in front of Jason, who had asked her to marry him. Virginia was all for the marriage.

The saleswoman looked at Jason, shifted her gaze to Virginia, and said, "Oh, you must be the girlfriend." She smiled at them. "I know your exact bra size," the clerk told Virginia. "He buys things here all the time."

"That's my son," Virginia told the woman.

When they walked out of the store, Jason was flushed with anger.

"Why did you tell her I was your son?" he asked. "I told everybody there that I was buying that stuff for my girlfriend."

Kris thought it was kinky for Virginia to send Jason out to buy sexy underwear for her, but she was used to odd behavior between the two. One of the weirdest things Kris observed was that Jason dressed Virginia in the mornings, laying out his mother's clothes, and even helping Virginia put on her bras.

The problems between Doc and Jason were coming to a head, in part because of Jason's close relationship with his mother. Although Doc did his best for Jason, he could never overcome Jason's jealousy of him. Nothing Doc did diffused the hostility Jason had for him.

Kris was riding with Jason in his car in May of 1990 when he said, "I'm thinking about getting a gun. Can you help me?"

"I don't know how, and I don't want anything to do with it," Kris told him.

On several other occasions Kris told police Jason said, "I want to hire someone to kill Doc. My mother deserves better. I'm tired of her being hurt."

Jason also wanted to know if Kris had knowledge of any poisons or drugs that could kill someone, but go undetected in an autopsy. "I could make my father's death look like an overdose," he said.

When Jason graduated from high school, a horrendous argument erupted between Doc and Virginia. Virginia had mailed a typed letter to Doc's parents and sisters, telling them to stay out of Doc's life. She signed her husband's name, but it didn't fool anyone: they knew the letter was from Virginia, who had also written to them previously under her own name, telling them that Doc was abusing her and the children.

"She had this distinctive way of typing, using all capital letters," one of Doc's sisters said.

After the fight ended, Norm went to the garage to stare at a boat he had built. He was pale, shaken, and in emotional torment. In spite of everything, he loved Virginia, but he couldn't let things continue on such a destructive path. He loved Jessica, Benjamin, and David . . . and even Jason, but the emotional conflicts were tearing him apart. The fights with Virginia were becoming more frequent, more explosive, and Jason's physical attacks were fierce.

Jessica, who adored Doc, went to the garage to be with him. Then, fighting back tears, she returned to the house where Virginia was. Her mother looked up with brown eyes that blazed with anger.

"I can't stand your father," Virginia said. "I hate how he looks, how he acts, everything about him. I want to get rid of him."

Ten

A few months before he left the DeLand house in 1990, Jason was in an automobile accident. He took *Becky Smith* to his senior prom at Calvary Christian Academy in Ormond Beach, after picking her up in Altamonte Springs, several miles away. They returned to the house in DeLand where they remained until it was time to leave for the prom in Ormond Beach, a twenty-six mile distance.

There had been thunderstorms in Central Florida all day, but the weather had cleared before Jason left to pick up Becky. He drove her home without incident, and started back to DeLand about 3 A.M. Jason got off Interstate 4, for some unexplained reason, and was driving on U.S. 17 (known as "Bloody 17" because of the number of serious accidents that occur) when he saw amber warning lights flashing ahead of him.

Just as Jason saw the lights, he said that a shadow, possibly a dog, darted in front of the car. As he swerved to miss the dog, Jason said, he lost control of the car, plowed through the warnings, and hit a storm drainpipe.

Here, the story gets confusing. The Florida Highway Patrol said the accident wasn't serious, that the car was moving slowly when it hit the drainpipe. Jason remembered that a Florida State Trooper told him it looked as if he should have been able to regain control of the car and avoid an accident.

Later, Jason said he had been knocked unconscious when the accident occurred, and had remained in a coma for three to four hours at a hospital. Virginia immediately got into the act. Over the next several weeks, she shunted Jason from hospital to hospital, trying to find a doctor who would diagnose him as having suffered disabling motor trauma. At least four hospitals refused to give such a diagnosis. Undeterred, Virginia acquired medicine used to control the epileptic seizures Jason said he was experiencing and started medicating him. Both Virginia and Jason said the epilepsy was caused by a blow to the head he had suffered in the accident.

According to Jason, Doc worried more about him than his mother did. Furious battles took place between Doc, Virginia and Jason over Jason's care. Jason described the aftermath of his accident as a time of closeness with his adoptive father.

Doc, Jason said, spent a great deal of time with

him planning a fishing trip, which would include Benjamin and David, who was not yet two years old. "We were going to go on a fishing trip because Dad and I haven't been fishing together in a year and a half or so," Jason said. He also said he and Doc formed an alliance against his mother. Virginia, he said, wanted Doc to set an 11 P.M. curfew for him, while Doc successfully pointed out that Jason was old enough to stay out later. Doc's decision was accepted, Jason said, because Virginia rarely disputed Doc's authority. Given the history of hostility and jealousy in the Larzelere household Jason's story seems highly unlikely.

Jason said his epileptic seizures were not frequent at first, but accelerated over the passing months. It was Doc, Jason said, who demanded that he be admitted to Shands Hospital, which is affiliated with the University of Florida School of Medicine, for more extensive tests.

When Jason was released, with no diagnosis for epilepsy, Virginia continued to dose him with Phenobarbital, Mycillin and Dilantin, supposedly to control the seizures, without Doc's knowledge. The medication didn't work, Jason said, even when he took Dilantin intravenously, and the seizures became more frequent. Jason blamed the failure of the medicine to stop the seizures on the potency of his immune system, which he inherited from his great-grandfather, a Cherokee Indian, Virginia's

110

mythical grandfather in charge of the make-believe oil wells on the mythical reservation.

"At first, I couldn't even walk," Jason said. "I had to have physical therapy and nurses."

Virginia admitted Jason to the Peninsula Medical Clinic in Ormond Beach for additional tests. While he was there, Kris visited him and Jason admitted that he wasn't taking his medication. He became angry when Kris told him he should.

"I don't need it!" he yelled. "I'm not an epileptic. I'm not sick. It's just for the insurance."

Phil Langston's living room at his home in New Smyrna Beach, just south of Edgewater, was a riot of living color. *Literally.* A dealer of parrots, Langston always had a dozen or so birds in his house, as well as an aviary outside, while he waited for the best market to sell them. From his physical appearance, Langston appeared more suited to wrestling alligators than dealing in birds. He was 6 ft. 6 in. tall, ruggedly handsome with wide shoulders, a thick chest, and slim waist.

Even giants have to take care of their teeth, and Langston was no exception. Edgewater was just a short drive from New Smyrna Beach, and Langston's dentist was Dr. Norman Larzelere. Over the course of Langston's visits, Virginia became especially friendly with him. Langston didn't know Virginia was attracted to tall men.

"She just seemed like a nice, friendly lady,"

111

Langston said. "We became very good friends."

In late May of 1990, Virginia told Langston that Jason suffered epileptic seizures, following an automobile accident, and was paralyzed. Virginia was suing an insurance company for damages, she said, and was pursuing it vigorously. Langston was surprised when, following an appointment to have his teeth polished, Virginia asked him to take Jason to a hospital and then bring him home. Jason was so debilitated, she told Langston, that he couldn't walk, and even needed help getting dressed.

Langston agreed, picked Jason up like a baby, plopped him in a wheelchair, wheeled him outside, put him inside the car, and folded the wheelchair and put it in the trunk. He repeated the process when he took Jason home, where Virginia was waiting for him. Doc wasn't there.

Virginia made an overt play for Langston's sexual company: She offered him $1,000 to go to bed with her. Langston, who thought Virginia had been coming on to him, agreed. From then on, Virginia paid the big man $1,000 each time they had sex. But after that first time, Virginia started to criticize her husband, claiming he was bisexual, and was trying to have her killed.

"Come on, Doc's not that way," said Langston, who liked Virginia's husband.

Virginia insisted that Doc had hired people to run her car off the road, shoot at her, and try to break into the house, all with the intent to kill her.

"He wants to kill me because I'm a millionaire and he wants my money," Virginia said.

Langston often had free time between visits to Managua, Nicaragua, where he bought his parrots. Once the birds were imported to the United States, they were in quarantine for three months. With this time on his hands, Langston agreed to Virginia's request to help take care of Jason and aid in his physical therapy.

"I'm hoping against hope that he'll be able to walk again," Virginia said.

For weeks Langston went about his unpaid job without complaint. He dressed and undressed Jason as if caring for a baby, carried him to and from the wheelchair, and drove him to his various appointments. To help Jason regain the use of his legs, Langston had Jason grasp one of his massive arms for support, and take feeble, uncertain steps. Frequently, Jason staggered and Langston had to grab him so he wouldn't fall.

During this time, Langston was growing sick of Virginia, even though she spent thousands of dollars on him, in addition to the fee she paid him for sex.

"She created so much turmoil that you just couldn't stand to be around her," he said. "Even at one thousand dollars a time, it wasn't worth it."

Ominous and sinister overtones developed in

what Langston considered nothing more than a dalliance, except for his sincere desire to help Jason recover. Sometimes Virginia telephoned Doc from Langston's house and screamed vicious insults at him. Often she was so angry that she lost complete control.

"I hate you!" she screamed into the phone. "I wish you were dead!"

When she hung up, Langston said, "You don't mean that."

"Yes I do. I hate him and I wish he was dead."

Langston didn't take her seriously at first, but he was beginning to think that Virginia was "crazy-mean." She told one lie after another, and was unable to keep them straight. Still he continued as Jason's nursemaid and Virginia's lover.

The affair with Langston followed the basic pattern as the one Virginia had with Norman Karn, the tall Californian. She convinced Langston she was a millionaire and Doc wanted to kill her so that he would inherit her fortune. Urgent telephone calls from Virginia were similar in content.

"Someone ran me off the road," she told Langston on a late night telephone call. "It's Norman trying to have me killed."

But the next day, when Langston examined the car, there were no dents or scratches to indicate it had been forced off the road.

Another time she telephoned to say someone

had driven up beside her car and fired guns at her.

There were no bullet holes in the car when Langston examined it.

This woman is seriously weird, Langston thought.

On yet another occasion, Virginia telephoned Langston late at night and told him someone was trying to break into the house. She asked him to help. After telling her to call the police, Langston went to Virginia's aid, carrying a loaded shotgun, but found no sign of an intruder.

It was only later that Langston realized he had walked into a potentially life-threatening situation. What if Doc had been home and saw him approaching in the darkness carrying a shotgun?

Yet Virginia maintained a grip on Langston, largely because of her free-spending ways. Virginia lavished gifts and money on Langston, even more freely than she had on Karn. She bought him clothing and expensive jewelry during their time together, which amounted to $70,000 in just three months.

Throughout the short relationship, Virginia continued vicious attacks on her husband that Langston overheard. Virginia, far from loving Doc, continually said she hated him. Langston began to believe Virginia was crazy, perhaps not in a clinical way, but she just didn't make sense to him. She seemed to be a pathological liar, and was so hard to please that she was constantly replacing babysitters to stay with David and Benjamin when she went out.

Langston thought Virginia changed babysitters the way most people change diapers.

"Virginia, maybe it's you," Langston told her once. "When you think everybody in the world's wrong, you've got to stop and ask yourself, 'Hey, maybe it's me.' "

Virginia didn't think the comment deserved a reply.

Even though Virginia had convinced Langston she was a millionaire, she confided to him that she was siphoning off Doc's money from the dental practice. She consistently flashed big stacks of one-hundred dollar bills. Langston asked her where she got the money. Virginia showed him bills from various businesses.

"He thinks he owes money to all of these people," she said.

"Doesn't he know you're taking this much money?"

"No," Virginia said. She drew his attention to the list. "See all of these people and their bills? He thinks he owes that money, but he doesn't. He writes the checks and I cash them."

Langston, by this time, believed little of what Virginia told him, and chalked it up as another lie. The thousands of dollars she carried and kept in her home were real enough, and it worried him because Langston thought it made her a prime target for robbery.

"If you're going to be carrying that much money, you need protection," he told her. "You need to have a gun in your purse."

Virginia agreed and Langston took her to New Smyrna's Shooter Supply where Virginia looked at various types of handguns. Virginia decided she wanted a .44 Magnum, the powerful gun used by "Dirty Harry," the character played by movie actor Clint Eastwood. When Langston told her that the weapon was too big for her, she balked at his criticism, but never bought the gun.

Throughout the affair, Virginia continually reiterated that she hated her husband and wanted to get rid of him. Langston frequently was present when she screamed at Doc over the telephone, telling him "I wish you were dead" and threatening to kill him.

After one fight with Doc, Virginia was with Langston in his car, parked outside his house.

"Do you know anybody who's a hit man?" she asked.

"No."

Then Virginia went into a rage, cursing Doc and calling him all kinds of names.

"I'd pay fifty thousand dollars to get rid of him," she said.

"Don't look at me," Langston said. "That's not my style."

"I was surprised that she asked me," Langston said later. "Big guys like me usually have the softest hearts because they don't have anything to prove. It's the little guys who like to be tough."

This was near the end of the affair and Langston was beginning to believe the whole purpose of Virginia's relationship with him was to maneuver him into killing Doc. The expensive gifts she bought Langston, and the offer to buy him a sports car that cost $200,000, he viewed as tests, seeing just how far he could be tempted into committing murder.

Virginia once asked Langston to marry him.

"It'll just be for two weeks," she said. "We'll get married in Reno. That way Doc can't get any of my money because I'll already be married."

The proposition made no sense to Langston and he refused. But even if Virginia wanted a legitimate marriage, he would say no because he didn't think he could stand to be around her for more than a few months, even part-time. Just having an affair with Virginia wore Langston down. He couldn't understand why she wasn't happy with her husband. She had a Mercedes, an expensive sports car, an airplane, jewelry, clothes, a nice house, and a seemingly endless supply of cash.

Besides that, being married to a dentist gave her access to prescription drugs, especially Valium, which she swallowed like candy. Virginia kept a bottle seven inches tall, filled with 10 milligram tablets of Valium, on a dresser in her bedroom. Langston saw it when they had sex at her house.

Playing nurse to Jason came to a sudden end less than a month after Langston agreed to help out. It happened when he took Jason grocery shopping. Langston drove to a store and, as usual, lifted Jason into the wheelchair, and took him inside. When they finished shopping, Langston picked Jason up and put him in the car. Langston was putting the wheelchair in the trunk when Jason suddenly bolted out of the car toward the store.

Jason ran to the entrance before he realized what he had done. He stopped in his tracks, slapped his forehead, turned toward the startled Langston, looked sheepish, and walked into the store. On his way back to the car, Jason trembled and stumbled.

"Oh shit," Jason said. "I blew it. Please don't tell mom."

"You little shit," Langston said. "You've been faking it."

Langston was disgusted. For weeks, he had changed Jason's underwear and socks, carried him everywhere, and treated him like the invalid he thought he was. When he knew Jason had been faking, Langston wanted to punch him.

"I'm not carrying you or wheeling you around anymore, son," Langston said. "If you want to go someplace or do something, you're going to walk."

When they got home, Langston told Virginia what had happened.

"Oh, I can't believe how much good you've done him!" Virginia said. "It's a miracle!"

Langston finally broke off the affair after three months. Shortly after that, Doc telephoned and left a message on Langston's answering machine, asking him to call back. When Langston did, Doc was almost in tears.

"What did you want?" Langston asked.

"It's too painful to talk about," Doc said. "I know you've been sleeping with my wife."

"Don't worry, that's over. That woman you're married to is insane."

"I know, she probably asked you to have me killed, didn't she?"

Langston said that was true and started to tell Doc about Virginia's plan in the past to have him killed by a man in California. Doc beat him to the punch.

"She tried to have me killed by somebody in California," Doc said. "She has a gun out there."

Dumbfounded, Langston listened as Doc explained that Virginia needed counseling, and how much he was afraid of her. As he listened, Langston thought there seemed to be no way out for Doc. He was afraid Virginia would have him killed if he divorced her and would have him killed if he didn't.

When the telephone conversation ended, Langston was glad Virginia was out of his life. Doc was obviously intimidated by Virginia, and Langston believed she was serious about having him killed. But he didn't notify the police. What could he tell them? It would be his word against Virginia's about a crime that hadn't even been committed, and then he might have to worry about being killed himself. He decided it wasn't any of his business and let it pass.

Doug Cook despised Virginia from the very start. A contract animal trainer, he was nearing forty, was a little stout, and had spent so much time with Langston's birds that he moved into Langston's house. Sharing Langston's house was advantageous to both men. Langston, who was a citizen of both the United States and Nicaragua, was often out of the country looking for birds, and Cook took care of the property when his boss was gone. On the plus side for Cook was the elimination of a commute to and from work.

Virginia came into Cook's life in June 1990 when she started visiting Langston's house, sometimes three times a day. Her visits were unpredictable; she would stay for a few hours on one visit and all day the next.

"She thought she was better than anybody," Cook said, adding that Virginia tried to make him feel inferior.

To Cook, there was never any doubt that Virginia wanted to have her husband killed. "It was all she ever talked about," he said. "She wanted to get rid of him. She would say it in general conversation with a room full of people."

On one occasion, Cook said Langston told him Virginia had offered him $5,000 to "hit" her husband, and that Langston had declined, saying "there is no way in hell that I'm going to kill another human being."

Cook's dislike of Virginia was abundantly reciprocated. She aggravated Cook by telling Langston he was stealing birds. More specifically, two birds every day. With each parrot selling for $600 that would have meant Cook was stealing $1,200 a day and, in a week, he would have stolen fourteen birds, something his boss would certainly notice. Langston just laughed at Virginia and told her he trusted Doug.

Infuriated with Cook, Virginia began telling his friends he had AIDS. The accusation angered Cook, who could not defend himself against the rumor, which delighted Virginia since that seemed to be her whole point. The animosity between Cook and Virginia heightened when Cook refused to buy Valium from her. Cook never doubted that, for some reason, Virginia was trying to get him in trouble with Langston. He didn't know why, but he considered Virginia a destructive force. Fortunately for Cook, Langston didn't believe any of Virginia's charges against him. In fact, they reinforced Langston's growing conviction that it was impossible to believe anything Virginia said.

In late August, Langston walked to his car and saw Virginia scrambling around inside Cook's vehicle. Virginia was startled when Langston peered inside.

"What in the hell are you doing, Ginny?" he asked.

"Looking for stolen birds," she replied.

Langston's expression darkened and he told Virginia to get off his property and never come back, then he stormed back into his house.

"I don't want that woman ever to set foot on this property again!" he told his small staff. "Use force to keep her out if you have to. Call the cops. I don't want anything more to do with that woman."

In late August, when Langston was still out of the country, Virginia telephoned to tell Cook she had made an arrangement to buy half of the business for $200,000. There would be no place for Cook, she said, once the transaction was completed.

Cook, who could hardly bear hearing Virginia's

voice, packed his bags and was ready to leave when Brian Booth, a casual laborer at Langston's operation, told him Langston had informed him Virginia was lying. There was no way Langston was going to get involved in a business arrangement with Virginia. Cook unpacked his bags and stayed on.

Eleven

In October, Jason said he needed a quiet place to recuperate, and Virginia rented him a place in Winter Park. But he'd lived there only a few weeks with Heather Fox, a friend whom Virginia called his nurse before his mother moved him alone into an expensive apartment in Orlando, which she furnished lavishly.

Jason, who was supposedly unable to walk, hit Orlando like a whirlwind, and started to party. Big time. At night, he partied at various night-clubs on Orange Blossom Trail, or OBT, a street which proves that whoever said you can't make a silk purse out of a sow's ear had never seen neon.

At night, the OBT is ablaze with colored lights in the shape of champagne glasses, female forms, and the words *Girls! Girls! Girls!* written in script. There are girls on the streets, ranging from teenagers with young faces and weary eyes, who have run away from home, to prostitutes who have grown old too soon, and use all the tricks in the book to land a john.

There are Yuppies with fresh faces, designer clothes and expensive cars who have money to spend and plenty of takers. Male and female hustlers cruise the street and wait inside bars where girls wearing only a swatch of cloth writhe suggestively around metal poles, in flashing strobe lights, or on tables while men tuck dollar bills in their G-strings.

Steven Heidle was a slim, blond, 19-year-old homosexual, who knew this world well. He had fake identification saying that he was twenty-one, and he used it to gain entrance to various bars, including The Big Bang, a popular nightclub on the OBT. Barnett Bank had fired Heidle for getting the names and Social Security numbers of large depositors and passing them on to a company affiliate that sold stocks and bonds. It wasn't illegal, but it was against company rules. At the time, Heidle lived with his mother, Patricia Ann Heidle, in the small town of DeBary, some twenty miles from Orlando.

Jason was at The Big Bang the night of October 27, 1990, and was introduced to Heidle by *Tim Richardson,* one of Heidle's friends and former lovers. Two things were immediately apparent to Heidle: Jason fell in love with him at first sight, and the guy was rolling in money.

The next day, Jason arrived at Heidle's house in DeBary with a word processor. At The Big Bang, Heidle had told Jason he was working to finish an assignment for one of his community college classes. Heidle was impressed that Jason had bought him such an expensive gift. Jason also sent flowers to Heidle, accompanied by cards that pledged his undying devotion.

"He was in love with me then," Heidle said.

Jason wanted Heidle to move into his apartment with him, and promised that he could have anything he wanted. Heidle would never again have to worry about money, Jason promised.

Heidle didn't know Virginia, Doc or Kris, but he heard about them often. Jason didn't like Doc and rarely spoke about him, but he talked constantly about Virginia, whom he described as a doctor, a contractor, and an heiress worth millions of dollars.

"He made her sound like this great, wonderful person," Heidle said. "He loves his mother to death. He worships the ground she walks on."

Heidle had a one-time sexual fling with Jason, but he spent a great deal of time at the apartment, and noticed that Virginia called several times a day to leave messages on Jason's answering machine. Jessica called several times, as well, but Doc didn't call once.

To Heidle, Jason was a welter of contradictions. "He could be so sweet, buying everyone drinks and dinner, and breakfast if they stayed out all night," Heidle said. "Then he would turn ugly."

Jason's radical mood swings were an enduring part of life for Heidle and the crowd that hovered around Jason for free food, drinks, and nights out on the town. Although Heidle never saw Jason use anything but prescription drugs, he believed those drugs accounted for Jason's erratic behavior. One moment Jason would be joking around with friends while he cooked dinner. The next instant, he would start screaming, throwing things, cursing them, and ordering them to leave.

Jason told Heidle he was an athlete before his automobile accident. Despite his assertion of disabling motor trauma and epileptic seizures, Jason walked without help, partied, and drove his car. Heidle never saw him have a seizure, but he was present one time when Jason seemed to have a problem.

Jason stopped and sat down on the floor at his apartment and said, "I'm in pain." He injected himself with Dilantin and slept the rest of the day. That same night, though, he was ready to party.

From the beginning, Jason warned Heidle his mother didn't like gay men, and he should be prepared for a very cold shoulder. That was exactly what Heidle received the first few times he met Virginia. She walked inside, didn't even look at him, said hello, then ignored him while she visited with Jason. This went on for weeks. Heidle was amused at Virginia's attitude toward homosexual men, and thought she obviously didn't know about Jason's sexual proclivities.

Only a month or so after Jason moved into the Orlando apartment, Virginia had rented a house for him. She hired a moving company to take the furnishings from the apartment to the house, but when they were delivered, no one was there. Virginia had taken Jason back to a hospital for tests in an attempt to prove he was epileptic. The movers just piled the items randomly around the house and left.

Heidle, unable to stand clutter, threw himself into the task of getting the house organized as a surprise for Jason when he returned from the hospital. It was a tough job, but Heidle was undeterred. He arranged furniture, organized the kitchen, put clothing in drawers, hung pictures, and had the house almost picture perfect when Virginia brought Jason home.

When Virginia walked into the house and saw what Heidle had done, her attitude toward him did a complete turnabout. She told him what he had done was wonderful, and she beamed at him, and couldn't compliment him enough, or express her gratitude adequately. After Virginia gave Heidle money for the work, she asked if he would stay in the house, keep it neat, and run errands for Jason. One of the most important jobs Virginia charged Heidle with, was to be Jason's chauffeur.

No mention was made of a salary, but Heidle wasn't concerned because Jason always had lots of cash. Heidle accepted the job, and although he had been hired to run errands for Jason, and keep the house neat, Virginia referred to him as Jason's nurse, a title that infuriated him.

"I don't administer medication and I don't have a nursing degree," Heidle said. "I was not Jason's nurse."

The job title of chauffeur didn't fit well, either, since Jason loved to drive, and wheeled about even though he was supposed to be totally disabled. Sometimes Jason refused to let Heidle drive as punishment when there were spats between himself, Heidle, and *Richardson*.

Heidle and *Richardson* had an off and on lover's relationship and Jason was jealous because he was in love with Heidle, and they had enjoyed one sexual encounter. It was what Heidle described as "kind of" a sexual relationship that occurred during one of his break-ups with *Richardson*. "Jason was right there, being a good friend," Heidle said, and that was when the sexual encounter took place. Then Heidle got back together with *Richardson*.

"He (Jason) would say, 'I'm so happy for you,'

but it was all bullshit," Heidle said. "I thought he was my friend . . . but he was trying to get at me again."

Back in DeLand, Kris wondered how Jason could afford a house and furniture, not to mention living expenses. The answer became somewhat clearer when Virginia had Kris make wire transfers to Jason's Orlando bank account. Virginia, in the meantime, wanted another car, a white Nissan 300ZX. Doc told Virginia that, if she bought the car, she should use her Mercedes sedan as a trade-in. Virginia agreed.

Instead, Virginia drove the Mercedes to Orlando and left it with Jason. Now, Jason not only had his own yellow 300ZX, but Virginia's Mercedes.

The free-spending ways of both Jason and Virginia caused Heidle to wonder where they got so much cash. Jason had so many hundred dollar bills he forgot what he did with them. He put hundred dollar bills under the floor mats in his cars and left them. More often than not, when Heidle took Jason's clothes to the cleaners, he found several hundred dollar bills in the pockets. Sometimes Jason let Heidle keep the found money and paid him an additional hundred dollars just for going to the cleaners.

Heidle had been around wealthy people before,

131

but he had never seen anyone who had as much cash as Virginia and Jason. Their life-style was lavish, too, and Heidle didn't think a dentist earned enough to pay for a sixty thousand dollar Mercedes, two ninety thousand dollar sports cars, a Suburban, Jeep, airplane, and several boats.

According to Heidle, Jason, who liked having others look up to him, first boasted about being a major drug dealer who sold cocaine, and said, "the reason I left home is because I had too much money to stay there."

Heidle heard that Doc had kicked Jason out because of their fights, and mentioned it.

"No, he found one of my briefcases with twenty-five thousand dollars in it," Jason said. "We both thought I should be on my own."

Referring to all of the cash Jason and Virginia had, Heidle asked, "Where does all of this money come from? Is it all drug money?"

"Drugs are too well publicized now," Jason replied. "There's more money in guns."

But Jason was inconsistent with his stories about dealing in drugs. Although Jason claimed to make more money in guns, Heidle recalled that he talked constantly about being a dealer. Sometimes he would be specific about his activities, as when he told several friends he was going to Indiana to establish a pipeline for the hallucinogen LSD, because it would bring a higher price up north.

Whether the trip had to do with drugs or not, Jason drove to Indiana in November, ordering Heidle to call him periodically on his car telephone so he wouldn't fall asleep at the wheel. Jason told Heidle he was going to see a girl named Heather. The trip made Heidle nervous and he was careful not to ask for details. The less he knew, the better.

Both Kris and Heidle had told police that by November, although neither wanted to admit it, they had come to the conclusion that Virginia and Jason had made sinister plans.

Virginia had bought Kris's Toyota and was co-owner on the title. In November she wanted to change things.

"You have to get another car," Virginia said. "I don't want this in both our names."

"I can't afford to buy a new car," Kris replied.

But Virginia was not to be deterred. She insisted, and found another car for Kris that required a trade in, plus a five thousand dollar down payment.

"Virginia, I can't afford this," Kris said.

"I don't want you to have a car in my name," Virginia replied, and paid the five thousand dollars.

Doc knew nothing about the transaction.

Virginia began a campaign to make the police

133

in Edgewater and DeLand believe that the lives of herself and her family were endangered. Doc, it seemed, was particularly at risk. An extraordinary number of complaints were received by both police departments, with Virginia charging harassment and threats.

Virginia reported intruders on the grounds around the house at night. She said people tried to break into the house and the dental office. Virginia assailed one of Doc's women patients in front of witnesses and accused her of threatening her husband because Doc wouldn't divorce Virginia.

In DeLand, Jessica opened the refrigerator door and recoiled in horror when she saw the bloody heads of her kittens lined up on a shelf and looking out at her with dead eyes. Jessica was certain Jason had killed them and chopped off their heads. It was a horrible blow to the teenage girl.

"They were really smart cats," Jessica said. "They would only come to certain people they knew. I think my mother called them to her and that Jason killed them and cut their heads off."

Jessica said when her mother looked into the refrigerator, she discovered the heads were placed on a copy of the petition for divorce that Doc had filed in 1989. Virginia fired off an angry letter, accusing Theodore Doran, who had represented Doc in the earlier divorce proceedings, of killing the kittens and putting their heads in the refrigerator to frighten her. She gave no logical reason as to why Doran would do such a thing.

Not long after the heads of the kittens were found, a dead possum was discovered at the front door to the dental building in Edgewater. The animal's throat had been slit and a knife had been plunged through the body and left there. Jessica said this was more of Jason's work, although Virginia presented it as concrete evidence that someone was out to kill her husband.

The complaints about intruders, the severed kitten heads, and the dead possum, police believe, were part of Virginia's master plan to make police think Doc faced death threats from several unknown sources.

Later, when Detective Gamell asked Jessica about the dead possum, she said, "Jason did that. They were trying to stage it to look like . . . a threat. . . ."

The pressure mounted on Doc. He knew that Virginia had tried to hire yet another person to kill him. Yet, although he was squeezed and frightened, Doc felt that, as Virginia's husband, he had a responsibility for getting psychiatric help for her. However, she refused to get counseling.

Not long after the incidents with the kittens and possum, Doc and Virginia agreed that Jessica should be sent away from the turmoil at home. The strain at home was affecting every aspect of the girl's life. Virginia was away a lot, but even when she was home, she virtually ignored Jessica, David, and Benjamin. Doc thought Jessica would be fine if Virginia provided a nurturing environment, but Virginia wanted to send her to a boarding school. Eventually, Jessica ended up staying with Virginia's sister, Jeanette Atkinson, in Lake Wales, as she had on previous occasions.

Jessica had developed a crush on Heidle, who pretended he wasn't gay, so he wouldn't hurt her feelings. She wanted to date him but Heidle made excuses, saying she was too young. The teenager told him her life was pretty bleak. "I know from talking with Jessica that she's been pawned off on her own for many years," Heidle said. "Every time her mother goes in search of a new man, or goes on a rampage, or another affair or something like that. She (Jessica) was contemplating suicide."

The teenager confided in Heidle during her telephone calls. "She told me that (Jason slept with Virginia) and that's when I about got sick," Heidle told police. "Because she (Jessica) told me that she had heard that David, the youngest, was actually Jason's child. Until Jessica told me that, I knew they were weird, but I didn't think they were that kind of weird. When Jessica told me that, I just about hung up on her."

Equally incredible and disgusting to Heidle was that Jason told him that he and Virginia did cocaine together.

"You do coke with your mother?" Heidle asked, astonished.

He didn't believe it until Virginia was leaving after a visit to Orlando, and handed Jason a small, brown bottle.

"I have to drive fast and I don't want to get stopped and have this in the car," she said.

When Virginia left, Heidle asked, "What's that?"

"Cocaine," Jason said.

Heidle noticed that Jason carried a ring with a large number of keys on it, in addition to the chain with the keys to the house, the Mercedes and the Nissan 300 ZX.

"What are these?" Heidle asked one day.

"Those are my work keys."

"What does that mean?"

"When I have to do things for my mother, those are the keys to all of our storage houses."

According to Kris, Virginia kept hundreds of files on past employees, paychecks, bankruptcies, insurance papers, properties they owned, the V-LAR Construction Company, lawyers, and medical bills. The file boxes were kept in the dental offices, at the house, Jason's house, and in rental storage warehouses.

In late November, Jason started to shop for a

Japanese sports car that cost almost $100,000. It was far too extravagant, so far as Heidle was concerned.

"It's nice that at age eighteen you have a $30,000 300 ZX," Heidle said. "This is a $99,000 car. You're not that rich."

"Around March, I'm gonna be coming into some money," Jason replied.

Twelve

Virginia initiated a frenzy of activity in late February of 1991. Doc apparently was so psychologically disoriented that he didn't know how to help himself. In fact, he was still trying to figure out a way to get counseling for Virginia and to keep the family together.

On a yellow legal pad, he started to sort out his thoughts. *How far must a man go to protect his wife?* he'd written, but wouldn't find the answer. If he had, it might have saved his life.

The arguments with Virginia, and his knowledge that she had attempted to have him killed, increased the pressure until Doc was at the point of emotional explosion. For almost five years he had been isolated from his friends and family, was fed lies and disinformation, until he didn't know what to do about Virginia. Frightened and nervous, Doc, who had never smoked before, became a chain-smoker. Virginia, although working busily on various schemes, was as calm as her personality and mood altering drugs allowed her to be.

Virginia wanted to be rid of Doc, and her plans with Norman Karn, Ron Hayden, Ted Goodman, and Phil Langston to have Doc killed had not worked out for her. By now, both Heidle and Kris had some knowledge of the plans to kill Doc, but claimed they didn't believe Virginia and Jason were serious. However, they said later that they didn't go to the police because they were afraid Virginia would have them killed.

During the last week of February, 1991, Virginia told Kris to move out of the house in DeLand for awhile.

"Don't go home," she said. "Find someplace else to sleep."

"Why not?"

"Just don't."

Kris alternated between staying with a friend and her parents. The involuntary gypsy life Kris found herself in didn't keep her from going to De-Land occasionally. Having been given such short notice, all of her clothing and personal belongings were still in the Larzelere house. Every few days, Kris went there to pick up things she needed. Although Kris was temporarily banished from the house, the edict didn't apply to the office, where she still showed up for work. Virginia never explained why she had banned Kris from the house.

In late February, Kris stole one of Virginia's Walking Liberty gold coins and hocked it at The House of Gold in Edgewater. Virginia confronted her about the theft and Kris confessed. Kris wasn't fired, but Virginia, having rescinded her exile from the house, ordered her to stay away from the office.

This time there was a turnabout in the way things usually worked: Kris said Doc telephoned her in DeLand.

"It's okay, you can come back to the office," he told her.

Events in Orlando, with Jason and Heidle, accelerated with sinister intent. Jason held a cocaine party and Heidle saw one of the young men in Jason's bedroom clowning around with a shotgun.

"Put that thing down!" Heidle said.

On another occasion, Heidle found a .45 caliber semiautomatic pistol under a pillow, when he made Jason's bed.

Heidle's grandfather died on March 3 in Massachusetts, but he didn't receive the news until March 5. Then it came to him in a roundabout way. Heidle's mother, Patricia Ann, was in Massachusetts already, and had several telephone numbers to call if she needed to reach her son. There was no answer at the first number, but she reached Jason when she tried the second one.

"You've got to get hold of Steven, because he needs to come up," she said.

Jason drove to Patricia Ann's house in DeBary,

where Heidle sometimes lived with his mother, but Heidle wasn't there. The two young men had scheduled a previous meeting at the DeBary house for 11 A.M., and Heidle was racing to get there on time. From past experience, Heidle knew Jason was too impatient to wait for people who were even a minute late, so he was surprised when he drove up at about 12:30 P.M. and saw Jason waiting outside for him.

Instead of being angry, Jason, who hadn't been pleasant to Heidle for a while, hugged him. Heidle thought that was strange, and wondered why Jason was being so nice.

"There's something I have to tell you," Jason said, then gave him the news about his grandfather's death.

Uncharacteristically, Jason, never one to do menial labor or wait patiently, had washed the deck, the patio furniture, and cleaned the pool filters while he waited for Heidle. Heidle went inside, lit a cigarette, and wept while Jason sat in his car, using his mobile phone to get Heidle a ticket on the next flight. Jason even packed for the trip, while Heidle sat and braced himself with a drink. Even through his grief, Heidle was surprised at Jason's thoughtfulness.

Jason drove Heidle to the airport to catch the next available flight. Heidle returned from Massachusetts late on Thursday, March 7, and Jason spent that night with him at Patricia Ann's house.

They stayed up late to watch television, then went to a doughnut shop. When they returned, Virginia telephoned to tell Jason he was stupid for driving around DeLand the previous night, when he was supposed to be in Orlando with people who could verify it.

Early in the next morning of Friday, March 8, Jason and Heidle drove to the storage units Virginia rented in DeLand. The units were filled with filing boxes. Jason took life insurance policies on Doc out of a filing box, and Heidle's attention was caught by one policy for $1.5 million. All total, Heidle said he saw $3 million dollars in life insurance on Dr. Norman Larzelere.

"God, is he worth that much?"

Jason grinned and said, "Well, he won't be around much longer."

"What's going on?" Heidle asked.

Jason grinned. "Nothing's going to happen. I'm just getting some files together for my mom."

"Whatever it is, I don't want to know."

"Don't worry."

It was mid-morning when Jason and Heidle arrived back in DeBary, driving separate cars. Heidle drove his mother's gray Nissan Maxima and Jason followed in his yellow Nissan XZ. Jason parked the sports car, which contained the files he had taken from the storage units, in the garage at Patricia Ann's house. At 10 A.M. Jason said he was taking Patricia Ann's Maxima to be detailed, and recited a list of things for Heidle to do while he was gone.

First he was to pick up dry cleaning and keep the receipts, making certain the attendant remembered him, then get lunch for two at a Burger King and to save those receipts, too. The Burger King receipts would have the date and time recorded on them, giving Jason an alibi. After that, Heidle was told to go to Jason's house in Orlando and wait for him to return, which was to be around lunchtime.

After giving Heidle instructions, Jason drove away in Patricia Ann's car, leaving his sports car containing the files inside the garage at DeBary. Heidle bought two lunches at Burger King, saved the receipt, picked up the clothes from the dry cleaner, and arrived at Jason's house at 11:30 A.M. Then, to protect himself in case *he* needed an alibi, he ordered a pizza, and when it was delivered at 1:57 P.M., he kept the receipt.

Jason arrived around 3 P.M., driving the XZ, which he had picked up after leaving the Nissan in DeBary. Heidle said Jason was so excited "he was bouncing off the walls."

"He seemed excessively overjoyed," Heidle said.

Heidle had plans for the evening and wanted to know when he could leave.

"I'm supposed to go over to Scott's," he told Jason. "What's going on?"

Jason said, "I have to wait here until my mother calls to tell me that my father has been murdered, because then I need to go to Edgewater or DeLand."

Fifteen minutes passed, with Jason growing increasingly impatient. "Why doesn't she call me?" he asked. "What's going on? Did you get the receipt from Burger King?"

When Heidle was able to leave, he returned to DeBary to look at his mother's car. Heidle had developed a habit of turning the mileage counter of cars he drove back to zero whenever he finished a trip. After arriving in DeBary from Deland that morning, he had followed the usual procedure. The meter was on zero when Jason told Heidle he was going to have the car washed and gassed up. Now the meter on his mother's car registered two hundred and thirty miles, and Jason had been gone five hours. The car had been cleaned and the gas tank was full, but it was obvious that Jason, or someone, had driven the car two hundred and thirty miles.

Had Virginia and Jason killed Doc and set him up to take the rap? Heidle wondered. The thought frightened him, but he was too scared of Virginia and Jason to run.

Kris didn't work at the office the week before Doc's death. She did errands at the Larzelere house, then went to Kissimmee on March 5 to celebrate her father's birthday.

On the morning of March 8, Kris was late as she drove back to Daytona Beach from Kissimmee, intending to go to her college classes. She was caught in heavy traffic and was running behind schedule, so she called Virginia on her car phone.

"I'm going to be late, so I might as well come to the office," she said.

When Kris arrived at Doc's office, Virginia was nervous and excited.

"Is something wrong?" Kris asked. "Is something going to happen?"

"Go run your errands so you'll have an alibi," Virginia said.

Kris finished the errands and returned to the office, but Virginia ordered her to go to the post office, make a bank deposit, and buy flowers for the nanny. Kris was nervous and called Virginia several times on the car phone to ask what was wrong. Virginia didn't explain, but ordered her to stay away.

"Go to lunch," Virginia said. "Take half an hour."

"I'm not really hungry."

"Take a lunch."

"I'll take half an hour."

"That'll be fine."

It was unusual for Virginia to tell Kris to eat out. None of the employees ever did: someone would pick up food, bring it back, and they would all eat at the office.

When Kris drove back to the office, she saw a police car and a fire truck in the parking area. Suddenly she started to tremble. She drove slowly around the block and then parked on a street in front of the office.

Doc had been killed.

Virginia was screaming hysterically, trying to climb into the EVAC ambulance to be with Doc. The paramedics gently persuaded Virginia that it would be best if she met them at Fish Memorial Hospital.

A crowd had gathered, and Kris saw Barbara Herrin, president of the Edgewater office of Sun Bank, just across the street from Doc's dental offices. Kris gave Barbara the keys to the office building, then drove Virginia to the hospital.

Once inside the privacy of Kris's car, Virginia's hysteria vanished.

"Jason screwed up," Virginia said, according to Kris. "He was half an hour late and there was a patient in the waiting room. I had to fake a robbery."

At the hospital, while she waited for Doc to be pronounced dead, Virginia gave orders to Kris when nobody was around. The moment someone showed up, she wept hysterically. A chaplain didn't leave right away and Virginia whispered to Kris: "Get him out of here." Then she told Kris, "Don't jump around so much. Act sad."

When Doc was officially dead, Virginia wept and staggered out of the hospital, with Kris's "help" and got into her car. They drove to the Sun Bank so Virginia could make a withdrawal, but was stunned that the accounts had been frozen by the police. Virginia was furious, but couldn't show it. Instead she drew three hundred dollars out of an account she held jointly with Kris.

After they arrived at the house in DeLand, it was afternoon. Virginia telephoned Heidle and told him to drive Jason's car to DeLand, and she dispatched Kris to pick Jason up in Orlando. The car telephone rang when Kris was just outside the city. It was Virginia.

"How far away are you?"

"Not far."

"Steven, his nurse, isn't going to be there," Virginia said. "It's just going to be Jason."

Jason was agitated, but quiet, when Kris picked him up and returned to DeLand. He was to become even less talkative by the time detectives from the Edgewater Police Department arrived around 11 P.M. Virginia took Jason upstairs and gave him heavy doses of Darvocet, a pain killer, to put him to sleep.

"I don't want him talking to the police," Virginia explained. Then she told Kris, "Be sure to tell the police that you called Steven and spoke with him at Jason's house."

Kris and Heidle had never met before they saw one another that night, but they had heard of one another. Virginia had told Kris that Jason needed nurses around the clock, and had referred to one of them as "Steven." A young man Virginia called Steven arrived, but Kris didn't know he was Jason's "nurse."

Heidle approached her in a hallway.

"You must be Kris," he said.

"How do you know my name?"

"Jason tells me everything."

Kris replied, "Virginia said for me to tell the police that I called and spoke to you, and we're supposed to stick to that story."

"Okay," Heidle said.

Kris was leery of Heidle, believing he had known about the plan to kill Doc for weeks. Perhaps he was even involved. It apparently didn't enter her mind that she was involved, too, however unwillingly.

After she brought Heidle's things in from the car, Kris put on a pot of coffee. Virginia was calling her sister, Jeanette, in Lake Wales, to have her bring Jessica, Benjamin, and David home. And then the police were to arrive.

It was going to be a long night.

The telephone rang on the evening of March 8, 1991, at the Atkinson's double-wide trailer in Lake Wales. Jessica answered it to find her mother on the other end of the line. Virginia was exceptionally calm and Jessica had no indication that anything was wrong. When Virginia asked to speak with Jeanette, Jessica handed her the telephone and went outside.

Twenty minutes later, Jeanette came out on the porch.

"Jessica, your father's dead," Jeanette said.

"I went haywire," Jessica recalled.

They didn't leave for DeLand immediately. First Jeanette telephoned the Edgewater police to ask if Norman Larzelere had been killed. The police verified Doc's death. Leaving the boys with her husband, Jeanette tried to calm Jessica, got her into a car, and headed toward DeLand.

When Jeanette arrived, it seemed like an ordinary visit from Kris's point of view. No one would have guessed that Virginia's husband had been killed, judging from the way they acted. Kris didn't see Jeanette show any emotion, and the two sisters didn't hug, console one another, or even say

150

they were sorry. Instead, Kris saw Jeanette simply walk in and say hello to everyone, followed by Jessica, who appeared to be dancing. All of them went straight to the TV room.

Otherwise, the Larzelere household was tense, but controlled. Jessica thought things were bizarre. Kris, Heidle, Jason and Virginia were there, but Jason was upstairs sedated on the drugs his mother had given him.

"He was out of work," she said. "Doped up."

"I can say he's on his medication for epilepsy," Virginia explained.

Virginia had taken so many drugs herself that she was almost incoherent. She discussed Doc's shooting with Heidle and Kris to develop a consistent story to tell Detectives David Gamell and Cheryl Osborne when they arrived. The story developed in fragments: Someone had entered the business, shot Doc, and had driven away. Then Virginia began to improvise; offering different versions of what happened, to see which played best.

The first scenario Virginia conceived was that there was no robbery. Whoever killed Doc had not stopped at the safe to steal gold coins, cash and bottles of Valium. The masked gunman had come inside and shot through the waiting room door, unaware that Doc was behind it.

Virginia then offered a second version. The gunman wasn't wearing a mask. She had seen his face and could identify him, and he *had* robbed the office safe before killing Doc. Apparently Virginia didn't remember she told Gamell previously she had not seen the gunman's face. Just his boots, boots that were indelibly burned into her memory.

Virginia didn't like her third version of the shooting, and modified it. In this story, the gunman ran into the office and shot Doc while shouting that "they" knew who he was and "they" were "getting even."

At last Virginia decided on a story: the gunman had shot Doc, wasn't wearing a mask, she had tried to restrain him, and he had sped off with a motorcycle escort. Having decided on a story, Virginia tried to orchestrate the interviews that she, Heidle, and Kris would have with the police. Jason, too, would be coached later.

Virginia told them what to wear and what to say when they were questioned by the authorities. Jessica was also given instructions on how to behave when the police interviewed her.

"Just don't say how much we fight," Virginia said. "Don't bury me, don't make me look like a bad person."

Thirteen

Detectives Gamell and Osborne arrived at the Larzelere home around 11:30 P.M. on the day of the murder. It would be a long time before Gamell's workday ended before midnight. He and other Edgewater police officers had gathered important, and sometimes confusing, information at the scene of the shooting, but there were no suspects yet.

Gamell parked and looked at the house, which was ablaze with light. Directly across the street from the house was an empty, untended lot with a small circular dirt road and, beyond the weeds, a light manufacturing plant. The Larzelere house seemed out of place both in the neighborhood and its own yard.

Inside, Virginia, the grieving widow, was surrounded by friends and family. Virginia explained that her sister, Jeanette, had driven up from Lake Wales with Jessica who had been living with her for a few weeks along with David and Benjamin. Kris and Heidle were present, as was Jason. Virginia explained, however, her son had suffered a seizure and was upstairs asleep. Jason, Virginia told the detectives, had been in a car accident a few months earlier and his injuries caused epilepsy that made it impossible for him to walk without help.

One of the first things the detectives noticed when they stepped inside the house was the smell of cat urine and rotting flesh. Next, they noticed the fleas. Fleas were everywhere, leaping in small black clouds, getting all over their clothes, biting them. Virginia and the others didn't seem to mind.

"They weren't clean in that house," Gamell said. "They were very dirty people."

Gamell and Osborne interviewed Virginia, who could barely keep her eyes open. She slurred her words and was almost incoherent. Gamell concluded Virginia was stoned on drugs or medication. "She could barely open her mouth, she was so toasted," he said.

In spite of her earlier rehearsal, Virginia was unable to keep her stories about the shooting straight. She was confident when she made a general statement, but when she was asked for specifics, her answers were slurred and incoherent.

Gamell asked if the shooter was wearing a mask.

"I was trying to grab his arm," Virginia said. "I

didn't look at his face. Or if I did I don't remember looking at his face. I remember he was dark and I remember grabbing his arm."

"So you saw his fingernails?" Gamell asked. "He didn't have gloves on?"

"I don't know why he didn't . . ." she mumbled incoherently. "I know I remember seeing . . ." Again she mumbled ". . . fingernails."

Virginia told the detectives Doc had been to K-Mart to buy a calculator and had just returned when a patient, who had caused trouble previously, checked in.

"He (Doc) got (the calculator) for nineteen dollars and we were laughing about it," Virginia said. "And he kissed me and we were talking about Jason, and then the patient came up."

Virginia said another woman patient came in while she was talking to the troublesome patient.

"Is he the one we were talking about that came in yesterday and gave them a hard time?" Kris asked.

"Uh-huh," Virginia said. "He gave them a hard time before. Paul Katyz."

It soon became apparent that Virginia had little regard for the Edgewater Police Department, Detective Leo Booth in particular. When she spoke of those grudges, she didn't mumble or become incoherent. She was clear and forceful.

Gamell asked Virginia if they had other disgruntled patients or if there were arguments within the family. Virginia said no, but there had been numerous threats.

"But they were all laughed off by Booth and the Sheriff's Department," she said bitterly.

"We're not laughing this off," Gamell said.

"Yeah, but if you hadn't laughed the other one off . . ."

"It was a head of something that somebody left on the back porch," Kris interjected.

"It was a possum with his throat slit and a knife in him," Virginia said. "A death threat and we gave it to him (Booth) and he just dismissed it." She added that the Sheriff's Department had also not taken it seriously.

"I kind of figure you have a bad taste in your mouth toward police officers," Gamell said.

Virginia admitted that was true. "Lieutenant Booth, when we were broken into . . . decided upon his own that I was a drug abuser and I had stolen our drugs," she said. "It almost cost Norm his license."

Again, Kris spoke up. "Virginia. What about . . . a couple of weeks ago when I was coming home from school and you had called me about the three guys and Norm had had to threaten them off the property?"

"Norm had problems with . . ." The name she gave was incoherent. Virginia said a patient had

156

come into the parking lot to threaten Doc, and then she became incoherent about the time, day, and identity of the patient.

According to Virginia, Doc was having an affair and being threatened by both the mistress and her husband. Gamell and Osborne asked several questions concerning identities and other specifics, and Virginia's answers were all incoherent.

Gamell asked if she and Doc argued.

"We got along fantastically," Virginia answered. "We have our ups and downs and argued over the kids because I want to raise them one way and he wants to raise them another, but we also stick by each other."

"Have you ever had an affair?"

"No. He thought I did, but he found out differently."

Virginia said when the gunman fired, she chased him and broke a fingernail when she scratched him. She had saved the broken fingernail in case the police wanted to examine it for skin scrapings. The gunman jerked away from her, she said, and jumped into the passenger side of a Toyota. Then, to the astonishment of police, Virginia said two motorcycles started up and raced away with the car carrying the gunman. One was riding a Harley-Davidson and the other was mounted on a Honda.

Virginia couldn't remember where she had scratched the man, on the hand, arm, or face. "I did like this," she made a motion, "and I broke this nail here." She held up a finger for examination.

According to Virginia, the safe at the office, which was used to store prescription drugs, about three thousand dollars in cash, gold coins, and gold for teeth, was locked. She told the detectives Doc was the only person who had the combination.

But when the police arrived, the safe was open. There was no gold, no cash, and only a partially filled bottle of Valium. Virginia said that the gunman must have robbed the safe, even though there was no evidence it had been forced open.

From nowhere, Virginia made the startling statement that the Department of Professional Regulation, which had investigated Doc, might have been involved in the murder. Detective Booth, Virginia's number one villain, had helped the DPR with its investigation. Thinking about it, Virginia launched into a tirade.

"I understand an investigation, but I don't understand Lieutenant Booth taking our money and freezing it," she said. "Explain that to me. Knowing I have to come home and feed these kids, how does he have the audacity to keep my checkbook?

How does he have the audacity to call Barbara Herrin and freeze all the accounts, knowing I got these kids to feed?"

"I can't answer for Detective Booth," Gamell said.

"Apparently nobody can."

A little later, still speaking clearly, she asked, "Why didn't you take the fingernail today? After I repeatedly said I broke it. Why? I have it. Do you want it?"

Gamell said he had asked officials from the Florida Department of Law Enforcement, who conducted forensic studies at the scene of the crime, if they wanted the fingernail. They told him it wasn't necessary.

"But I brought blood," Virginia insisted. "How is that not necessary? You've got blood type."

The detectives promised they would have the fingernail tested in a laboratory. "I saved it," Virginia said, then retrieved it.

Gamell was prepared to close the interview, when Virginia asked, "Did Jeff Harding really see him (the gunman) at McDonald's afterwards?"

"I beg your pardon?" Gamell asked, startled.

"He was seeing the family at the hospital and they said they saw him at McDonald's."

"Saw who?"

"The guy at McDonald's, eating."

The detective explained that a bag lady claimed she had seen a man, whose appearance was opposite of the gunman Virginia described, come into a McDonald's restaurant, waving a .45 pistol around, then holding a gun to an employee's head while he ordered a hamburger to go.

"I just wondered if the guy had stopped to eat afterwards," Virginia said.

Gamell explained that McDonald's had not reported such an incident, and that it wasn't likely that the killer would stop to get a Big Mac while fleeing the scene of a murder.

"Did Emma (the dental assistant) tell you about the motorcycle guy?"

The detectives had not yet questioned Emma Lombardo, but Gamell promised they would. The things Virginia questioned, or described, were getting stranger by the minute. Virginia said the biker had asked about Valium.

"Would you notice if he wore any colors, like the Warlocks?" Gamell asked.

Instead of answering yes or no, Virginia became incoherent once more, but said there was a girl with the biker. Asked to describe the girl, Virginia once more became incoherent. She became more specific when asked again about the biker. According to her he was clean shaven, had short, thinning hair that was pulled back into a ponytail about three inches long and held in place by a blue rubber band.

Virginia then launched another verbal assault

against Detective Booth, concerning a report he had made about an alleged break-in at Doc's offices when he was helping the DPR investigation. Although a burglary had been reported at the offices, Booth was dubious.

"The (sic) Lieutenant Booth decided that," she said. "The office was not broken into. He called DPR and let them know the office wasn't broken into. It was a hoax. And A.J. Ellis had been fired because she was stealing money, forging scripts (prescriptions) and he called her in, and she gave testimony, and I don't know what testimony, but anyway, Lieutenant Booth decided that the Larzeleres stunk and I was a drug abuser, and the DPR ought to be called in, and so A.J. Ellis was a very disgruntled employee."

"Booth's a detective, not a lieutenant," Gamell said.

"I don't care what he is."

Doc, she explained, sometimes became physically abusive to her when he erroneously thought she was having an affair. Gamell asked about the relationship between Doc and Jason.

"He and Jason got along beautifully," she said. "The DeLand police have a report about a tussle upstairs four years ago when Norm took a swing at me." She said there had been no trouble between the two until Jason had an accident that resulted in seizures. "Jason was gonna be a dentist like his dad and Norm felt guilty."

161

Virginia said Doc had a guilt complex because he initially believed the physicians who said Jason faked the seizures. Because of that, she said, Doc had Jason move out of the house. Time had healed the wounds between Doc and Jason, Virginia continued, then physicians discovered that Jason's seizures weren't faked.

"He had to have special medication because he'd suffered brain damage," Virginia said, "and they got along beautifully."

On medication, which was "enough to put a horse down," Virginia said, Jason was incoherent and dopey. Jason's doctor, James Ortoloni, she said, told her Jason would be on medication for years. She said Jason could walk, but only if he moved slowly. Virginia said Jason was unable to drive. She said he tried it once and had a wreck.

"Is there anything that we can do for you?" Gamell asked.

"As long as you conduct a very fair investigation, that's all I ask."

"We're doing that."

"We did not get it before (during the DPR investigation) and it caused a lot of dirt. It caused a lot of hard feelings. . . . And I would please like my money turned loose. We have to do that."

Gamell asked if Virginia had noticed whether or not anyone had been following them.

"We all have. Kris has. Norm has. That's all been reported."

162

"Followed by who or what description?"

"We even called Edgewater when the guy set [sic] across the office with a gun shining through the window, in a red pickup truck," Virginia said. "I called Edgewater Police Department and reported it."

"And they came about twenty-three minutes later," Kris interjected. "The guy was sitting and watching the office and she (Virginia) noticed it. And I was sitting at the typewriter, and I got up and I looked out, and the guy got out of his truck, he had a gun in his hand. I don't know if he was loading it or what he was doing with it. And he walked around the truck, and she (Virginia) got on the phone and called the police after I got up to see what the guy was doing."

Osborne said, "Never a dull moment."

No one with the police had ever been a problem before, Virginia said, except for Detective Booth.

"Have you had men making passes at you?" Gamell asked.

Jessica interrupted: "That's a stupid question. She's a beautiful woman."

Virginia attacked Booth again, and said that, among other things, he resulted in Doc losing twelve of his best Edgewater patients.

Just before he was killed, Virginia said, Doc had filed a complaint with the State Attorney

163

General regarding Booth and the DPR investigation and the Edgewater Police Department. Theodore Doran was also listed in the complaint, she said, which charged harassment, not following through with investigations, lies and slander.

"Let me ask you another question, Virginia," Gamell asked. "Do you have a boyfriend?"

"No, should I?" she answered.

"Don't get upset. I just asked you."

As the interview continued, Virginia mentioned that several bikers had spoken to Doc while he was in the waiting room. Gamell's antenna went up.

"Bikers? Were there more than one?"

"Yes, yes," Virginia said. She explained that Emma had put Katyz in the room where the safe was, before she went to another room to work with Doc. Katyz, Virginia said, asked her what kind of drugs were in the safe.

Virginia said she mentioned this only because the safe had been robbed, Doc had been killed, and two motorcycle riders escorted the murderer's getaway car from the dental office. She thought the biker was from Chicago.

"Ask me anything you want to. I can describe him to a 't.' He's a Warlord."

"Warlord or Warlock?" Gamell asked.

Virginia laughed. "Warlock. I'm sorry. I like Warlords."

Until a few months previously, the Warlocks, which are headquartered in Volusia County, had a very low profile. The club had been in the news just recently because its president had been killed in what appeared to be an execution. The murder had been in the newspaper headlines and on television news broadcasts.

When Gamell asked Virginia to describe the biker's colors, Virginia was more certain. She said the man wore a black vest with WARLOCK printed on the back in white letters.

Virginia's description of the biker all but eliminated him as a suspect, even if he had been there when the murder occurred. "He's five foot four," she said. "He has black hair, balding at the temples. He had a teeny, tiny, little ponytail with a teeny, tiny, little blue rubber band in it. He had dark eyes, olive complexion."

"Muscular?"

"Yeah. Tattoos."

"Was he grayish? Starting to gray?"

"Thinning at the sides and at the top very thinning. He wanted to remain young. So instead of having it short, it was all brought back so that it was joined by this teeny, tiny little ponytail that stuck out approximately three quarters of an inch from the rubber band. He had a white T-shirt."

The man had a terrible cigarette habit, Virginia said, and his hands were calloused. He wasn't an attorney or CPA who had come to Daytona Beach for Biker Week. She said his fingernails were dirty, his hands greasy, and that he had black hair growing out of his nostrils. He had brown eyes. He had a gold earring in the left ear.

According to Virginia, the biker had a face scarred by acne, wore blue jeans and biker boots. The man's girlfriend, Virginia said, was a brunette with no makeup, stood five feet three inches tall, and weighed one hundred and forty pounds. "(She'd) pass for a man except she had some tits."

Gamell asked about her relationship with Norm again, and Virginia answered, "Everything has been so beautiful."

Already rumors were swirling about, maintaining that Virginia had had Doc killed to collect on his life insurance. Virginia said she had already heard the rumor from one of Doc's patients.

Virginia told the detectives that Doc got a million dollar life insurance policy, and they were going to get one on her, but they couldn't afford premiums on two such large policies. Since the policy hadn't been in effect for at least a year, it was worthless. The fact that Virginia held other policies on Doc's life in the amount of $2.1 million was something she didn't mention.

At the conclusion of the interview, Virginia said, "I want to tell you that you have been more than nice and more than fair. You really have."

Gamell and Osborne left with no firm conclusions. Virginia could have been on prescribed sedatives to calm her after such a traumatic event. In that case, her confusion about what had happened was explainable. But it seemed more than coincidental that her incoherency coincided with questions that dealt with details of her broader statements. Even so, Gamell still considered Virginia a victim and felt sorry for her.

Fourteen

It was still dark outside in the early morning of Saturday, March 9th, as Virginia, Kris, Jason and Heidle sat around a table with papers, purses, and files laid out. They were working like beavers to destroy evidence that could link them to the killing.

It was strenuous for Kris and Heidle because they didn't know or trust one another, even though Virginia used her formidable persuasive powers in an effort to have them become friends. Kris seemed nice enough, Heidle thought, but she talked too much. For her part, Kris didn't trust Heidle at all.

The most incriminating records were in Kris's Daytimer. In it, she had records of her activities before Doc's murder, and had cataloged the errands she ran for Virginia, amounts of money she received from Virginia, and money Virginia gave her to FAX to Jason.

No one had slept, except for Jason, who had been knocked out from Darvocet, and they were red-eyed and tired. Virginia orchestrated the emptying of Daytimers, purses and wallets, examined the contents, pulled potentially damaging records out, and burned them. And she repeated this process frequently over the next few days.

All four in the group had been drinking heavily since the Edgewater detectives left, and Jason, roused from sleep, was barely able to sit in his chair when Virginia brought up a risky piece of business.

"Jason, you and Steven go and get rid of the library book," she said. "Library book" was the code name she had for the shotgun that was used to kill Doc. "Kris and I are going to the lawyer's office and to some insurance companies."

Jason conveniently chose that moment to pass out. Virginia told Heidle he would have to take care of the "library book" by himself.

"No, I don't want to do it alone," Heidle said adamantly.

"Kris, you go with him."

Heidle drove Kris's Toyota Celica to his mother's house in DeBary without speaking much. Kris claimed she didn't know they were going to pick up a shotgun, and thought it was typical of Virginia to worry about an overdue library book. "Virginia was a woman who would panic about leftover ham in the refrigerator," she said.

Kris saw a Nissan in the driveway when they arrived at Patricia Ann Heidle's house to pick up guns, cement and muratic acid. The automobile gleamed from the previous day's detailing, and Kris mentioned that it was a good-looking car.

When they arrived at the house, Heidle went to the attic and retrieved a carrying case for a shotgun or rifle. Then he placed a jug of muratic acid (a powerful, caustic chemical routinely used in swimming pool maintenance) in the car, plus a bag of cement. It was almost dawn when they returned to DeLand.

"Go upstairs and take care of it," Virginia said to Heidle

Kris was ordered up to help, and started by wiping down a handgun with muratic acid to remove fingerprints, while Heidle did the same with the shotgun. Virginia explained that the handgun belonged to Jason "and I don't want the police to find it."

Previously, Doc's murder hadn't seemed real to Kris, but more like a nightmare. Now the reality crashed down on her, leaving her terrified. Kris wanted nothing more than to run and hide, but she thought her only choice was to follow Virginia's orders. There was no doubt in her mind that Virginia would have her killed to protect herself.

After the guns were washed with acid, Heidle mixed cement in the tub in Virginia's bathroom. Concrete splashed around the room and on the tile walls. Something that looked like a long plant container was in the bathroom. Kris found out that it was a glue vat used by wallpaper hangers.

Virginia ordered Kris to pass the guns to Heidle, who put them in the container. Kris held the guns in a towel to keep from getting fingerprints on them, and Heidle put the guns in the vat before covering them with cement. They both wrapped the container in plastic, and put it in the trunk of Kris's car. Then Virginia ordered Kris to give the bathroom a thorough cleaning.

At first, Virginia thought the container could be buried in a hole dug in the cellar, where the concrete was broken. Kris got a shovel and started to dig, but found a metal grating just beneath the ground.

"There's no way you're going to break that up," she said.

"Just get rid of it," Virginia said. "I don't want to know where or how. Just get rid of it. Just make sure it won't be found and don't get rid of it anywhere in the vicinity."

At 10 o'clock, Heidle and Kris drove north on Interstate 95, looking for a secluded body of water to dump the cement-encased guns. Along the way, they stopped to get something to eat, then pulled into a Wal-Mart Store.

"I'm going to buy some towels," Heidle said.

"Why?"

"If I'm going to wade into water to dump this, I'm going to need something to dry off."

In addition to towels, Heidle bought a map and

masking tape to secure the plastic around the container of guns and cement. Then they drove to St. Augustine, some twenty miles south of Jacksonville, and about ninety miles north of Edgewater. They stopped at a public telephone and Kris called Virginia to say they still had the guns.

"Can you tell me in a roundabout way where you are?" Virginia asked.

Kris said, "The Fountain of Youth," referring to the quest of Ponce de Leon, the Spanish explorer.

Virginia exploded. "Don't be so specific! Get Steven on the phone."

Heidle talked to Virginia for a long time, and when he hung up, he said, "We have to go back to find some place to dump it."

They drove south on the less traveled U.S. 1 until Heidle spotted a bridge over a tidal pool. He pulled over and stopped.

"We're going to get rid of it here."

The plan was to make it look as if the car had a flat tire that was being changed. Heidle opened the trunk, put the spare tire on the ground, and positioned the jack so it seemed to be in use.

"We'll wait until there aren't many cars, then you can take it out and dump it," he told Kris.

When there was a lull in the traffic, Kris retrieved the container with the guns and concrete and dropped it over the railing into the tidal pool. The container sank to the bottom, and Kris and Heidle drove back to DeLand.

* * *

It had taken about six hours to get rid of the guns. Kris was scared, dirty, tired and exhausted, and wanted to take a shower and get some sleep. Virginia said there wasn't time, and ordered Kris and Heidle to meet her at a restaurant for a talk before the police conducted additional interviews with them.

Virginia didn't want anyone to talk about the murder at home or in her or Jason's cars.

"There are bugs everywhere," she said. "People are taking pictures from across the street."

"What?" Heidle asked.

"The FBI's in on it," Virginia said.

"It's not an interstate case, how would they know?" Heidle asked.

The FBI was not involved, but it added to the complex web Virginia was weaving. Kris and Heidle were already frightened, not only because of the roles they played preceding Doc's death, but of what Virginia had them do after the murder.

Kris was scheduled for her first interview by the Edgewater police on Monday, March 11th. At the restaurant, Virginia coached her on what to say.

"Tell them that Doc and I didn't argue," she said. "Be sure to say that Jason and his father had a good relationship. Make sure that the family seems happy, that there's nothing wrong with the family unit. Tell them that we're happy-go-lucky."

When Kris returned from the police questioning,

Virginia was anxious about what she had said.

"Did you tell them the things I told you to say?" Virginia asked.

Because of her fear of Virginia, Kris had done exactly as she had been instructed.

Heidle was afraid Virginia had ties to organized crime, making him afraid to tell the truth to the police. Virginia had told him about her "Uncle Ray," supposedly a powerful underworld figure who kept a hundred-plus foot yacht at a harbor in New Smyrna Beach.

"That's who I'm afraid of," Heidle said.

When they watched a television news broadcast that night, a reporter mentioned that the man who killed Doc had used a blue Toyota. Heidle remembered that Jason had driven his mother's car in DeBary, returning it with two hundred thirty miles on the odometer. Virginia suddenly became concerned for Heidle's mother.

"Is your mother okay?" she asked. "Maybe we should do something nice for her."

Jason agreed, and Virginia suggested that she buy her a new car.

Although it would be nice for his mother to find a new car waiting when she returned from Massachusetts, Heidle foresaw problems. "What are you trying to do?" he asked. "Set her up as the hit man?"

Virginia brushed his objections aside, got the Massachusetts telephone number from Heidle, and dialed. On the other end of the line Patricia Ann was surprised to hear from Virginia, whom she had never met. Patricia Ann was even more surprised when Virginia said she wanted to buy her a new car.

Thinking the proposition was pretty weird, Patricia Ann declined the offer. That made Virginia furious.

"She just went completely wild," Patricia Ann said. "She was screaming and yelling like a madwoman. Fuck this and . . . I just couldn't believe it."

Patricia Ann thought Virginia was a nut case and couldn't help laughing. This made Virginia even angrier.

"Don't you snicker at me!" she said. "Because I'll see to it that you'll go right along with the rest of them."

"Just exactly what are you talking about?"

But Virginia hung up.

Heidle was certain his mother's car had been used in the murder. Since Patricia Ann had laughed at an offer to buy her a new car, Virginia decided the old car should be painted a different color and have new tires put on. But Heidle was only given enough money to buy a mask for the

175

grill; he and Jason decided to tell Patricia Ann that her car had been in a minor accident.

When he picked her up at the airport, using her car, Patricia then remarked, "There's something wrong with this car."

"No there isn't," Heidle said.

"No, it isn't riding smoothly," she said.

She took the car to a service station to have the brakes checked because she thought the problem stemmed from there. The mechanic told her the problem wasn't with the brakes, but that the front right wheel was bent, as if the car had been driven over a curb at high speed.

Things weren't going smoothly with Jason and Virginia in the aftermath of Doc's death. Jason complained that he wanted $200,000 immediately, and Virginia told him that he couldn't have it.

"You're selfish and you screwed things up," Virginia told him, according to both Kris and Heidle. "You were fifteen minutes late."

"I've done everything you asked me to do," Jason yelled. "I've devoted my entire life to you. You have no right to say that I'm selfish and involved in it just for the money."

"You never do anything you're told," Virginia yelled back. "You don't know when to keep your mouth shut. If you had kept it shut like I told you, things wouldn't be as bad as they are."

Jason screamed at his mother, picked up a vase and threw it against the wall, where it shattered. Then he stormed out of the room.

The Edgewater Police Department was small, but astute and determined. Detectives were quick to discover evidence that contradicted Virginia's statement the night of March 8, and found enough irregularities to confuse the investigation.

The day after Doc's murder, Gamell spoke with Patricia Ellis, who had started to work at Doc's dental office about two or three weeks before he was killed. Virginia hired Patricia merely because she had made a passing comment that if there was anything she could do to help, regarding Jason, to let her know.

Patricia never dreamed it would go further than that, and was surprised to find a message from Virginia on her answering machine. Virginia asked her to fill in for her, and she would be repaid by having her dental work done at no charge. Although she was more than a little surprised, Patricia accepted.

Then Kris called to remind Patricia about an appointment, and seemed aggravated that Virginia had not told her Patricia had been hired. "I'm only the office manager," Kris snapped.

When Patricia went to work, she overheard mysterious telephone conversations between Virginia and Kris. Virginia said, "Did you get in touch with the source in Orlando that we talked about?" It seemed strange that Virginia would say "source" instead of mentioning a name.

Patricia liked Doc and thought he was a nice man who was thoroughly dominated by Virginia. She told Gamell that Doc had fired Kris several times and didn't want her at the office, but Virginia kept countermanding him.

"He told me once that the reason he didn't want her (Kris) in there anymore," Patricia said, "is because she had ties with organized crime from up north. Virginia didn't want to fire Kris because she was afraid of the consequences.

"And I said 'I don't know that much about that, Doc.'

"And he said, 'We had dead animals on the doorsteps and things like that.' "

A former employee, Grace Cash, told Patricia that Virginia was responsible for making Doc believe Kris had mob ties. "She said, 'She keeps pumping this stuff into Doc's head,' " Patricia said. " 'She's training Doc to believe this and he does.' She (Grace) is totally terrified. So am I. I started to think that maybe the stories about Kris's Uncle Vito and the mob were true.

"I believe Doc loved Virginia," Patricia told Gamell. "He just seemed to dote on her. The whole thing just blows my mind." On the other hand, Patricia said, "Grace said that Virginia just makes a fool out of him (Doc). She just uses him."

The business community in the vicinity of Doc's dental practice had few kind feelings toward Virginia. Barbara Herrin of Sun Bank said: "Virginia was known in the community as a troublemaker. She would sue anybody at the drop of a hat." Furthermore, Barbara said, people in the area believed the marriage was shaky and Virginia was ruining Doc's practice.

"When they were separated, he would come into my office to talk," Barbara said. "He told me he had left the house and moved to Edgewater with David and Benjamin and was hiding. He said that he feared for his life, that he was afraid of Virginia."

Emma Lombardo, Doc's dental assistant, was terribly shaken by the murder. The murderer had stood just a few feet from her, and she said he wore a dark ski mask, dark, long-sleeved shirt, and dark trousers. He was tall and skinny, she said, "like Jason."

According to Emma, Doc fell to the floor and cried, "Jason!" Then he looked at her and said, "Help me."

Virginia asked, "Jason? Is that you Jason?"

Then, Emma said, Virginia put her mouth over Doc's, to keep him from saying more. She smothered him until he bled to death in seconds.

The information from Emma was gathered while she was still stunned by the violence she had seen. There was a great deal of investigating to be done. Virginia was not yet considered a suspect because things were confused. The Edgewater Police Department was careful about what facts it told the media. Gamell and the other detectives in the Criminal Investigation Division continued to search for evidence.

"There were no preconceived opinions," said Detective Sergeant Bill Bennett. "We approach every case with open minds. We go where the evidence leads us. At that point, Virginia Larzelere was considered a victim."

Fifteen

On Monday evening of March 11, Kris and Heidle were in the house in DeLand but not present
when Detective Gamell, accompanied by Osborn,
interviewed Virginia again at home.

The story about Doc buying a calculator during
his lunch break was repeated. Virginia took pains
to point out that although she, Jason, and Doc
had had their problems, everything had been resolved within the past few months. Virginia's contention was supported by Jason, Heidle, and Kris.

After Doc bought the calculator, Virginia said,
"We started talking about bringing Jason home
and moving him into Kris's room because he was
doing so much better."

"Where was Kris going to be?" Gamell asked.

They never resolved that, Virginia said, because
Emma came back from lunch, and Hilda Levezinho, a patient, arrived for an appointment. "She
leaned across the desk and was gonna say her
name and I said, 'Hi, Hilda,' and she said, 'You

have a good memory,' and I said, 'Yes, I never forget a face.' "

This was not the case when it came to the man who killed Doc.

"I heard shots or a shot. I can't tell you," she said. "I just heard the boom noise and I turned around and a guy was running. He had a gun and I grabbed for his arm."

Did you see anybody that had a mask on?" Gamell asked.

"I didn't look at his face. I looked at his pants and shoes and his belt."

"What did his shoes and pants look like?"

"He had on black combat boots and they had mud, dirt on them. And he had dark clothes."

Although Virginia couldn't remember the color of his clothing, she said that his skin was dark. She pointed out once more that she had scratched him and broken two fingernails. Previously, she said she had broken only one.

Virginia said the gunman shoved her back and she chased him outside, screaming the license plate number to Emma Lombardo. The man leaped over a four-foot metal bannister from a landing that was two feet off the ground, and didn't miss a step. He jumped in a waiting car and sped off with a two motorcycle escort.

"He got in the car so fast," she said.

"Where was the gun?" Gamell asked.

"Still in his hand. He didn't drop the gun."

"For him to leap over that, he'd have to put his hand down, and he'd have to brace himself."

"He just leaped. He just leaped. I remember thinking, God. I thought how fast, how agile he was." Virginia said she was amazed at the speed the gunman got inside the waiting car.

"Just 'whoof' and he's in," she said.

"Do you remember what side he was on?"

"He went in on the passenger side."

"Are you positive?"

Virginia said she was, and added that the car took off, without screeching its tires, before the gunman had time to move to the driver's side.

"The motor was running," she said. "I was going to chase him but the car took off immediately. The motorcycle took off immediately."

"One or two?"

"The first one and the one behind him."

Virginia set the scene up in detail, the waiting compact Japanese car, with the motor running, and two children about Benjamin's age playing at the end of the driveway on red tricycles.

A shooting such as Virginia described would have required precise planning. As the interview continued, Gamell noticed flaws in Virginia's story. According to her, Doc had gone out to buy a calculator and returned, and had noticed nothing unusual. Then, Virginia said, she had gone to the bank, and had not been back long before the gun-man burst in.

The detective saw several things that didn't seem right. The fact that both Doc and Virginia left the office, according to Virginia, represented two random breaks in normal office routine. A precisely planned operation such as Virginia described could not have taken these variables into account. Certainly, if such a precise operation occurred, the vehicles would have been in place when Virginia said she returned to the office.

Virginia seemed to improvise her story as she went along, as if covering inconsistencies. She said she heard someone inside the building when she went to the bank. Virginia said she didn't give it a second thought.

"Do you think he was already in here?" Gamell asked.

"Uh-huh."

The detective pressed the point. "For him to commit the crime and go out the door, and the car to be waiting at exactly the same time," he said. "How would they know to be there? And how were the motorcycles in position without you seeing that? And something startled Norman to make him run hurriedly to get away."

"Uh-huh," Virginia said.

Virginia was unable to address this inconsistency, and Gamell noted more holes in her story:

her various descriptions of the gunman, his escape by motorcycle escort.

He steered the interview to people Virginia thought might have motives to murder Doc. On this, Virginia named Doc's alleged mistress and her husband, disgruntled patients, carpenters and paving contractors, among others.

She even included a policeman and a delivery man for United Parcel Service.

"You want me to go all the way back?" she asked. "Tell me how far you want me to go back. The last year's been pure hell."

"That's where I want to go," Gamell said.

"We've had problems with *Tom Epson.*"

"Did he ever threaten to kill your husband?"

"Yes. And against me also."

It was during Doc's affair with *Pam Epson,* Virginia said, that the dead possum was found on the doorstep of the dental office, the severed heads of kittens appeared in the refrigerator, and dozens of threatening letters appeared, along with unknown parties shooting at her in her car, parking outside in broad daylight with guns, and trying to run her off the road.

"It started then and it went on for months and months," Virginia said.

Virginia said *Pam* came to the dental office to tell her she was having an affair with Doc. According to Virginia's story, the following happened.

Doc came in eating a breakfast sandwich and was surprised to find Virginia and *Pam* together.

"He asked 'What's going on?'

"I said, '*Pam* is letting me know that you're having an affair.'

"He got real angry. She left. I walked her out to her car and I said, 'By the way, he's not a piece of cake. He's a hard man to live with and you ought to just leave him alone.'

"She had a white dress on and she was on her way to the office. And I said, 'That dress makes you look very virginal but I think you're a god-damned bitch!' and she got in her car and left.

"And then I went back in and Norm threw me against the wall and we had words, et cetera, et cetera."

"Was there anything physical other than that he threw you against the wall?" Gamell asked.

"Norm was real physical during the time that he was seeing *Pam*."

"Did he batter you in any way?"

"Yeah."

"In the office?"

"In the office. In front of people."

Once, Virginia said, a patient with dental pain was left sitting in a working room after Doc injected his gums and gave him a Valium. Doc "was beating" on her, then left the office to see *Pam*, before he returned. She said the patient wouldn't leave because he wanted to protect her from Doc.

"When Norm came back and he was still beating on me, this guy leaned across and told me that he wouldn't do anything unless I asked for help," Virginia said.

"Do you know his name?"

"I can't think of it." But before the patient left, Virginia said the patient confronted Doc. "He told Norm that if he ever hit me in front of him again, he would break his hand because he didn't believe in a man hitting a woman. He was very upfront and honest."

So far as *Pam* was concerned, Virginia said, the affair ended on September 24, 1990. But, she said, Doc received blackmail letters from *Pam,* claiming she had incriminating pictures.

"And the threats kept coming and coming and then they kept telling me that they had films and slides . . ." Virginia said.

The affair with *Pam,* and the attempted blackmail, Virginia said, caused problems between her and Doc, but they put them aside and went to Anna Marie Island to patch things up. But, Virginia said, *Pam* came to the island in a further attempt to blackmail Doc.

"We argued the whole weekend," Virginia said.

After they returned to Edgewater, Virginia said *Pam's* husband, *Tom,* came to the office. "He told

187

Virginia and Doc shortly after they were married
in 1985. (Courtesy of *The News-Journal*)

The former Larzelere home in DeLand where Virginia slept
with some of her lovers when Doc was at the office.

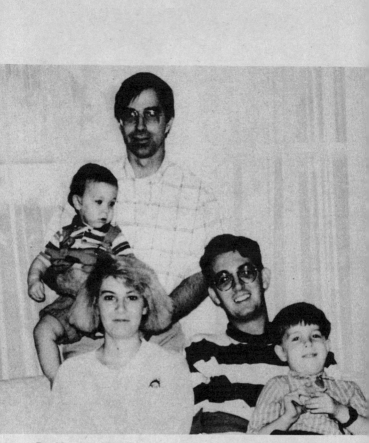

Dr. Norman "Doc" Larzelere with his children shortly before he was murdered. From the left: David, 1; Jessica, 13; Doc; Jason, 17; and Benjamin, 4. (Courtesy of *The News-Journal*)

The building in Edgewater where Dr. Norman Larzelere had his dental practice, and where he was killed. (Photo by Roger Simms, courtesy of *The News-Journal*)

The side door through which the gunman fled from the building and the railing he supposedly vaulted over as he made his escape. (Photo by Roger Simms, courtesy of *The News-Journal*)

Jason and Virginia during a pretrial hearing. (Courtesy of *The News-Journal*)

Wearing her prison jumpsuit, Virginia laughs during the pre-trial proceeding. (Photo by Roger Simms, courtesy of *The News-Journal*)

Leo Booth, a narcotics undercover agent, testified for the state. Photographers and TV cameramen were not allowed to picture him inside or outside the courtroom.

Detective David Gamell testifies at a bail hearing where he played portions of a taped interview with Jessica, who said that Jason and Virginia "were like man and wife." (Courtesy of *The News-Journal*)

Dorothy Sedgwick, assistant state attorney for Orange-Osceola Counties, was the chief prosecutor in Virginia's trial. (Photo by Sam Cranston, courtesy of *The News-Journal*)

John Howes, one of Virginia's two defense attorneys.
(Courtesy of *The News-Journal*)

Jack Wilkins, one of Virginia's defense attorneys, listens as a state witness testifies. (Photo by Roger Simms, courtesy of *The News-Journal*)

Emma Lombardo, Doc's dental assistant, was only six feet away when the gunman fired the shotgun that killed him. (Photo by Roger Simms, courtesy of *The News-Journal*)

Claude Murrah, one of Virginia's many lovers, testified that Jason was not disabled. (Photo by Roger Simms, courtesy of *The News-Journal*)

Steve Heidle, one of two star witnesses for the state. Heidle led police to the murder weapon and was the first to tell police of the conspiracy to kill Dr. Norman Larzelere. (Photo by Roger Simms, courtesy of *The News-Journal*)

Jurors, accompanied by a police officer, visit the building where Doc was killed for an on-site inspection. (Photo by Roger Simms, courtesy of *The News-Journal*)

Virginia in tears after breaking down during a tour of the murder scene. She is accompanied by two bailiffs.
(Photo by Roger Simms, courtesy of *The News-Journal*)

Virginia reacts as she hears the jury recommend that she be sentenced to death. (Photo by Nigel Cook, courtesy of *The News-Journal*)

me to quit calling his house and harassing him," she said. "Or he would do me in."

"He said that?"

"Yeah. I let him know I hadn't called his house. I didn't know what was going on. And then he and Norm had words outside a couple of times."

Virginia said she tried not to listen, but that the threats continued. The kittens' heads in the refrigerator, she said, were placed on a copy of Norm's petition for divorce. Those papers had been locked in a barn, to which only Doc and *Pam* had keys.

Another threat occurred, Virginia said, when a Blazer, just like *Pam's*, pulled up beside Benjamin and tried to lure him inside in a kidnapping attempt. *"Pam* was trying to take the child."

"Never a dull moment," Osborne interjected.

Virginia said there had been threats from two carpenters, a paving contractor, a lawyer, a United Parcel Service driver, and even a policeman, whose name or description she couldn't recall. There were constant threats, she said, but the police didn't take her seriously, all because of Detective Booth.

"I do not have a good moral character in Booth's eyes, and it's tarnished," she said. "Therefore, anything I say has to be a lie or fabrication."

Although threats and family arguments continued almost to the end, Virginia said things had been much quieter. "Our life was nice," she said. "Norm and I patched things up. We had not had any arguments. Things were great. Christmas was beautiful."

Gamell mentioned that Emma Lombardo and a patient who had been in the waiting room when Doc was shot had heard Doc call Jason's name. Virginia said it was because Doc and Jason had been estranged, and had just recently resumed a close father-son relationship. But Doc felt guilty, she said, because he was the one who had approved Jason's late curfew on prom night and blamed himself for Jason's accident.

"I didn't know they had become so close again," Virginia said. "Norm confided in Jason a lot, told him things, he didn't tell me because he didn't want me to worry. I can understand why he would say 'Where is Jason.' " According to Virginia, it was a cry of remorse because Doc loved his adopted son so much.

As for Jason, Virginia said he was "an artist, a beautiful artist, multi-talented. He was surrounded by girls. Women of all ages found him a very, very, very handsome man." Before the accident, Jason weighed 199 pounds and was in great physical shape, Virginia told the detectives. It was his weight loss that alerted her mother's intuition that he was sick, in spite of so many doctors saying that he wasn't.

Virginia said, after going to more than half a

dozen hospitals, Jason was admitted to the Peninsula Medical Center in Ormond Beach, was in intensive care, and stayed at the hospital three
weeks. Gamell had already checked this out.

"He was only there three days," he said.

"That's not true."

"We called twice and both times they said three
days."

"He was in intensive care. That's not true."

Gamell let it go and had Virginia talk about Jason and Doc again. Virginia said, after Jason was
stabilized on medication, he and his father became
even closer than before the accident.

"They used to have lengthy, lengthy conversations," she said. "It was like one intellect on top
of another."

"Did they argue? Or become physical one time?"

"Yes. About four years ago. Norm took a pot
shot at me . . ."

"You better explain pot shot. We think of a
gun."

"He threw a punch at me and Jason took his
arm and, like I said, Jason was very big."

"At that time?"

"Yeah, even back then."

"Did he punch Norm?"

"Nope. They tussled."

According to Virginia, Norm had a terrible temper and patients were always storming off because
of his tirades against them. Once, she said, he

threatened to shoot a workman because of shoddy work. In Edgewater, he told three men on his property that "he was going to get his shotgun, just blow them off."

"And after that everything has been so nice and smooth and easy, easy times," Virginia said. "Oh, God, it's beautiful."

Gamell said he had heard about trouble with Kris, and that Virginia had fired her. Virginia sluffed it off.

"Kris and Norm, and Kris and I, and Norm and I argue constantly," she said. "I have fired Norm, Norm has fired me. I have fired Kris. Kris and Norm had an argument and had been telling tales back and forth, playing one against the other."

"Did you think they were having an affair?" Gamell asked. "Did that run across your mind?"

"Yes, it did and I was not gonna go through what I did before, okay?"

"I'm glad you're honest with me."

Virginia said she had it out with Kris and Doc, that Kris was fired for a week, then everything was fine, and Kris came back to work on March 8 to get her paycheck.

"Paid her for the whole week," Virginia laughed. "But that's me. Because if I like you, I like you a lot, and if I've got a beef, I do say it."

The gossip about Doc and *Pam* had wounded Virginia badly, she told the detectives, and she had decided not to be stung again. So she had not believed the rumors that Kris and Doc were having an affair.

"Was she coming on to Norm?" Gamell asked.

"Yeah, yeah, yeah."

"She made passes at him?"

"Yeah, and he threw her out of the office like Tuesday or Wednesday of last week," Virginia said. "He told her to go home because I had left, and he didn't want her there after I left, because he knew that she upset me."

"She was still fired Friday when this thing happened?"

"No, she'd already been to work."

Gamell reviewed what he considered Kris's strange behavior, such as returning to the office, being sent back out, then driving past the building twice after Doc had been shot before she stopped. Only Kris could answer that, Virginia said, but told Gamell what he already knew: Kris had telephoned Virginia on her car phone.

"She called . . . because I forgot to tell her how much to spend," Virginia said.

"Why wouldn't she call you from the flower shop?"

"I think it was right before or right after . . ."

Gamell could see no reason why Kris would call to find out how much to spend *after* she had bought the flowers. Something else was strange, too.

"I wonder why she didn't call from the florist

instead of running up your phone bill in the car phone," he asked.

"She loves that damn car phone."

"I have to pick everyone apart," Gamell said. "I have to play the devil's advocate."

"Do, do. Even if it's tearing me apart, that's okay. Because Norm didn't deserve what he got. He had quirks, and we all do things wrong, you know, but Norm didn't deserve what he got."

The interview ended with Virginia saying Doc was the only person who had the combination to the safe. "He was the one that opened (it), come hell or high water," she said.

In fact, the police had discovered the combination to the safe was written on a sticker beneath a counter. Several people had access to the safe.

There was little traffic after the rush hour when Gamell and Osborne stepped out of the office into the mild evening. It was cooler than usual and less humid. The lowering sun streaked the sky with hues of orange, peach, and red; a seaward breeze made palm trees sway.

Doc would never see another sunset, or take his boat out on the swells of the Atlantic. Gamell was determined to bring his murderer to trial. Virginia had been inconsistent in her statements, and her explanations weren't plausible, but she was supported by Jason, Kris, and Steven Heidle, who corroborated her stories or offered alibis.

She was still considered a victim, but evidence was mounting that could make her a suspect.

Sixteen

Virginia ordered fifty copies of her husband's death certificate as soon as they were available. She also ordered a copy of the death certificate for Ted Goodman, the man who had been one of Virginia's lovers before she steered his attentions toward Kris.

While purging her files, Virginia was busy coaching Jason, Heidle, and Kris on what to say in their inevitable statements to the police. Kris and Heidle were both afraid of Virginia and Jason. They listened carefully to Virginia's instructions, since they were often complicated, and at variance with the truth.

Neither of them doubted that they would be killed if they didn't cooperate. Kris was also worried about her parents' safety. Her nerves were frazzled because each time she met with the police, she feared she would be arrested and charged with murder.

When Kris and Heidle returned from questioning, Virginia thoroughly grilled them about what they had told the police. She had them write their statements down in detail so she could make necessary revisions. When either made a statement she didn't like, Virginia became a heavy-handed editor.

"You have to change it," Virginia said. "This is what I want you to say."

The tension in the house was thick. Virginia and Jason snapped at one another, and even got into fights where they kicked and bit one another. Kris, who had never even seen them argue, was shocked at Jason's temper tantrums.

According to Kris, Jason became infuriated when newspapers and television newscasts quoted Chief Lawrence Schumaker, of the Edgewater Police Department, as describing Doc's murder as the work of an amateur. The only purpose of the incident was to kill Doc, Schumaker said, not robbery and not drugs.

One morning Jason had a temper tantrum and locked himself in his bedroom just before Virginia left for an interview with the police. Concerned about him, Kris tapped on his door. Jason screamed at her: "Get out of my sight! I don't want to see you or Virginia. I don't care what happens to any of you!"

Fearful, Kris wrote a note for Virginia, left the house, and walked to a gas station where she called a friend to pick her up. Kris stayed at the friend's house until Virginia telephoned to ask what had happened.

"He told me to get out and I got out," Kris said.

Kris wanted to leave Virginia's house, but was afraid of what would happen if she did. Virginia obviously wanted her and Heidle under her direct control, where she could monitor everything they said and did. Kris felt like a prisoner, and was so concerned about the danger posed by Virginia that she warned a friend to stay away from them.

A male homosexual friend Kris knew from community college had met Jason and developed an almost obsessive sexual attraction to him. He talked about Jason constantly.

"Don't get involved with Jason or Virginia," Kris told him.

But he was smitten and didn't heed the warning. The two men saw one another regularly, prompting Kris to speak with her friend again. She told him everything she knew about Doc's murder.

"The best thing you can do is stay away from him," she said. "I don't know what I'm going to do. I have to make a decision about whether I'm going to say anything or not. But you should stay away from him."

Kris already believed her life was in danger, and she became convinced of Virginia's duplicity, when she overheard an argument over Doc's insurance money. Virginia told Jason the money was only going to be split three ways. To Kris, this meant either she or Heidle would have to be killed, and perhaps that was in store for both of them.

Virginia walked out of the room following the argument and saw Kris, who had obviously been close enough to overhear.

"Steven isn't to be trusted and won't be getting any money," Virginia told Kris. "I'm only interested in Jason, myself, the kids, and you."

Heidle became increasingly nervous, and suspected he was being set up as the killer. Now he understood why Jason wanted him to order two dinners from Burger King and keep the receipt, and the visit to the dry cleaners. It was all to prove that Jason was in Orlando at the time of the murder. Heidle could claim he was in Orlando, too. But if Jason disputed him, it would be his word against Jason's, who was supposedly too sick to drive.

Other signs made Heidle think he was to be the sacrificial lamb. Virginia kept him and Jason apart, and when he returned to his mother's house in DeBary, she tried to persuade him to drive Jason's sports car around town, and when he went to his interviews at the police station.

"I'm not driving this banana mobile around,"

Heidle said.

"People are watching your house," Virginia said. "They have a search warrant for your house. They're going to come and break down your door. They're going to take you off to jail if you don't do this."

"I'm not gonna be driving the yellow 300 ZX around," Heidle said. "It's a pretty obvious car."

"Drive it for one day and then bring it back to the DeLand house," Virginia persisted. "What do you have to worry about?"

Heidle knew he had a lot to worry about, including Virginia and Jason, who were not the least of his problems. But Heidle drove the sports car from DeBary to DeLand in time to hear Jason and Virginia get into a riotous argument. That was the end of Heidle's driving the sports car, as much as he liked it. Things were too tense and he was afraid something might snap.

Heidle listened closely as Virginia coaxed him on the answers he was to give his police interviewers. Jason was with them at the Red Lobster restaurant in Daytona Beach.

"Tell them that Doc often called Jason in Orlando," Virginia said. "Tell them that they got along beautifully."

Heidle nervously agreed. Virginia leaned forward and seemed to have a need to explain what she was doing.

"Business is business," Virginia said. "Kris has

gone in to be questioned. They seem to think that she knows something and they seem to think that you know something."

Heidle was worried. "Am I a suspect?" he asked.

Virginia described the person who shot Doc.

"I want to let them see that I don't weigh whatever he weighed," he said. "I want them to see that it wasn't me."

Virginia was firm. "Well, you know, business is business," she said. "If something should go wrong, the same thing that happened to Norm could happen to you and Kris."

Virginia made it appear that she was strapped for cash after Doc was killed. Doc's accounts were frozen until it was determined positively that Virginia had nothing to do with his death. The insurance policies, which totaled $2.1 million, were withholding payment for the same reasons. Virginia had money in numerous other accounts but feared having money she couldn't account for.

Having already filed claim on Doc's insurance, Virginia wanted to raise money by selling his dental practice. The building, which resembled a Mexican adobe hacienda, had already started to mildew when she arrived there one Saturday with a prospective buyer in tow. Jason, Kris, and Heidle also accompanied them. They waited in another room as Virginia showed the offices.

The following conversation took place in that room as recounted by both Kris and Steven in sworn depositions.

Jason mentioned that, following Doc's death, he wanted to commit several burglaries in Edgewater and New Smyrna Beach to make it appear that a burglary ring was at work. He thought it would bolster Virginia's story that Doc was killed in the course of a robbery.

"Did you tell your mother about this?" Kris asked.

"Yes, but she didn't like the idea."

"Have you ever killed anyone before? Did you do it for your mother?" Kris asked.

"Yes, but it wasn't directly for Virginia. She asked me to do it because I'm good at it."

"Virginia told me this wasn't your first time," Kris said. "She said there were others."

"All I'm good for is pushing drugs and killing people," Jason said.

Then, according to Kris and Steven Jason stated that he had killed his adoptive father.

"Let me tell you about it," Jason said.

"I don't want to know," Heidle said.

"I walked in the back door. What a fucking wimp. He got up and ran."

Jason showed Heidle how the shot from the gun had spread.

"Look how far it went," he said. "That door is solid wood. I shot right through. You wouldn't believe how that gun shot. I'm glad I didn't hit my mom."

Jason walked to the waiting room. "My mom was right here and I'm glad I didn't shoot her."

According to Jason, the shot had spread out because he had sawed off the barrels of the shotgun he used.

"Why didn't you have Uncle Ray do it, or have him get it done professionally?" Heidle asked.

Jason looked at him. "It may sound mean, but I wanted to do it."

"How do you and Virginia expect to get away with this murder when all of those people in Orlando you do drugs with have seen your guns?" Heidle asked.

"I give them free drugs," he said. "You don't have to worry about them because they do drive bys."

"What the hell's a drive by?"

"When somebody drives by and kills somebody."

On March 10, Virginia accompanied Kris and Jason to Sam's Wholesale Club, but waited in the car while the purchases were made. Virginia wanted a new Daytimer and briefcase to replace her own which she'd given to the police, plus legal folders and boxes for her files. When they returned with the supplies, Virginia sent them in for additional purchases.

Virginia was tearing things out of Kris's Day-timer when she and Jason returned.

Heidle said later to the police that Kris was asked to go along so that Virginia could further purge her Daytimer while she was shopping.

Virginia's energy level was manic. She continued to perpetuate the myth that her life was in danger. Once, during her second interview with Gamell on March 10th at the Edgewater Police Station, she claimed to see a gunman outside, stopped the interview, and had the detective check for an intruder, before continuing.

Late that same night, Virginia telephoned the DeLand police and claimed an intruder was trying to get into the house. Several police officers arrived at the house within minutes, while Virginia stayed on the phone.

"He's downstairs," she said, then later, "he's upstairs." Eventually she had him all the way up in the attic.

Sergeant M.R. Melton surrounded the property with police officers and, along with Patrolman Joel Hancock, decided to search the house. But the six-foot hurricane fence was locked and they had to climb over it. Melton climbed a part that was covered with vines, got his feet tangled, and fell on his back from the top of the fence.

"I'm afraid to come down and unlock the door,"

Virginia said, and threw her keys from the bedroom window onto the lawn. "You'll have to break the chain on the door."

The two police officers searched the downstairs and basement but found no one. On the second floor, all of the bedrooms were made up and Jason was in Virginia's bedroom, which had the only bed that had been slept in.

Having found no one on the first two floors, the policemen searched the attic. Outside, Sergeant Evelyn Paterno stayed in touch by radio. She heard a dull, crashing sound from inside the house. "What was that?" she asked. "Hancock just fell through the ceiling," Melton replied. The subflooring had broken under Hancock's feet and he had fallen through the ceiling, hurting his right leg.

There was no sign of an intruder or that anyone had tried to break in. Virginia had left a second-story window open but there was nothing to indicate that someone had scaled the wall to enter it, as Virginia suggested. The police finally left, after finding no evidence of an intruder.

Detective Gamell had put in a long day and was in a fitful sleep when Virginia telephoned him around 4 A.M. on March 11th to report the incident. He told her that the information would be reported to him as a matter of routine if she had contacted the DeLand police. Virginia said she just wanted to be sure he knew.

Just before midnight on March 11th, Gamell's beeper went off again, and he roused himself from sleep to call Virginia. She had a strange story to tell.

She told him that she found a shotgun in her closet and suspected that somebody had climbed up the wall and put it there, after the police had left.

Gamell thought the case was becoming more bizarre with each passing hour.

"Did you touch it to leave fingerprints?" he asked.

"Well, I kind of touched the wood part," Virginia answered.

"What about the barrel, did you touch the barrel?"

"I sort of touched it and then I began stroking it, and I started crying and rocking back and forth with it, because I thought it was Norm."

She thought a shotgun was her husband? "Just put the gun under your bed and I'll pick it up." He went back to bed, but was too wound up to sleep. Everyone in the CID had been working around the clock since Doc's murder.

But Virginia didn't keep the shotgun. Claiming she was too nervous and didn't want the gun in the house, she had Kris telephone the DeLand police. Patrolman Steve Wilson arrived to investigate around 1 A.M. on March 12. Virginia and Kris were up but, in spite of all the excitement, Jason was in bed asleep.

Virginia said she was going through her closet, trying to find something suitable to wear at Doc's funeral, when she saw two gun cases, a big one and a small one.

"They weren't in there last night," she reiterated. "I beeped Dave."

Virginia told the police she put the larger case on the bed, opened it, and saw a gun inside. "I read the label 'Remington' and touched the gun by the wooden part," she said. "I didn't recognize the gun or the pistol case. Would you take the gun and the pistol case? And would you look inside the closet to see if you can find anything else?"

Wilson checked the closet and found two yellow .20 gauge shotgun shells located far back on a middle shelf. Kris peered in and discovered a rifle case rolled up in a blanket.

"I don't recognize them," Virginia said. "Would you take them, too?"

Sergeant John Bradley arrived to aid in the investigation and had Virginia sign a "consent to search" form. He looked inside the closet and found not only three more shotgun shells, but a .20 gauge single-shot shotgun.

"That one belongs to Norm," Virginia said. "You can leave it."

Virginia said the only people who had legal access to the house were herself, Kris, Heidle, Jason and Juanita Washington, the nanny. Nothing else in the house was missing . . . or had been brought in by prowlers.

"Would you write a statement about this incident?" Wilson asked her.

"Yes, but I can't write. I'm shaking too much."

Virginia dictated a statement that was brief and to the point, and signed a shaky signature. Kris made a similar written statement, then the police left, taking the gun cases, shells and the mysterious shotgun with them.

The police asked themselves, why was Virginia looking through her closet for something to wear at midnight?

Seventeen

Doc's funeral was held at Baldwin Funeral Home in New Smyrna Beach on March 14, 1991. It was a tragic day for Norman and Lucy Larzelere, Doc's parents, who had lost their only son in an explosion of violence. But Norman and Lucy had grieved long before because, in a very real sense, they had lost their son through the manipulation of Virginia.

Even though they were shattered by Doc's death, they still had to plan a suit to gain custody of David and Benjamin, who had been brought to the funeral by Virginia's sister, Jeanette.

Kris was psychologically numbed, and still couldn't fully accept the reality that Doc had been killed, much less her own unwilling role in the murder. Virginia felt the ground shaking under her feet, too, and was fearful the police would arrest her at any moment. She shared her angst by confiding in Kris. As Virginia felt her defenses crumbling, she said that Kris could be the star witness against her.

"I didn't see anything," Kris said. "And why are you their prime suspect?"

Virginia just smiled.

The police had interviewed dozens of people whose stories were at odds with what Virginia had said, and she was right to believe that she was a suspect. The police had literally hundreds of leads, but were several weeks away from finding probable cause to arrest either Virginia or Jason. Virginia's natural paranoia and cunning prompted her to take steps to protect herself from the police at Doc's funeral.

She persuaded one of her sisters, Diane Waters, to impersonate her by wearing one of her wigs, stuffing one of Virginia's bras to make her bust appear larger, and wearing a dress identical to Virginia's.

"Indictments are going to be handed down and I'm going to be arrested at any moment," Virginia said. She handed Kris a large makeup bag containing a bottle of Valium and tens of thousands of dollars in cash and told her, "Don't let that bag out of your sight."

The plan was for Diane to go into the funeral home first, and if the police tried to arrest her, they would swoop down on Diane, and Virginia could escape before they realized Diane was a decoy. The scenario called for Kris to hand Virginia the makeup bag and she would be out of danger before the police gathered their wits.

When the plans were set, the family entered black

limousines and were driven to the church where services were held. On the way, Virginia scolded Kris for her behavior: "Don't smile so much. Don't act so happy. You're smiling, joking around too much, and being too friendly. Try to act more distraught and upset."

Then she told Jason, "Be sure that you have to be assisted in everything. Don't do anything on your own."

Jason had been given drugs by his mother, and was so sedated he could barely sit up straight. When they arrived at the chapel, Kris helped Jason toward the casket where the body of his murdered father lay. Benjamin clung to Jason's hand, and when they arrived at the casket, he began to weep loudly and repeat over and over, "I want my Daddy! I want my Daddy!"

The scene was so emotional that everyone started to cry, including Jason. Jeanette took Benjamin and David out of the chapel and tried to keep them calm as the services continued. Through it all, Jason lay his head on Kris's shoulder and wept.

Detective Gamell was at the funeral and the cemetery, trying to be as unobtrusive as possible. It might seem insensitive but experience has taught homicide investigators to gather as much information as they can in the shortest time. The police had moved quickly in this investigation, and even though they had chased false leads, Virginia and Jason were now considered suspects.

Gamell approached Heidle at the cemetery and said, "I need to speak to you."

When Heidle was inside the limousine, Virginia asked, "What did he want?"

"He said he wanted to talk to me and I told him now wasn't the appropriate time."

"Are you going in for questioning?"

"Of course. You made out that I'm so close to your family, that I needed to speak with them."

Following the funeral, it was business as usual. Virginia and Kris had an appointment with a lawyer, regarding probate, then acquired medical records from a doctor in the hope of showing that Jason was disabled. The arguments Virginia had had with Jason since Doc's death worried her, and she didn't want him to talk with the police.

"Where would you like to go to lay low for a while?" she asked him.

"Texas," Jason replied.

Virginia bought two airline tickets to Dallas so he would be accompanied by one of the two "bodyguards" she had hired to protect them from what she insisted were constant death threats and they left on March 16. However, Jason had only been gone two days when Virginia yearned for him to come home, but didn't want him to return by air.

"It's too dangerous for him to fly," Virginia told Kris. "I don't care how you get him back here, but

211

get him back safe."

The woman who carried thousands of dollars in cash gave Kris only one hundred dollars to drive to Dallas and back. Kris decided she would have to drive straight through because there was barely enough money for gasoline, let alone meals, and certainly not enough for motel rooms. Weary and sleepy from long hours of driving, Kris had a minor accident. She wasn't hurt, but both headlights on her car were smashed, making it impossible for her to drive after dark. Luckily for her, she was only a few hours from Dallas.

Kris was exhausted, hungry, and flat broke when she arrived at Jason's hotel. She spent the night in Dallas and left with Jason for Florida early the next morning. The trip was easier this time because Jason picked up the expenses, including motel rooms, gasoline, and meals. He didn't help with the driving, keeping up the charade of being incapacitated. They arrived back in DeLand on March 23.

Doc's murder and all of the mechanizations after it had dulled Kris's senses. She was almost as psychologically overpowered by Virginia as Doc had been, and she was afraid she might be killed at any time. She couldn't sleep or eat, and after living in fear for about a week, she couldn't stand being around Virginia and Jason any longer. Kris planned her escape so Virginia wouldn't think she was moving out.

The next time Virginia sent her on an errand, Kris called her parents from a pay telephone.

"Call Virginia and tell her you're coming to pick me up," Kris said. "Act nonchalant. Don't do anything that will make her suspicious."

Two hours later, Kris's parents arrived to take her home. They had read newspaper stories about Doc's murder, but asked Kris no questions. To avoid suspicion that she was leaving for good, Kris left most of her personal items at the house, hoping to convince Virginia she would be back. But she had no intention of living in Virginia's house again. Kris felt a little safer, being around her father, but she was still scared because she believed Virginia had strong underworld contacts.

The media was hot on the trail of the story. They published and broadcast allegations made by police and other witnesses of incest between Virginia and Jason. There were published allegations that Jason and Heidle had an affair, and that Kris was intimate with both Jason and Virginia. It was a hard thing for Kris to live with, since the stories concerning her were false, but she had other things on her mind. Kris knew she could be in trouble with the police, and she was edgy and couldn't eat or sleep.

Oddly enough, Kris couldn't make a clean break from Virginia. She saw her each time she reported to the Edgewater police station for an interview. Kris felt that she was caught in a web Virginia had spun that involved her in Doc's murder and the cover-up. She feared having murder charges filed against her and worried about the threat to her life posed by Virginia. Kris had good reason to be afraid of Virginia. She had been threatened before, and now, just before Kris left for her second interview with the police, Virginia telephoned to say they should meet at a restaurant first. Kris was too confused and frightened to say no.

"You're the police's star witness against me," Virginia told Kris. "It's your fault that everything has gone wrong. If you think you're smart enough to choose the other side of the street, you'll be sorry. If you think your family is powerful, I know enough people to have you wiped out."

Heidle, who was also afraid, was either in his mother's house in Orlando, with the lights off and the drapes pulled, or staying with friends. He didn't want Virginia or Jason to know where he was. He had received a bone-chilling threat from Jason on his telephone answering machine that reminded him "you know what the consequences are for screwing up."

Things were not going well for Virginia. The police had interviewed witnesses whose stories differed from Virginia's concerning the shooting. Four days after Doc's murder, Chief Lawrence Schumaker told news reporters that the investigation was ongoing, but focusing on two suspects whom he refused to name.

"We have got to find out why (Doc was killed),"
Schumaker said. "When we find out why, we'll be
closer to finding out who killed him."

The police had been busy. Virginia had told Detective Gamell she had seen what appeared to be a
Georgia license plate on the getaway car, and that
the last three numbers were either 278 or 478. Already the Edgewater police had obtained the names
of more than three hundred Georgia automobile
owners whose final three license tag digits were 278,
and expected to receive some three hundred additional names of car owners with license plates ending with the numbers 478.

By March 28, Virginia had grown weary of the
police investigation, and how it was upsetting her
life. She called a press conference that day, explaining to Kris and Heidle that she was trying to get
sympathy from the public in an effort to generate a
ground swell of support. She wanted to generate
enough pressure to have Doc's bank accounts unfro-
zen, and to force the life insurance companies to
pay up the $2.1 million because of Doc's death.

"I want them to think, 'Well, there's this poor
widow and the police are treating her badly,' " she
said.

At the press conference, Virginia was angry with
a newspaper article quoting the Edgewater police as
saying that Doc was killed "for the specific reason

that someone wanted him slain." Gamell and other investigators had said there was no motive, at that time, for Doc's killing.

That contradicted one of Virginia's stories (the one she was sticking with now) that her husband was killed by a robber.

"The motive was that somebody wanted to steal Valium," Virginia said. "He was surprised after he got a bag of it from the safe. He also got gold coins. The robber never intended to kill my husband, but he got in the way."

The press, eager to get news on a sensational case, were quick to contact the Edgewater police for their reactions to Virginia's charges. Chief Schumaker countered that Virginia's story wasn't credible, and Sgt. Bennett told reporters there was absolutely no evidence that anything was taken from the office.

And he reported what Gamell had said: "Her story changes so much, there's no telling what she's going to say next."

Virginia charged that the police completely discounted her description of the killer.

"They're telling me what the man looks like," Virginia said. "I know what the man looks like." She admitted she was confused, but blamed it on the police. "To be honest, I don't know which end is up anymore. Every time I turn around, the Edgewater Police Department has a different version."

The various descriptions, of course, came directly from Virginia, not the police. Virginia claimed that the police suspected Jason of being the gunman, something she said was clearly impossible because of his disabling epilepsy.

"He can hardly walk across the floor, much less pull the trigger of a shotgun," she said.

The press conference ended with Virginia saying what a warm, loving relationship she had with Doc, and how close her husband was with Jason. Kris was contacted by a reporter, and told him that she backed Virginia's story, and added, the Larzeleres were "just like family."

Information from other witnesses and good, hard detective work pointed to Virginia as the mastermind behind Doc's murder and Jason as the actual shooter. But suspecting someone of a crime is not reason enough for an arrest or a charge: There has to be "probable cause." Simply stated, it means there must be enough solid evidence to make a strong case.

The Edgewater police took statements from a number of people who disagreed with Virginia's claim about how well she got along with her husband. There were conflicting statements as to the shooter's description, how he came in and escaped, and what actually occurred in those brief, violent minutes inside Doc's offices.

It seemed to the Edgewater detectives that the case was a maze. People they interviewed mentioned a dozen others who should be questioned, and there were time-consuming leads that went nowhere, most of which had been provided by Virginia. The detectives knew they were being misled, but had no choice but to thoroughly investigate each new piece of "evidence."

Gamell was besieged by people who wanted to talk. "They were dying to come in. And things were not as they seemed when Dr. Larzelere was killed," he said. "Things were getting stranger and stranger."

Other people who know Doc and Virginia provided the police with information that led to promising sources. A.J. Ellis told the police what she knew, and mentioned that Virginia had affairs with Norman Karn, a Californian man, and Phil Langston, who lived in New Smyrna Beach. Emma Lombardo, Doc's dental assistant, had a version of the shooting and a description of the gunman that differed from Virginia's.

But Virginia had been a genius at confusing things through lies, obfuscation, and subterfuge. "Virginia was a master of deception," Bennett said. "She pulled the strings. She knew how to make things so confusing that they went off in all directions. But she knew exactly what was going on while everyone else just scratched their heads and wondered."

Gamell had been steered on his share of wild-goose chases in the investigation, but he and other detectives were gathering a considerable body of evidence. Virginia felt the pressure, and now ranked the entire Edgewater Police Department as being no better than Leo Booth, the detective she despised because of his work with the DPR regarding substandard practices at Doc's dental practice.

At a press conference, on March 20th, Virginia told the press of additional problems. She claimed that because of police harassment she had been financially ruined. "I think I'm going to lose the Edgewater office, my home, and my car," she said. Worse, Virginia said, someone had shot at her and Jason three times at about 10:40 P.M. the previous night of March 19th, as they stood outside their home with Charles Sylvester, a private investigator she had hired. According to her, unknown parties were still trying to kill her.

"There were three shots," Virginia said. "After the first shot, Chuck threw me back, drew his gun and told us to get in the house. We could see three men in front of the house and they fired two more shots."

Under the circumstances that anyone had shot at Virginia was preposterous. Police cruisers from DeLand were parked in front of the house. If someone shot at Virginia while she was framed at the front entrance, they would have been standing next to the police.

Commander Steve Edwards of the DeLand police said there was no evidence of a shooting or prowlers. Sylvester admitted the sounds could have been firecrackers instead of gunshots, but Virginia didn't give up so easily. Although the police didn't look for bullets, she said, "I found one in the fence and I'll try to find the others." Virginia never produced the bullet, but she used the incident to criticize the Edgewater police again.

Just a few days after Doc was killed, Virginia said she received a telephone call from a man. "He said, 'You saw the hit. You're next.' "

Virginia told Pat LeMee of *The Orlando Sentinel* that the Edgewater police didn't believe anything she said. "They won't listen to me because I once spent three weeks in jail on a bad check charge because my ex-husband depleted our checking account."

Doc's will, she said, was an issue, too. "I know he changed his will last September to make me sole beneficiary, but that was because he knew I'd take care of the kids. Police say I did it for about $1.5 million in life insurance, but I had nothing to do with his death." And she claimed neither did Jason. "He has to have help walking, and he can't drive a car, go to school or be active in any way. There's no way Jason could have or would have shot Norm."

Virginia expressed dismay at "rumors of incest and bizarre love triangles" that had been reported in the media.

The stories would get worse.

Eighteen

One of the people who was anxious to talk with the police was Rebecca Goodman, from Fort Lauderdale, the sister of the late Ted Goodman. Rebecca had telephoned the police and told them she had important information regarding Doc's murder.

Leo Booth, the Edgewater undercover narcotics detective, was due to be in Fort Lauderdale to speak with a man called Dirt, who belonged to a motorcycle club, on another matter. But Booth stopped by Rebecca Goodman's house to hear what she had to say.

"Virginia kept calling and calling for Ted," Rebecca said. "Once Ted told my daughter that Virginia had asked him to kill the doctor. When I heard about that, I just kept hanging up on her."

Rebecca mentioned that two men she knew only as Tony and Dana were close associates of Goodman's, and they said they would kill for a price. "Ted was manic-depressive and you couldn't always believe everything he said. But I wouldn't take any more of Virginia's telephone calls."

The Edgewater police followed up on Rebecca's

leads but were unable to locate Tony or Dana. They established that Goodman had an AT&T calling card and he had used it frequently to call Virginia's telephone numbers in her car, at the office, and at her home. In a matter of days, the police discovered Kris had spent a weekend in West Palm Beach with Goodman, and the intention of the trip was to find Tony.

And pay him to kill Doc.

On April 7, Lieutenant Bucky McEver and Sgt. Bennett called Kris to police headquarters to ask questions about her trip with Goodman. The story Kris told was completely unbelievable. She told McEver and Bennett that Goodman had made unwelcome advances toward her, but had convinced her to spend a weekend in his hometown.

"He said I didn't know him, that I only saw what he was in Daytona Beach," she said. "He said I would like the real Ted Goodman I would see in West Palm Beach."

Kris told the detectives that she had agreed to the trip, but only after Goodman promised to stop bothering her if she didn't have a good time.

McEver and Bennett knew there was far more to the trip than Kris was telling. Even if they hadn't known, the story made no sense. Why would she spend a weekend with a man she admittedly despised? The two police officers listened to Kris's story, then gently applied pressure in an attempt to have Kris open up. They reminded her she would be held accountable if she didn't reveal everything she knew.

Even with that dark cloud suddenly looming over her, the interviewers had to coax the truth from Kris, who first told the police a lie, then was reluctant to tell the truth. She finally admitted that she heard Goodman talk about killing someone, but thought he was "only joking around." She admitted that Goodman had a bad temper. At a bar where people had greeted him with cries of "Hi, Teddy Bear," a man went to buy her a drink, and Goodman, who had left for a few minutes, was back when the man returned.

"Ted made a major thing out of it," Kris said. "He said, 'If you don't keep your hands and eyes off of her I'll beat the shit out of you.' He was very short-tempered. He would get upset if a guy went by and cut him off the road. He would chase after them."

McEver told Kris the police knew of Goodman's temper, and he had been diagnosed as being manic-depressive. There were more than a few unsavory clouds that had hung over Goodman's life. McEver made it clear to Kris that the Edgewater Police Department was not composed of ignorant small town cops. Rather, they were competent, had technology, and would do whatever it took to find Doc's killer . . . or killers.

"This is a capital case, Kris," McEver said. "It won't go away, there's no statute of limitations. Talk to me, Kris. Talk to me."

Kris complained that she was being drawn deeper and deeper into the murder. She said the situation made her so sick she had to quit school, but she felt compelled to stand by Virginia. "I don't want to desert her now," Kris said. "She needs me."

223

Kris was worried about her own safety, and said she felt safer with Virginia than anywhere else. McEver thought that was odd, but everything about the case was. Kris obliquely alluded to the fact that she feared for her life and the lives of her parents. Her father had urged her not to become involved in the investigation because he didn't want her to get hurt.

McEver agreed there was reason for her to be afraid. "This is the scary part. The person who did this will do it again." He emphasized how important it was for Kris to tell the whole truth. "If there's anything that you aren't sharing with us, you become an accessory to murder. You're too young and too nice-looking to get caught up in this triangle crap."

"I know."

McEver mentioned the press conferences Virginia had called, and reminded Kris that Virginia regretted them because she contradicted herself so often. And he told Kris some of Virginia's comments along with other information had led the police into directions that surprised him.

"One of those directions was West Palm," he said.

Kris was obviously shaken by how much the police knew, or how much she *thought* they knew. Even so, she was unwilling to tell the whole story. McEver knew Kris was being squeezed from both sides and tried to persuade her that cooperating with the police served her best interests. He compared the case to a jigsaw puzzle, and said the police had put half of it together and knew where the other pieces fit. McEver mentioned statements that incriminated Kris and emphasized how serious her situation was.

"We're having to reach out with long, long arms and bring in people from everywhere," he said. "So what I'm saying right now is that being an accessory to murder or principal to murder carry life in prison or death sentences."

Kris paled. "Are you saying that's what I am?"

"No. I'm going to leave this in your mind. I need you to search your mind to tell me everything."

"It's a fog bank," Kris said.

"You're twenty-two," McEver said. "Twenty-five years should not be spent in an institution."

Kris still wouldn't talk in specific terms, but the first cracks in her story appeared. "I know I didn't do anything," she said, "but somebody might have said something in front of me. A lot of times I don't pay any attention to gossip or conversations."

McEver disagreed. "If it was devastating enough, you would remember it," he said. "It's not going to be hard to convince a jury if somebody says 'We're going to kill somebody.' "

Anything that "blatant" would definitely stick in her mind, Kris said, even if it was said in a joking way. McEver assured her that he appreciated her help, but said the police expected to have the case solved soon with or without her cooperation.

"Too many people just know too many things," Bennett said.

"It wasn't a good job," McEver added. "This was not a pro job. That's what's helping us out."

This unsettled Kris even more. She claimed she

didn't understand anything that happened and she was worried about newspaper stories and rumors saying she was a witness to Doc's slaying. "A witness to what?" she asked. "I wasn't even there."

"I saw you there," McEver said.

Obviously nervous and uncertain of what to say, Kris continued to procrastinate. It appeared she wanted to talk but was too afraid.

"Kris, what do you think happened?" McEver asked gently.

There had been so many versions of the story that she wasn't sure anymore, Kris said. The only thing she was certain of now, she said, was that Doc wasn't the kind of man to run if he thought his wife or family were in danger.

"I cannot see Doc running if someone drove up and got out of a car with a gun," she said. "I know how personally protective he was over her and the children." She said Virginia once called Doc on his car phone to tell them three men had broken through the hurricane fence and were pounding on a door to the house.

"Instead of calling the police, he drove back and chased them off the property," Kris said. "He's not afraid, and he went out there unarmed. They keep saying that he ran 'cause he saw a guy coming. And whether or not he knew he was in danger or knew what was going to happen, I can't see him leaving Virginia sitting there. I can't see him running away. I can't understand that part."

* * *

Whether she knew it or not, Kris had just implicated Virginia in Doc's murder. If he ran, he must have known Virginia was involved, or he would have stayed to protect her.

The detectives played along with Kris, but McEver said he wanted to know more about what really happened when she was with Goodman in Palm Beach, and if she had heard a conversation with anyone concerning murder. McEver paused and stared hard at Kris. "This is the six million dollar question," he said, "so you have to think long and hard."

Kris was scared but still held back. "See, the hard part for me right now is trying to remember what happened in Palm Beach," she said. "A lot of it is going to be fuzzy because half the time he was smoking."

"You're not a pro," McEver said. "You're not a person that does bad things."

"No. But . . ."

"You're not even good at it, so what I want you to do is search your memory."

"When you said Ted Goodman and I was down there and everything I found out what he was into," Kris said, "I just didn't want to be involved in all the stuff he was doing."

"Kris, think. Other people have thought and I seriously think there's been some conversation you've been a party to."

At this point, Kris made the first admission that she knew more than she had said.

"I wouldn't have been a part of them (murder plans)," she said. "I might have overheard them."

McEver reassured her that she wasn't considered a

participant in Doc's murder, and he wanted her to search her mind to remember things she had heard. Kris said she needed time to think.

"You don't have to think about hearing something that devastating," McEver said. "This isn't 'Colombo.' It's up to you, Kris."

"I consider Virginia a good friend and I want to help her, but then I don't want to be in jeopardy," Kris said. "My butt's going to be on the line and I'm the one that's going to get shot, or something's going to happen to me."

After that, Kris's resistance broke concerning her relationship with Ted Goodman. She still withheld information she had before and after Doc's murder, but she shed new light on her trip to Palm Beach with Ted Goodman. It was far from being a "test drive" to determine whether or not she would become Goodman's girlfriend.

Kris said Goodman called Virginia repeatedly from the bars they visited, but she didn't listen to what they talked about. Sometimes, she said, Virginia telephoned a bar to speak to Goodman, indicating that she knew exactly where he would be.

Kris and Goodman met with people who made her uneasy, including a woman who warned her not to believe everything Goodman said. The woman had lunch with them and, while Goodman was in the rest room, Kris asked, "Is he really going to die?"

"You never know with Ted," the woman said. "It could be the truth or it could be a lie."

After leaving the restaurant, they drove around for a long time with Goodman and the woman talking a lot. Kris said she tried to tune it out. But she remembered the woman telling Goodman to shut up because she didn't want to know anything.

"It had to do with a big, black guy that ran a limousine service," Kris said. "I'm trying to remember."

At that point, Kris began to stumble and backtrack, talking about how Goodman drove her crazy, Virginia's telephone calls, and getting sick and throwing up on Goodman.

"I feel there's something you want to tell us, Kris," Bennett said.

Kris said she was trying to remember the conversation with the woman in the car. Goodman and the woman were in the front seat, Kris said, and she was in back. "He was saying something about how Doc used to beat up Virginia," Kris said. "She asked me, 'Is that true?'

"I said, 'They argue a lot but I've never seen him hit or abuse her.' "

McEver had enough of Kris's waffling. He looked her straight in the eye. "I have reason to believe from seven statements that you were around when he was talking about somebody being killed," the detective said. "Now if you do not recall, then you're the only one in the entire conversation that did not know. And that ain't gonna look good for Kris."

Kris fidgeted but said if any such conversation occurred, it was the one she mentioned. For several minutes, she insisted she didn't remember anything more.

"You need to get your young little rear end off a

wringer right now and speak to me," McEver said.

McEver's bluntness caused Kris's fog to lift a little, and she remembered additional details. The woman in the car was Goodman's sister, and he told her he had come to West Palm Beach to find somebody to bump off Doc.

There it was at last.

"Let's talk about that," McEver said.

Kris said Goodman didn't want Doc to abuse Virginia, and the children didn't deserve a father like that. "He said he was gonna make everything all right, and that he was gonna see some black guy that had a limousine service that owed him a debt."

Finally, she also admitted she was with Goodman when they met a tall, blond man in someone's house.

"He (Goodman) asked him something about what he used to do . . . hurt people or break their bones. I don't remember exactly. But he (Goodman) said he knew somebody that needed a lesson to be taught. And the blonde guy said, 'No, I don't get into that.' "

Kris claimed she couldn't remember anything else, and said she had not even thought about how odd it was that Virginia knew which bars to call to locate Goodman. The weekend was a nightmare for her, Kris said, and she told Virginia on the telephone she didn't know if she could get through it.

"Have you ever thought about what you're getting into here?" McEver asked. "You're getting into a minimum of twenty-five years in prison," McEver said. "That means when you get out you're gonna be well into your forties."

"For doing what?"

"For just being involved with this situation."

"As far as I knew, the purpose for us going down there that weekend was for him to show me what kind of life he could provide for me."

"Right, right. Somebody you despised. Somebody you don't even really like. Do you want me to play the recording back?"

"I know it was stupid."

"It's not *stupid*. It's not *true*."

A few minutes later, McEver said, "Right now we're not worried about nobody's ass but Kris's," he said.

"I have been worried about mine since the beginning."

"And you should, you very well should. Because this isn't a game. Somebody is really dead."

Kris promised she would be available for other interviews. She left the police department a very shaken young woman.

Nineteen

Gamell had a delicate task ahead of him on April 16, and he wasn't looking forward to it. He was to have an interview with Jessica Larzelere at Lake Wales High School, the location she selected. Conducting interviews was one of Gamell's strong suits, and he was so good at it that the other Edgewater detectives nicknamed him Pastor Dave. They even bought him a clerical collar.

Regardless of how hard he tried to make it otherwise, Gamell knew the interview would be unpleasant for Jessica. She was bound to have psychological wounds from living in a severely dysfunctional family, not to mention the brutal murder of her adoptive father. He knew Jessica thought of Doc as her *real* father, and couldn't have loved him more if they shared the same blood ties.

Jessica was composed when she and Gamell went to a private room, accompanied by Keith Windham, the school principal, who had been asked to sit in on the interview, which was eventually entered into evidence at

Virginia's bail hearing. The detective was gentle with Jessica. He knew she had moved to Lake Wales to stay with her Aunt Jeanette, Virginia's sister, a few weeks before Norm was killed. This was only the most recent in a series of flights from the tension at home.

Gamell saw an attractive, but sad, teenager, who looked older than her years. "I felt like she had been robbed of her youth," he said.

Virginia said she had sent Jessica to Lake Wales for her own safety. To hear her tell it, the Larzeleres were targets and all of Volusia County was a shooting gallery. In spite of her claims to the contrary, the police learned that Virginia told several people Doc had done his level best to have her killed.

"Why are you living in Lake Wales?" Gamell asked Jessica.

"Because I don't get along with my mother," Jessica said. "I don't like her lying. I don't like what goes on in there."

"What goes on?"

"Everything. She's involved in a lot of drugs. Jason sells and he does a lot of coke." Jessica said she had no personal knowledge of where Jason obtained cocaine, but when another aunt asked him where he got it "he said, 'My mother gives it to me.' "

Jessica said Virginia ignored her and her little brothers, but lavished attention on Jason. David and Benjamin were in Lake Wales because Jessica didn't want them in the environment at home.

Gamell asked how the relationship was between Jessica's parents, and was told it was volatile, contrary to the closeness Virginia had portrayed between herself and Doc. "Sometimes it was really good, like he sent her flowers all the time, and the other times she could care less if he was there or not. The majority of the time, they fought a lot."

Gamell asked if Jessica had heard anything to make her think her father's murder was being planned.

"I heard different things," Jessica said. "A couple of times my mom would call me and she'd be crying and saying stuff like, 'I can't stand your father anymore. I got to get rid of him.' And then she'd call back the next day and say everything's fine now. And then she called up my aunt one time and she said, 'He's ready to divorce me. I know he is. He's going to leave me.' My aunt asked, 'Why is he going to leave you?' Mother said, 'I don't know, he's just gonna leave me . . . I think he's gonna leave me because of all the fighting and stuff that goes on and I think he thinks I'm lying to him.' "

"Was she?" Gamell asked.

"Of course."

Gamell asked Jessica if she had heard her mother offer money to Ted Goodman, Phil Langston, or anyone else to harm her father. Jessica said she knew nothing firsthand but Ted Goodman, who her mother had an affair with before guiding his ardor to Kris, had dropped a hint.

"The only thing he really said to me was that he didn't like my father and wished he could do something to get rid of him so he could go ahead and marry my mother," Jessica said.

Jessica laughed when asked about Virginia's relationship with specific people. She knew about her mother's affairs with Phil Langston, Norman Karn, Ted Goodman, and others whose names didn't come to mind.

"She had one in Orlando, too," Gamell said. "I'm not sure who with. I think it was Steven Heidle."

Jessica laughed. "I'm not sure of that."

Heidle made no secret that he was a homosexual, but had tried to hide it from Jessica because she had a crush on him. Since then, Jessica had seen newspapers and television broadcasts portraying Heidle as gay.

Jessica told the police that it wasn't unusual for Jessica to attend nightclubs with her mother and her lovers. Virginia made no attempt to hide her affairs from her children, and flirting was something her mother did all the time. Less than a month before Jessica fled DeLand for Lake Wales, she had gone with Kris and her mother to Attitudes, a night club in Daytona Beach. Virginia managed to get her underage daughter into the adults only club without any problems. They left late and Kris fell asleep in the car. While Kris slept, Ted Goodman called on the car telephone to say that he had asked Kris to marry him.

Jessica said her mother started to flirt with Goodman and said, " 'Just wait. Just wait.'

"Her voice changes dramatically when she's flirting," Jessica added. Virginia continued talking with Goodman on the telephone after they had dropped Kris off at her car.

A few nights later, Goodman dropped in unexpectedly at the house, bringing roses for Virginia and gifts for Jessica and the two little boys. "He just sat there and ranted over her (Virginia)," Jessica stated, adding that Virginia sent her upstairs, where she remained for about an hour. When she came downstairs, Virginia and Goodman were still talking.

"I didn't know what they were doing," Jessica said,

"so I just left them alone. Then Dad came home and Dad was like, 'Hey!'," Jessica said. "Dad didn't like him at all."

Instead of causing a scene, Doc took Goodman out to the garage where he kept his boats, leaving Virginia behind. "Mom was kinda worried about what they were talking about," Jessica said.

"Why would she be worried?"

"Probably because he would be telling Dad something that she didn't want him to know," Jessica said. "So she went out there to see what they were talking about."

Jessica described a seemingly endless parade of problems in the family. Kris lived at the house even after Doc was killed, but Jessica never liked her, considered her a "floozy." She thought there was more to her relationship with Virginia than met the eye. "My mom bought her a car," Jessica said, adding that Virginia also gave Kris her own room in the house.

"Dad didn't like Kris," Jessica said. "Dad fired Kris from the office three times and each time my mother hired her back. Kris and my mom are good friends and Kris knew everything about my mother. When my mom was having that little fling with Phil Langston, Kris knew about it, I knew about it. The only thing is that Kris didn't want to tell anybody and I told Kris I was going to tell my Dad. And Kris told my mom.

"My mother has Kris on a rope. If my mom says do something Kris will do it. I know that my mom gives Kris a lot of money to keep her mouth shut. The same with Jason and Steven."

"Keep her mouth shut as far as?" Gamell asked.

"Everything. If they know the slightest little thing, she pays them to keep their mouths shut. She tried to do that with me this summer. I can't be bought."

"My theory is if you have nothing to hide, why run?" he said.

"That's my thought," Jessica said.

"Did your mom have knowledge of this?"

"She's the one who set it up."

Several months before the murder, Jessica said she listened in on a conversation between Phil Langston and her mother, who said she wanted to buy into Langston's exotic bird business. Then the conversation took a different turn. Jessica said, "She said, 'If you can just hold on, we'll be together in six months.'

" 'Because that's when everything will be okay and we can get married.' "

Jessica said she was in the TV room, sitting on the floor, and listening in on an extension phone. When Virginia hung up on Langston and came into the room, Jessica asked, "Why six months?"

"She said 'Because that's when I'm going to get rid of your father,' " Jessica said. "I thought she was talking about a divorce."

Another problem Jessica described was drug abuse by both Virginia and Jason. She said Virginia forged Doc's name to get prescription drugs, and on bills for dental work that was never done. "She loved to forge Dad's signature," Jessica said. "She signed for diet pills, Valium, or just on stuff that she could use. That was her favorite high. . . . She's not any good."

Virginia and Doc argued most of the time, usually about Virginia's love affairs and her activities at the dental practice, Jessica said. Sometimes her mother got so angry she became irrational.

"Every time they would get into a fight, Jason would just voluntarily push himself into it and start hitting my father," Jessica said, "and then just going all out on him. Beating him up."

"His father was not a fighter?" Gamell asked.

"He fought back, but it was his son."

Gamell asked Jessica to describe the relationship between Jason and Virginia.

"Sometimes they're relatively close and then times he'll rebel against her and they'll be really far apart and they'll hate each other."

"How close would you say they were when they were close?"

"Like husband and wife," Jessica answered. "I know that she (Virginia) and Jason slept together a lot. I know that . . ." Jessica stumbled, embarrassed.

"You can tell me," Gamell said. "About your mom . . ."

"I know so much that it's hard to just spit it out," Jessica said. "We (Jessica and Doc) would always talk about how Jason was getting too close to my mom and how we thought maybe they should just separate. So I came over here for a little while and my father threw Jason out of the house."

Gamell asked, "Tell me about your mom."

"Do I have to?"

"You don't have to but if you want to you can."

238

The activities Jessica described made the Larzelere household seem to be a continuing game of musical beds. Kris, she said, was bisexual and had a sexual relationship with Virginia, and that Jason had sex with his mother. (Kris has adamantly denied having sex with Virginia) Jessica said Virginia not only had sex with Jason and Kris, but with Heidle, Goodman, Langston, Karn, a plastic surgeon, a swimming pool contractor, and others. "All of them," Jessica said. Jason, Jessica said, also had sex with Kris, other young men, and a brief homosexual encounter with Heidle. Both Jason and Heidle had other homosexual boyfriends. Jessica even hinted that Benjamin, Virginia's next to youngest child, might be Jason's son.

Jason often fondled his two younger brothers, Jessica said. Doc tried to put a stop to it, and ordered everyone in the family not to leave Jason alone with the two boys.

Doc knew about many of Virginia's affairs, Jessica said, but he had no idea about her lesbian relationships.

"Did he (Doc) suspect them (Virginia and Kris) of having an affair?" Gamell asked.

"No, he was blind when it came to things like that. The only thing he really looked out for was my mother. He really didn't look out for who was sleeping with who. He just wanted to make sure no one was hurting her . . ."

"So he loved your mom?"

"He loved her a lot." She added, "Mom was never true to my father."

239

The detective had heard previously about the alleged sexual activities, but they seemed even more shocking when they came from a girl just barely in her teens. That she even suspected such things was almost inconceivable to him. The alleged incest between Jason and Virginia had been stated publicly in an earlier pre-trial hearing, and one reporter had dubbed Doc's murder "The Oedipus Case."

"Do you feel Jason had knowledge of this homicide before it happened?" Gamell asked.

"Yes, I do."

Jessica said she believed Jason knew about the murder for several reasons: Virginia had rented a house for Jason in Orlando and gave him strict orders on how to furnish it because she intended to live there. Virginia also bought Jason an expensive sports car and a car for herself that cost over $100,000.

"She was making sure that she was going to be well set up." Jason received large sums of money from Virginia just before the murder, Jessica said, which he used to buy clothes for himself and gifts for her.

Jason lived in Orlando and rarely visited the house in DeLand until just before Doc was killed. In the two weeks before Doc was gunned down, Jason came to DeLand regularly, when his stepfather wasn't there, to talk with Virginia. He wore splendid new clothes and jewelry, but he was mean tempered.

"When Jason has something on his mind he's really grouchy, mean, and ugly," Jessica said, "and I thought he had something heavy on his mind 'cause he was a real bear."

"Do you think that if your mom had asked that (killing Doc) be done that he would do it?" Gamell asked.

"Yes. He would do anything for my mother."

Did Jessica think Jason had knowledge of the murder or that he might have planned it? Jessica said she believed Jason was involved with her father's murder, and suggested that Ted Goodman could have been involved. Goodman had been diagnosed with terminal cancer and the doctors told him he had about two years to live. Instead, Goodman died just about a month before Doc was killed.

Allegedly, Virginia had offered Goodman $50,000 to kill Doc. From the stories Gamell heard, Virginia had told him the same lies about being a multimillionaire, and convinced him that Doc was trying to kill her. In addition, Jessica said, Virginia told Goodman that she had millions of dollars stashed in secret bank accounts. This last bit of information rang a bell: Gamell was following up on reports that Virginia had at least one bank account in California.

"Who do you think masterminded this plan?" he asked.

"My mom."

"Just her alone?"

"Probably my brother."

Jessica told Gamell that Virginia had taken out a $1.5 million life insurance policy on her father without his knowledge. She suggested that, if you planned to kill someone for insurance money, it made sense to increase the amount of the policy.

"Who do you think pulled the trigger?" Gamell asked. "Who do you think had the motive to do so?"

"Anybody that was associated with my mother or associated with her drugs or somebody she paid off."

"Do you feel this was a drug hit?"

"I think it was planned by my mom, Jason, and Kris. Jason had something to do with it," Jessica said.

"What leads you to believe that?"

"Because I know Jason, and I know that if it comes down to it he would do anything for my mother."

"Even kill?"

"Even kill," Jessica replied.

Although Virginia had said the family didn't own a shotgun, except for an antique that didn't work, Jessica said there were two shotguns in the house. She said Jason kept one in a closet and another under his bed. Virginia, Jessica said, asked Jason to move the one beneath his bed, which he did. Jessica didn't know what happened to it. So far as she knew, the one in the closet remained.

Those were the two shotguns that were removed by the DeLand police, Gamell thought, one of which Virginia claimed had been planted in the house by the man who killed Doc.

All of the turbulence in the house seemed to be building toward a violent conclusion when Jessica left. The fights between her parents increased, and they apparently fought after Jessica left. Five days before Doc was murdered, Jessica said Virginia telephoned her in Lake Wales and said: "Don't worry, we'll be getting rid of him (Norm) soon."

"She said that?" Gamell asked.

"Those were her exact words."

Jessica said Virginia called back the next day and her mother said that everything was fine. The more she thought about it, the less certain Jessica was that she had left DeLand of her own accord. The household tensions kept her from concentrating on her schoolwork, but she believed Virginia had sent her away. It could have had something to do with her father's murder.

"Why do you say that?" Gamell asked.

"Because my mother knows that if she had me out of the way then she could do what she needed to do and go ahead and get rid of all the things that she needed to get rid of."

"What do you think your mother's motives would have been?"

"Money."

"Anything else?"

"No. She's very greedy."

Norm had shown his will to Jessica the summer before he was killed. He had bequeathed the house to Virginia, and his boats to Benjamin, and had added David as a beneficiary of the boats when he was born. The will provided for Jessica and Jason to receive joint ownership of the house if anything happened to Virginia.

Gamell asked if Jessica could give him a more exact date when her father showed the will to her.

"July," Jessica said. "Because it was like right when everything was exploding, my mom and dad and Phil Langston. He had shown it to me because he wanted to make sure I knew that if anything happened to him I was gonna be well taken care of. And in the will, it said if anything should happen to my mother . . . I was to go live with my aunt."

Throughout the two hour interview, Jessica consistently portrayed her mother as devious and sexually promiscuous; a user and dealer of drugs; a forger of her father's signature on prescriptions and other important papers; and a liar who was willing to kill her father.

The interview with Jessica added to a body of evidence stacking up against Virginia and Jason Larzelere.

Were they capable of murder? It seemed they were.

Was there a motive? Yes.

Opportunity? Yes.

Means to commit murder? Yes.

Jessica had made powerful statements that implicated her mother and brother in her father's murder.

Twenty

Phil Langston was in Nicaragua, and temporarily out of touch, but the police talked to his employees. Gamell wanted to know more about the relationship between Virginia and the tall man who imported exotic birds. Just twelve days after Doc's murder, Brian Booth, one of Langston's employees, voluntarily arrived at the Edgewater police station to make a sworn statement. Gamell, Leo Booth, and Bob Darnell, from the FDLE, attended the interview.

Booth told them his job was to care for the birds, to feed them, and keep the cages clean. He worked under the supervision of Doug Cook, a contract animal trainer, who lived at the house when Langston was in Nicaragua. Virginia came to the house frequently for a few months, Booth said, and sometimes stayed half of the day. The thing that impressed him most about Virginia was that she constantly complained about her husband.

While Brian Booth and Cook were outside making stainless steel grates for bird cages, Booth said Cook told him Virginia had offered Langston five thousand dollars to kill Doc, and Langston had refused. It was a worrisome bit of information for Booth, but it really struck home when he heard Doc had been murdered.

He went directly to Langston.

"I said, 'I was told that you were offered five thousand dollars to kill her (Virginia's) husband.'

"And he said, 'Yeah. But I told her there wasn't no way. That wasn't my style.' And there's no way that he could do it, he said, no way in hell that he would do it.

"Did you kill him?

"And he just started laughing and said, 'No way. She knows better than to even think that. I wouldn't kill anybody.' "

About a month before her husband was killed, Virginia arrived at Langston's house, but Brian met her at the gate and stopped her. "Phil said not to let her in. He said she was just a crazy person and he didn't want nothing else to do with her."

Virginia handed him an envelope to give to Langston, and he passed it to Langston's secretary and discovered that it contained six thousand dollars in cash. Darnell asked how he learned there was cash in the envelope.

"When Phil came in, he asked Annette (his secretary) if she (Virginia) left six thousand dollars for him so he could go get some birds," Booth said.

It was difficult for Booth to remember exact dates, but under questioning, he said the money had been delivered about three months before Doc was killed. But Langston had repaid the money, he remembered, because Langston had made considerable profits on some of his birds.

Langston went to Nicaragua in February, but warned him, Cook, and his secretary that he didn't want Virginia around. "When he left," Booth said, "he told us, 'Do not let her in my house or on my property. If you have to, use force to get her out. If that doesn't work, call the police and have her removed.' "

"Are you scared of Phil?" Darnell asked.

"No," Brian answered.

"Are you scared of Doug?"

"No."

"Are you scared of Virginia?"

"I wouldn't put anything past her."

"Who do you think killed the doctor?" Gamell asked.

"I think she did it," Brian said.

"What makes you think that?" Gamell asked.

"Because she's crazy."

Gamell asked Brian to expound on what he meant when he said Virginia was crazy. Several examples came to mind, but they were weird and bizarre rather than insane. On one visit, Virginia told Brian someone was looking into the window at her and that he had a shotgun. He saw nothing, but Virginia insisted a man was there. Another time she said a man with a shotgun in a nearby field was watching them, and was annoyed when Brian saw no one. He told about a time when Virginia telephoned Langston at night and said a man with a shotgun was trying to get into the house. Langston rushed over with a shotgun of his own and, instead of

247

finding an intruder, discovered two Volusia County deputies looking for a phantom assassin.

Following the murder, Brian said his stepfather told him he should take a vacation, get out of town for a week or two. "I said, 'No. I do that, then they're really going to think I had something to do with it.' My stepfather said, 'Then stay the fuck out of it.'"

"Uh-huh," Leo Booth said. "The only unfortunate thing about that is that we're conducting a murder investigation."

Langston telephoned the Edgewater Police Department from Nicaragua just a few days later. After several minutes of slapstick comedy with a Central American telephone operator who kept asking for Mr. Edgewater, Detective Booth was finally connected with Langston, who apologized for not getting in touch sooner. He didn't want the police to think he was dodging them. Leo Booth assured him that was not the case, and told him they had decided to wait until he returned to the United States before questioning him.

"I was out at your place talking with Doug (Cook)," Leo Booth said, "and he shed a lot of light on things with Mrs. Larzelere."

"Oh, yeah. She's a real, real, real nut lady," Langston said. "The whole thing was a sick incident I wish I'd never got involved in it."

Langston described how Virginia had initially recruited his help in carting Jason around. "I'd get him ready, and carry him to the wheelchair, then put him in the car," he said. "Virginia seemed real sincere. I thought I was doing something good."

But Virginia initiated an affair, and Jason forgot he was supposed to be paralyzed and ran into a store. "She said that my rehabilitation had worked a miracle. I should have dropped it then, but I didn't have enough sense. Then, every time she would go somewhere, she would call up and say somebody shot at her or somebody tried to run her off the road. I feel like she was trying to get me to think that her husband was trying to do her in, so I would go after him."

Langston told Detective Booth that Doc told him Virginia had tried to have someone in California kill him. "She mentioned that to me, but I didn't take her seriously. But I heard her say it so many times that —"

"What'd you hear her say?"

"That she wanted to have him killed. She couldn't stand it with him, that he was a bisexual, and that he was trying to have her killed."

Langston's former secretary, Megan Francella Rojas, once received a telephone call from Virginia. She claimed there was a man outside the window who had tried to kill her, Langston said. Virginia claimed she had survived only because the man had given himself away by tripping over a sprinkler.

The DeLand police were at the house when he arrived, and there was no sign that an intruder had been there. "I stayed that night, thinking that somebody was trying to kill her. That was way back in September, so now the whole thing comes to light."

Leo Booth grunted.

"It was just like something out of a movie," Langston continued. "You don't take full face value when somebody says something like that. But it knocked me off the sofa when I saw it on the news."

Virginia routinely stated she was a millionaire and frequently presented herself as "Dr. Larzelere." Langston said Jason also called himself "Dr. Larzelere" sometimes. "He's the one I feel sorry for because he's a clone of her," Langston said. "Just a clone of her."

After assuring Booth once more that he wasn't avoiding the police, Langston told Booth he would cooperate in any way "because the people that were involved need to go down."

"There's no doubt about that," Leo Booth replied.

"She's got the idea that she is smarter than everybody else. She tells so many lies that she doesn't even know which one she tells. She can't even keep up with herself. She can't tell the same lie twice to anybody, anytime. I don't think she should go to a mental institution because she deserves worse than that. She probably didn't pull the trigger herself but she might as well have."

When Langston returned to the United States, he made an appointment to be questioned by Gamell at police headquarters. The detective went over much of the same ground as Leo Booth did. The information was mounting against Virginia.

They talked a while about Jason's faked paralysis, and Langston said he thought it was for a dual purpose. Virginia wanted to sue an insurance company for damages, but he suspected another motive as well. "After Norm's killed she could say, 'Well, Jason couldn't do it. He can't even walk.' "

"Did you ever see him drive after the accident?"

"Oh yeah."

Like others before him, Langston had noticed Virginia was a heavy Valium user, and gave the drug to Jason, too. She'd give them out like aspirins for a headache.

"Do you think Norm had knowledge of her activity with narcotics?"

"Yeah, I think he did. Because she had him under so much control that she could just about do anything."

"Did he just look the other way or was he scared?"

"I think he was scared and intimidated and just really at a loss as to what to do with her."

"Did you ever hear her say she loved her husband, or she didn't love him?" Gamell asked.

"I never heard her say she loved him. She hates him."

"Did she ever say she wished he was dead?"

"Yeah, she did."

Later the detective interviewed Megan Rojas, who had been lured away from Langston by Virginia after being offered a salary increase of two dollars an hour. Virginia sweetened the deal by bailing Megan's fiance out of jail. Although Megan was employed by Virginia four months (from April 1990 to August 1, 1990) she was never sure what her duties were. Essentially, she was a companion and confidante who became exceptionally friendly with her employer.

Megan said Virginia made an effort to get close to her and she responded because Virginia needed a friend. After all, her husband was trying to have her killed. Or so Megan thought. "She informed me that she was a multimillionaire of $30 million to be exact. She said that was the reason why Norman was trying to kill her.

"I expressed concern. 'Why do you live like this, Virginia?'

"She said, 'I'm just trying to survive with the kids. It's horrible living under this pressure.'"

"Did she say that he was trying to kill her and beat her up?" Gamell asked.

"She said that there were contracts out after her and that there were people across the street, around the house, around the office, following her, shooting . . ."

Gamell asked if Virginia said what weapons were used. Megan said Virginia told her a shotgun was used once. Another time, someone shot at her with a machine gun, smashing the windows when she was driving her Mercedes. The police checked and found the windows intact. Langston came over once and found no bullet holes in any of Virginia's cars.

"But she made you think Doc was doing all this?"

"Yes. I said, 'Well, Virginia, what are you going to do?'

"And she said, 'Unless I get him first, there's really nothing I can do but live in this fear.'"

Megan found it hard to believe Doc was trying to kill Virginia. She saw him as being passive, friendly, a wonderful father and a dedicated husband who would do anything for his wife.

"Would he try to hurt her?" Gamell asked.

"No. He'd laugh at that one."

"Do you think he loved her?"

"Deeply," Megan said, looking sad.

It wasn't a pretty picture Megan saw Virginia paint for her, Langston, and her children. Doc was portrayed as an evil man who was trying to kill her. Megan heard Doc and Virginia argue a few times but she recoiled at the thought that Doc could become physically violent.

"God, no," she said. "Norman's hands were like cotton."

During the time Megan worked for Virginia, she saw an unhappy household, to say the least. The relationship between Jason and his mother was far too intimate to suit her. She said Doc was worried about it, too.

"Their relationship is abnormal, don't you think?" Doc once asked. Megan agreed that it was. "Don't you think it would be better for Jason to leave?" Again Megan answered in the affirmative.

In Megan's mind, Jason and Virginia were much more than mother and son, and she thought it was blatantly obvious. "It was unbelievably noticeable," Megan said, adding that Doc tried to kick Jason out of the house, which proved none too easy. Jason was at home when Doc was at work, although he would disappear when Doc was present. Virginia told Megan she was hiding Jason, and urged her not to reveal Jason's visits.

Then Virginia confided that Doc was trying to kill Jason, too.

The strain in the household affected all of the children. Benjamin and David were both nervous. David, who was still a baby, had terrible insomnia and Benjamin bit his nails down to the quick. In the four months she worked for Virginia, Megan never saw Virginia pick up any of her children, except for the one time she lifted David briefly.

"They never really came to her," Megan said. "They were Norman's children. Norman was their mother and their father."

Virginia often sent Benjamin and David away, and Jessica was frequently banished to Lake Wales with Virginia's sister. "Poor Norman," Megan said. "She constantly used those little babies against him. She used to send them away. She said that Benjamin interfered with their marriage. I don't know what she got out of that. I never really understood."

When the children were at home, Megan said they were cared for by a series of "hired hands." Jason played the role of big brother and did it admirably in Megan's view. Although Jessica seemed to resent it, she was the one who cared most for the children between the hiring and firing of various hired hands.

Jessica seemed angry most of the time, especially where Virginia was concerned. "She was very much aware that her mother was ill," Megan said.

Although Virginia was decidedly strange, Megan didn't consider her crazy. She was like a whirling dervish who kept things stirred in a frenzy of accusations, suspicions, and unnatural relationships with her family. Virginia ignored Benjamin and David, tolerated Jessica, and treated Jason more like a lover than a son. And she hated her marriage.

"This marriage is a joke," Virginia told Megan. "It's lasted far longer than it should have. David isn't even Norman's."

Besides her strange behavior, Megan said Virginia and Jason were heavy drug users. She said they took amphetamines, known on the street as "speed," and Valium. Megan saw bottles that contained one thousand ten-milligram pills of Valium on dressers in the house and in Virginia's makeup kit.

After just a few weeks, Megan hated going to the Larzelere home to work. There was so much tension and so many lies that she found it difficult to maintain her own sense of proportion. At first she was afraid of Doc, because of the things Virginia said. Then she discovered he was a kind man who befriended both her and her fiance. Virginia, on the other hand, gave Megan increasing amounts of cash, which she implied were payoffs to keep her from ratting on her to Doc.

Virginia always carried hundreds of dollars in cash, but Doc was almost always broke. "He never had ten cents," Megan said. "I had to buy a pack of cigarettes for him."

"Was there an occasion where he asked for five dollars for gas?"

"He and Christopher (her fiance) went to Scotty's one day and he didn't have the money to buy something that was ten dollars," Megan said. "He asked Christopher for the money."

"How much did Virginia have?"

"She would hand me three hundred or four hundred dollars just to go to Wal-Mart. I've seen her with over four thousand dollars at one time."

"And Norm not having anything?"

"Right. She took all the cash from the deposits at the office."

"Did you actually see her do that?"

"I collected the money. I prepared the deposit ticket."

"You say she took the cash and you deposited the checks? And then you gave it all to her?"

"That was a big problem, because Norman wanted me to give the money to him," Megan said. "At this point he was questioning her about where the money was going. She forbid me to give it to him."

"Did you ever hear *divorce* come up?"

"Yes. Norman came over to my home and said that he and Virginia were getting divorced," Megan said. "I was no longer working for her, I was working for him."

Virginia, however, had different ideas. When Megan arrived at the office the next morning, Virginia called and said, "What the hell are you doing there?"

"And I said, 'Norman came over and told me to come here.' The next day, Norman's attorney called the office. Virginia intercepted the call. She got violent when she realized that it was his divorce attorney."

"She got violent in what manner?"

"She just exploded right in the middle of the office. I mean, 'I'll take half of everything!' This is *all* mine! This office is half mine. The business is half mine. It was a real scary situation. I excused myself."

"Did she ever tell you that Norman was a homosexual?"

"Yes. But I know it wasn't true."

After the interviews with Langston, Jessica, and Megan, Gamell felt the effect of the tragedy seeping into him. The major victim in a murder, of course, is the person who is killed. But it doesn't stop there. It affects family and friends; disrupts the lives of business associates, casual acquaintances, and the police officers who investigate, as well as their families. The detective felt sorry for Doc, Jessica, David, and Benjamin. Whether or not Virginia or Jason were guilty of murder was not a question for him to decide. Yet the whole episode was a horror.

Doc had been an abused husband, father, and stepfather. Jessica had been robbed of her childhood, and who knew what scars David and Benjamin would carry? Doc apparently had been too tolerant for his own good. He had known about Virginia's affairs and of at least one plot to have him killed, but had turned the other cheek.

Twenty-one

Norman Karn, Virginia's former lover in California, told Gamell a now familiar story. After meeting Virginia while picking up a blind date at Doc's dental office, she initiated an affair, had him believing she was worth $39.6 million, and that she was the daughter of a Cherokee Indian Chief. In the latter capacity, she claimed to receive monthly royalties from oil wells on the reservation.

Because of time constraints, Gamell conducted the sworn interview on the telephone, and recorded it. He had never met Karn but knew quite a lot about him.

After he had bedded Virginia in North Carolina, Karn said, Virginia spent a great deal of money on him, and they continued their love affair after he returned to California. "We had a back-and-forth. I ended up making three or four damn runs to Daytona and she did the same with me out here to California."

The fact that Karn had documented details of his affair with Virginia was more than Gamell could have hoped for. Details would be recorded that otherwise might have faded from memory with the passage of time. Virginia, Karn said, was consistent in saying she didn't get along with her husband.

"Did she ever lead you to believe that Norman and she fought and Norman beat her up?" Gamell asked.

"Oh, yeah. Yes, sir. One time she flew out of here in the middle of February. Boy, she had some bruises on her around her ribs and toward the middle of her back from just about halfway under her left bust line to around the middle of her back. I mean, she was green."

"Man."

"Black and blue and purple and this and that and the other. She said he (Doc) was beating her, that he was trying to have her killed. I had phone conversations that lasted all night long."

Virginia told Karn she got the bruises when Doc threw her down the stairs into the basement, but Karn didn't believe her.

"She wouldn't have any landing room. Then she kept saying, 'Boy, I don't want to give up half of my fortune to him. If only he would die.' "

Karn said it wasn't until the latter part of February 1989 that he finally realized Virginia wanted him to kill her husband. Virginia telephoned him from her car phone, he said, to tell him someone had forced her off the road. According to her, she was calling from her wrecked car. "She said that Norman was trying to get her killed."

Virginia also complained to Karn about prowlers, who were constantly trying to break into the house, and of others who tried to shoot her from ambush. There was no place where she could feel safe, she told him, because Doc was determined to kill her and she was afraid he would succeed. Virginia claimed she had hired bodyguards.

"Did she ever make hints to you that she'll get him first because he's trying to get her?" Gamell asked.

"Yes, sir. I don't remember a specific in that respect, but the general attitude was that whoever got done (killed) first would be the winner because it was like he was trying to kill her. I kept telling her all along, 'Well, goddamn it! That's against the law. Call the cops.' "

Virginia always made excuses for not getting the police involved, Karn told Gamell, then she started lying to him about that, too.

Karn said in the brief time he knew Virginia, she swallowed dozens of pills a day. The only pill he recognized in her assortment was Valium, which she also gave freely to Jason.

It was after she had taken so many pills that she had near death episodes after sex. "At least four different times, we would be in bed together and she went through a . . . like she died. I mean she would lay there and stop breathing. We'd finish making love or whatever and she'd lay right there and stop breathing. And I would grab onto her chest and I couldn't even feel a heartbeat.

"I'd start pumping on her darn chest, not pounding on her, but I'd just start pushing on her and figuring on giving her mouth-to-mouth resuscitation. It was scary to me."

After about five minutes, Karn said, Virginia would come to, as if waking from a dream. Virginia's lover was relieved, but confused because he didn't know what was going on. "I thought it was rather odd," he told Gamell.

Karn told Gamell about the telephone calls both Virginia and Jason made to him regarding her alleged kidnapping, and of the wreck she supposedly had when Doc had her run off the road. Although he considered Virginia more than a little strange by then, he told Gamell that he was thinking about her money. "Boy, I would have married her in a heartbeat, no matter how crazy she was. Just in order to collect alimony from her."

Although Virginia's behavior was often bizarre, and the way she presented things was confusing, Karn started to think of Doc as his personal enemy. Perhaps Doc really was trying to have Virginia killed. The fact that Jason and Jessica treated their mother's new lover well convinced Karn there was nothing wrong with having an affair with Virginia.

"I was totally convinced it was all right," Karn told Gamell. "Until Norm (Doc) called me."

"What did he say?"

"This was after the allegations of him beating her up and trying to have her killed and all that kind of stuff. And then, out of the clear blue sky, he called me up and was asking a bunch of questions. He was feeling out the territory. A.J. (Ellis) had told him that we were having an affair, and he didn't want to believe it.

"He was just trying to test the waters. He said, 'Has Virginia been out there?'

" 'Not to my knowledge.' "

At this point Karn thought Virginia was the injured party and didn't want to volunteer information.

"She was gone for a week," Doc said.

"Where did she say she was going?"

"She said she was going to Albuquerque."

"Did she go there?" Karn asked, knowing that she had been with him in California.

"I don't know."

"Why don't you ask her?"

After some preliminary questions about Virginia, Doc surprised Karn by breaking down and weeping. "He said, 'I think that she's crazy and that I ought to have her put away.'

"I really don't know her that well."

Hearing Doc's anguish, Karn had a hard time keeping his composure. It reminded him of how he felt when he thought his own wife was having affairs. And here was a man in the same boat, weeping on the telephone, and seeking comfort and reassurance from the man his wife was cheating with.

Following the tearful conversation with Doc, and considering Virginia's odd behavior, Karn started to think the unthinkable. On February 16, which was his birthday, Karn recorded the strange events and his suspicions in his log.

"God, it seemed to me like she was leading up to having me . . . somebody do Norm," Karn told Gamell. "And it started to make sense to me."

Karn concluded that the limousine driver he'd met in Daytona Beach who called her "weird" was right. "She is. Big time. I just didn't see how deep at that time. . . . She was making innuendoes around, hoping out of my true love for her and her true love for me that I would volunteer."

"To kill Norm?" Gamell asked.

"To kill Norm . . . to get him done out of the way."

Karn recounted the time Virginia brought Jessica and Jason to California on one trip. Along with Karn and his daughter, Stacy, they went to a restaurant called The Dixie Bell. They were joined by Ron Hayden, the featured country singer, on his first break. Karn's version of the story was that Hayden's van had conked out and that the singer was broke.

"Ron made this statement exactly," Karn said. "He said, 'Hell, I'd do anything for $2,000."

"Virginia said, 'You would?'

" 'Yeah.' "

Karn said he, Virginia, and Hayden moved away from the others.

"She said, 'I'd be willing to pay $20,000 to have someone killed.'

"He (Hayden) said, 'Who?'

" 'My husband Norman.'

"And he says, 'How do you figure you want to get it done?'

" 'A shotgun is the cleanest way and it's not traceable.'

"He says, 'Where do I get the shotgun?'

" 'I have one at the house.'

"That hit me right upside the head," Karn said. "Because she had told me prior that she would not allow any guns in the house."

"Would you say she was kidding or was she serious?" Gamell asked.

"I figured she was serious as a heart attack."

On March 8, 1989, Karn said he tried unsuccessfully to contact Virginia, and then received a four-page letter from her in the latter part of March ending their relationship. Virginia gave several reasons for breaking off the affair, but said her main excuse was that Hayden had told her Karn intended to marry her, divorce her to get alimony, then remarry his ex-wife. Karn wanted to punch Hayden out, thinking he had caused him to lose an opportunity to marry a multi-millionaire.

But Virginia's letter wasn't bitter. "She thanked me for showing her where her button was," he told Gamell. "You know, the button was . . . supposedly she'd never climaxed before meeting me, never had an orgasm."

Karn said he was surprised that the police hadn't contacted him sooner. He had been afraid Virginia would put a contract on his life because he knew too much.

"When Virginia dumped me, I wanted to look up Ron Hayden, look him in the eye, and give him hell," Karn said. "Now I'd like to look him up and tell him that he did me a favor."

The affair with Karn had lasted just under three months, ending March 8, 1989. The fling was so intense that it left Karn dizzy. To Gamell the lies and subterfuge reinforced the image of Virginia as a master of intrigue with an insatiable sexual appetite. He could not help being impressed with her physical and mental energy. He thought it must have come from the drugs she took.

Twenty-two

Steven Heidle felt the pressure mounting near the end of April, 1991. He worried about being framed for Doc's murder or disposed of by Virginia or Jason. Kris probably felt squeezed, but she had no intention of betraying Virginia, who likewise felt things closing in. Instead of withdrawing, Virginia reacted by holding additional press conferences.

Kris and Heidle were worried about Virginia's attempt to court the press since she invariably contradicted herself regarding the events and description of the gunman who killed Doc. When they knew Virginia had called a reporter for an interview, both Kris and Heidle ducked to safety. Heidle pleaded with Virginia not to put his name in the newspaper, but it did no good.

When Kris walked out of the Edgewater police headquarters after an interview on April 29, she found Pat LeMee, a reporter from *The Orlando Sentinel,* waiting for her. Virginia had telephoned the newspaper and asked that a reporter interview Kris, even though the police informed everyone involved it wasn't ethical to talk to the press about an ongoing investigation.

Nevertheless, Virginia, wearing five gold rings that she told LeMee were love gifts, was outside the police station talking to the reporter. Virginia told Kris to give LeMee an interview. Kris bristled and refused to answer LeMee's questions and became angry when the reporter persisted.

"I'm just an employee and I do not enjoy these interviews," Kris said. "You're being rude and asking sexual questions that are nobody's business."

Doc's murder was sensational news, but the press was eager for more information on the allegations of incest, homosexuality, bisexuality, and the three-ring sexual circus allegedly performing at the Larzelere household. It disgusted and embarrassed Kris.

The next day, Virginia called a reporter for another interview, and both Kris and Heidle hid. Heidle had asked Virginia not to put his name in the newspaper, but there it was in the next edition, spelled with the *i* before the *e,* which was a mistake Virginia always made with Heidle's name.

It was obvious to the suspects that the police were closing in, but Kris and Heidle had even more on their minds.

"Do you think they're gonna try to pin this on us?" Kris asked Heidle.

"What the hell do you think they're doing?"

They were both very nervous and tried to think of something else to talk about, but couldn't. "What do you think went on when you were driving by slow?" Heidle asked.

"I was just making sure everything was done with."

"That makes you a suspect."

Kris didn't say anything more at that point, but seeds of betrayal were planted in both of their minds. Heidle was particularly worried about being framed for Doc's murder, and that Kris might be helping to set him up. After all, she had lived with the Larzeleres for a year, and she might know much more than she admitted. He just didn't know.

On May 2, Heidle decided that, for his own protection, he should tell the police everything he knew about Doc's murder and of pertinent events before and after. His sworn statement was taken by Bennett and Gamell. Heidle was accompanied by his mother, Patricia Ann, who sat in on the interview.

"You previously made a statement to the police department," Bennett said, "and for whatever reason you neglected to give us all of the details."

"The point I want to start with is that the previous statements, however false or incomplete," Heidle said, "were made because of the hold Virginia had on me and the fear I had of her."

Since he knew Virginia had Doc killed, he believed she would have no qualms about killing him. Heidle wanted to tell the police everything he knew about the case, but he wanted protection — and not just from Virginia. Heidle was worried about a man Virginia referred to as Uncle Ray, who had ties to organized crime, and lived in a large yacht in New Smyrna Beach.

"We have no knowledge of him," Bennett said.

"I hope not. I don't want them in jail and have Uncle Ray after me."

The police had promised to protect Heidle, but they didn't have the authority to grant him immunity from prosecution. Bennett read Heidle his rights, which he waived, and he began telling a story that cracked the case wide open.

Heidle wasn't sure whether or not Kris had knowledge of the murder before it occurred, since he had never met her until the night after Doc was killed. But he suspected she had to know something.

"Kris told me that on the day of the murder, they said 'Go and be gone for a while.' And Kris said 'All right.' She (Kris) said Virginia told her to make sure she was in a public place where lots of people would see her.

"I'm sitting in this house alone ordering pizzas and making phone calls and they're all making sure their asses are covered. That should prove to you that I did not plan it. I'm sitting in this house all alone . . . and they told Kris 'make sure you have an alibi, make sure you're in a public place, and make sure you take a long lunch.' "

"Who told her that?" Bennett asked.

"Virginia. That's what Kris told me, at least."

The detectives wanted to know why Kris drove around the office before she parked.

"She wanted to make sure it was over," Heidle said.

"So she had knowledge that the murder was gonna occur?"

"I never directly asked her that question. I said if they

were gonna plan this big thing and then drag me into it, why would they screw me like this and leave me in the house all alone? I was a hundred and twenty miles from the murder. I didn't kill anybody but . . ."

"You didn't have an alibi?"

"My mother is my alibi and Domino's Pizza man is my alibi, the Burger King man and the dry cleaning lady."

"Did he like his father?" Bennett asked.

"No, but I did not believe he (Jason) would kill his father, or that Virginia would. There's bad people and there's truly evil people. And I believe she (Virginia) is a truly evil person."

Heidle told Bennett and Gamell about the cocaine party at Jason's house, and that he had walked into the bedroom and saw a young man holding a shotgun with gold filigree work on the metal.

"Was it sawed-off or was it pointed?" Bennett asked.

"It wasn't sawed-off yet. Jason waited to do that."

"Do you know where that shotgun is now? Or where he put it?"

"Yes."

"Could you tell us and show us?"

"I could bring you there but I couldn't tell you. I wanted to tell you that so bad," Heidle said. "I feel so much better now. I wanted to tell you so bad."

Heidle's mother said, "I'm gonna have to throw up."

Virginia and Jason had coached him on everything

269

he was to tell the police, Heidle said. He had done so out of fear for his life. "They (Virginia and Jason) told me to tell you that Jason and his father were on good terms and that he called all the time. I never spoke to Norman on the phone. Never, never had he called."

"Who told you to tell the police that?" Bennett asked.

"Virginia. Before I went in to be questioned by you, she was basically coaching me on what to say. I said, 'I'm not really comfortable with this.' She said, 'If you're not . . .' "

Heidle broke off and showed them an audio tape cassette. "I wanted you to hear this."

"Is this a tape of her?"

"I'll play it for you. This is my answering machine. One day when I was at home."

Heidle played the tape. Virginia spoke first in a firm voice.

Virginia: *Hi, are you home? This is Jenny. Pick up if you're home.*

Jason spoke, his voice articulating every word, heavy with menace: *Steven, it's Jason. If you're there you'd better pick up. If you're with Scott you're in trouble. Steven, it's Jason. If you're there pick up. Damn you! You better get ahold of me. You best get your ass somewhere where we know the phone number and stay put. Damn it all. Where . . . are . . . you? You checked your messages yet? Are you there? Steven, you know what the consequences are for screwing up. Where . . . in . . . the . . . hell . . . are you?*

"What was he referring to, 'You know what the consequences are for screwing up?' " Bennett asked.

Heidle told about the meeting he had with Virginia where she told him that "business is business," and said it meant he would be killed if he didn't follow their orders.

Later in the interview Steven described his first trip to the storage facilities in DeLand where Virginia kept various records. He and Jason had gone to them about two months before the murder. The storage areas were filled with several boxes and briefcases.

"Have you ever overheard Jason make statements in regards to the murder of (Doc) either before or after the murder?" Bennett asked.

"Yes."

"How long prior to the murder did he make that statement to you?" Bennett asked.

"Two months."

"Do you think he was involved in that murder?" Bennett asked. "Do you think he did the shooting?"

"Jason killed his father, period," Heidle told the detectives.

"He did the shooting?"

"Jason killed his father."

"How can we prove it?" Gamell asked.

Heidle said there was no way he could prove it, and that Virginia had told him, " 'Don't tell the police unless you can prove it.' And I said, 'I can't prove it.' I just know that he killed his father."

* * *

Steven then went on to relate his activities on the day of the murder including his second trip to the storage facilities with Jason, the complicated set of errands Jason had ordered him to do without explanation and the use of his mother's car by Jason.

Because he was afraid of Virginia and Jason, Heidle said he moved into a friend's house after the murder and hoped they wouldn't be able to find him. But he talked to Jessica almost every day on the telephone because he thought she needed a friend. Jessica had a crush on him, Heidle said, because he pretended he wasn't gay and told her the only reason he wouldn't date her was because of her age.

During one conversation, he reported that he asked Jessica, "Do you think your mother had your father killed? And she said, 'Yes.' " He was worried about Jessica's state of mind. "This girl is talking about suicide. When people talk about it, they're not kidding." The best advice he could give was that things would get better, and told Jessica to stay away from her mother.

Virginia and Jason got into an argument about money just a day or two after Doc was killed, Heidle said. "They sat down one day when we were looking over the insurance policies. I overheard Jason bitching about money, and she (Virginia) said, 'Don't worry. You'll get your two hundred.' And she hands him hundred dollar bills like they're water so I know she meant two hundred thousand from the insurance. So I'm sure Jason didn't just on a whim get up and say 'Let's kill my dad today.' I'm sure, him and his mother were as tight as they could possibly be."

Gamell asked if Virginia had talked about the insurance policies with Heidle. When she reviewed the insurance policies, Heidle said, Virginia made several comments. " 'Allstate is screwing me. They said I have to have it a year and it's only been a couple of months. I don't know if I'm gonna be able to collect on this.' Plus all the way through this she was playing poor so she wouldn't have to give anybody money. She won't even give money to Jessica or her own sister."

"Did she ever mention a will?"

"She told me that she forged the will."

"She told you that?"

"When I asked for the Power of Attorney for her, to buy her a new car, she said 'Forge it. I forge Norm's as well as I forge his Power of Attorney. It's easy to do.' "

Whether or not Kris had anything to do with planning the murder was something Heidle couldn't answer. "But I do know she had a lot of knowledge after the fact."

"What do you know that she had knowledge of?" Bennett asked.

"I'm sure she knows exactly what happened. She probably knows all about that other stuff that went on in Edgewater that I don't know about because I was in Orlando. I know what happened in Orlando. I know my mother's car disappeared for a long time and I know there were a lot of miles on it."

Gamell asked if he knew about the possum that Jason had killed, or the dead kittens. Although Heidle knew nothing about the possum, Jessica had told him about finding the disembodied heads of her kittens in the refrigerator.

When Heidle helped load files from the dental office

into the Suburban, he found a file marked "Newspaper Articles" that Virginia had saved. It contained numerous newspaper stories about the murder, one that mentioned dead animals and death threats. But what caught Heidle's attention was the number of times Virginia contradicted herself.

Heidle said he didn't receive a salary when he worked for Jason, but both Virginia and Jason gave him several hundred dollars just to buy groceries or pick up the cleaning, and told him to keep the change. "She was just good to me. She bought me clothes for the funeral and stuff, and new shoes. She'd take me to dinner."

"Does she have large sums of money hidden somewhere?" Bennett asked.

"I'm sure she does."

Virginia was still nice to him after Doc was killed, but she tried to keep him from seeing Jason. Then, after the funeral, Jason just disappeared. No one told Heidle where he was. It was only later that he discovered one of Virginia's bodyguards had taken him to Dallas. "While he was gone, I was with his mother, and she was spending money on me, pretending to be my friend, telling me what a mess everything was.

"She told me that the only problem with everything was that Norm was screaming for Jason in the ambulance.

" 'Were you there?'

" 'No, they wouldn't let me in the ambulance.' "

Heidle said Virginia called out Jason's name only because Doc did, and she couldn't decide how to cover herself. Now it was of real concern to her.

Another problem concerning Virginia was that Jason's timing had been off. "Jason was supposed to be at the office Friday afternoon at twelve o'clock. He was late and there was a patient there and Emma was there, back early from lunch. There wasn't supposed to be anybody there."

"Is that what Jason told you?" Gamell asked.

"Uh-huh."

Virginia became paranoid after the murder, or at least worried enough to concern Heidle that they might be picked up at any moment by police, or killed by unknown parties who had been threatening her. "She claimed that people were following me and that I needed to zigzag to lose them. She said all of the phones were tapped, that the houses were tapped, and that people were watching from across the street and taking pictures."

But even with the pressure of the police investigation, Virginia still had her wistful moments, although it was never certain whether Virginia was lying or telling the truth. When she and Heidle had lunch at a restaurant, "I asked, 'What are you going to do when all of this is over?' And she said, 'I'd just love to sit back and watch Jason and you graduate from college.' She never mentioned getting remarried, but she said she might like to travel. I thought she might not travel any farther than the nearest jail cell."

The interview verified the body of information the police had gathered: Jason was gay, he didn't talk about his father, Jason could walk *and* drive without help, and he had a one-time sexual encounter with Heidle.

But Heidle had no idea what Kris's sexual preferences were and he denied any sexual involvement with Virginia or Kris.

Returning to the shotgun used in the murder, Heidle said both he and Kris had disposed of it on Virginia's orders. Heidle told the detectives the gun was in Virginia's attic. At first, they tried to bury it in the cellar, but couldn't dig through the floor. Virginia told him and Kris to take it away. He protested, saying he wasn't going to get involved with anything like that.

"Did they mention that it (the shotgun) was the murder weapon?" Bennett asked.

"No. They just said . . ."

"They just asked you to get rid of the shotgun for them?"

"Uh-huh."

"And you and Kris got rid of the shotgun?"

Heidle's answer was confusing. "They didn't ask me to get rid of a shotgun. She (Virginia) didn't want this in the car anymore. That Kris and I were to go for a ride. And I didn't even know it until I walked out to the car and Kris was putting something wrapped up in a towel in the back of the car."

The shotgun looked like the one he had seen at Jason's house in Orlando except that it was shorter. Since he saw a bag from Home Depot (a hardware store), a blade, a bag of metal shavings, and a hacksaw, Heidle believed Jason had sawed-off the barrels.

"Are you positive the shotgun . . . was the same one

. . . or were they just identical?" Bennett asked.

"I'm positive."

"Did they tell you that it was the same shotgun?"

Heidle's answers about certain aspects of the gun were confused, even though he was supposedly coming clean. The detectives noticed discrepancies in his story, and he waffled on some points. Still this was riveting information and might be the break they had worked toward to put all of the pieces together. Gamell asked where they had hidden the gun. "She (Kris) threw it into the water." Heidle said he would show them where to find it.

There was hardly any traffic in Interstate 95 as the unmarked Edgewater police car headed north. Sgt. Bennett drove while Heidle searched in the 3 A.M. darkness to find the spot where the gun had been dumped. Gamell was on the radio as they entered different counties, alerting them to have diving teams ready if they were needed.

Florida has been developed to the point that its ecosystem is severely strained, but there are still large stretches of scrub palmetto and swampland that have no distinguishing features. The police drove almost all the way to Jacksonville, and Heidle had not been able to locate the spot where the gun was thrown over a bridge.

The police turned back. This time, Heidle recognized the bridge where he and Kris had stopped. "He had marked it in his mind so well that he counted off the pilings on the bridge where the gun had been tossed over," Gamell said.

Divers from St. Johns County, who had been alerted, showed up to look for the gun in the dark, murky water. This was dicey business because there were an unusually large number of alligators around. Gamell grabbed a shotgun and scrambled down an overgrown embankment to protect the divers in case an alligator decided to attack.

Fortunately, the search was over almost as soon as it began: Heidle had remembered the spot so well divers found the block of cement on the first try, and were out of the water within minutes. The detectives tried to restrain their excitement. They had been misled often and heard so many lies, and this could be just another wild-goose chase.

But they didn't think so. At last, they believed they were getting to the truth. If there actually *were* guns in the cement, they could start making arrests. The sun peeked out of the east, turning the sky red, pink, and gold as the detectives drove back from St. Augustine. They took the block of cement to the Radiology Department at Halifax Medical Center to be X-rayed and waited with anticipation for the few minutes it took to receive the negative. It was only a black and white negative but it was one of the most beautiful things Bennett and Gamell had ever seen.

The silhouettes of a shotgun and pistol were crystal clear inside the cement.

Twenty-three

Heidle's sworn statement had given the police enough information to allow them to piece together most of the events surrounding Doc's murder. But they need collaboration.

The next day, Friday, May 3, they decided to call Kris back to Edgewater for another interview. Kris still resisted telling the police everything she knew about the plots to kill Doc, the actual murder, and the things that occurred afterward. McEver and Bennett had applied pressure to her previously — but gently. Now it was time to try the nutcracker approach: Kris would have to decide whether to face charges or tell the truth.

But she didn't know that when she sat down with Bill Bennett and Leo Booth. Bennett advised Kris of her rights and she signed a waiver.

Bennett wasted no time getting to the heart of the matter. "There have been some new developments in the case, and when you talked to myself and Lieutenant McEver before, he said one of the things you have to do is be honest with us and tell us what you know." He told about new witnesses and the insurance policies on

Doc's life. "We know the reason why Dr. Larzelere was killed, we know who the trigger man was, and we have located the murder weapon."

Kris appeared nervous but not terribly shaken by the news that the guns had been found. "There are fingerprints," Bennett said. "Fingerprints are forever. That's one thing you need to understand. What I want from you is the truth. Because I've got you in lies. I've got you on taped statements and I've got you on lies. There are a couple of roads that you can pick. This thing is all over and it's winding up this weekend."

"What lies?" Kris asked.

"You told me that you didn't know anything else about this. You told me that you were not involved in this."

"I wasn't."

"I want the truth, and I want to know everything you know."

The things Bennett told her finally seemed to hit home and Kris looked scared.

"Am I gonna have to stand trial?"

Bennett didn't let her off that easy; he wanted the words to come from Kris's mouth. "Are you gonna have to stand trial for what?"

Kris didn't bite. "Am I gonna have to be in trial at any time?"

The detective told her again that she had two choices. "You have the avenue that goes this way, which is with us. Or you have the avenue that goes this way, which is gonna be where Virginia and Jason end up."

Thoughts ran through Kris's mind. "Understand this," Booth said. "Your cooperation is what makes you look that much better. Okay?"

"I understand that. But the thing is, I want to know if I'm gonna stand trial and I would sit there and be as she told me her, her . . ."

"Her little puppet?" Booth offered.

"No. Her, uh . . ."

"Her alibi witness was the word?" Bennett said.

"Her star witness."

Bennett told her that yes, she would have to testify in court.

"That's what I needed to know."

"I'm not going to lie to you and I don't expect you to lie to me," Bennett said. "But you're not going to be the only one to testify. That's why this is being wrapped up in this fashion this weekend. Because if the people are behind bars, they cannot hurt you. They cannot get at you or anybody else."

Kris made an unintelligible sound.

"Okay, right now, I want you to do all the talking," Bennett said. "And I want you to tell me Kris's story of what she knows. From the very beginning. How you met the Larzeleres and the whole truth is what I want."

Booth made his hands into a cup. "Hold your hands like this," he said. "You have your whole life right there in your hands."

"I know. In my hands. I know."

"Let's hear what you have to tell us," Booth said.

Kris said she didn't lie about her trip to Palm Beach with Ted Goodman. But even while she promised to tell the truth, she hedged. She said Virginia didn't hire anyone through Ted Goodman to kill Doc, but speculated that the weekend might have been a cover-up for something. Later, when she told Virginia that Goodman said Virginia had asked him to do "something," Virginia retorted that he lied.

Then Kris jumped ahead to the day Doc was murdered. She said Virginia sent her to lunch and wouldn't let her come back when she telephoned. When she did, everything had already happened. But she said she didn't know if Virginia had killed Doc, or if she had hired someone. She said she believed it might have been a robbery "because Doc was in a lot of things that I didn't know about."

She mentioned that after the funeral Virginia told her and Heidle to get "something" from Patricia Ann's house, which turned out to be guns. Kris talked about wiping guns with acid, and trying to bury the guns in the cellar. She then admitted to putting them in a plastic tray that was covered by cement, placing it in the car, and driving around until she and Heidle found a place to dump it into the water.

The homicide officers began to force Kris to rethink some of her story. They told her enough of what they knew to be the truth to squeeze her. They knew it would take a combination of tenderness and shock therapy to bring Kris out of Virginia's control.

"The day it happened, you drove around the office, turned around and drove back up," Booth charged.

"I did not. I was sitting at Wendy's. I had my lunch at Wendy's. I drove by the street and I went to the Gas Stop and bought a pack of gum. I did not drive down the street. I did not."

This was a lie that contradicted what dozens of wit-

282

nesses had said. But was Kris intentionally lying, or was her memory still fogged? The detectives let it pass.

"Since then, what has Virginia told you about?" Booth asked.

"Well, actually I didn't say anything to Virginia, and I guess Jason didn't think that I knew at the time all this was going on. And then after that happened, Virginia just said, 'You're in this as much as we are.' "

Kris had contradicted herself as she talked, but the nutcracker was working.

"Has she ever referred to the murder itself?" Booth asked. "Of Jason doing the shooting?"

"Jason came out and said it to me once or twice. In arguments."

"Has Virginia ever said that to you?"

"She said once that 'Jason never screwed up this bad before' or something like that."

"When did she tell you this?" Bennett asked.

"This was after everything happened."

"When did Jason tell you? How long after that did he tell you?"

"It was after . . . the second questioning . . . I'm not sure. It was before I moved out and after she had us get rid of that cement which I am now assuming was the gun."

Kris said following Doc's murder that things were so tense Jason and Virginia had violent arguments. Jason threatened to turn himself in because "he was sick of it, and shit like that. Then him and Virginia would get into it and Virginia would say, 'Okay. Go ahead. Say good-bye to your brother Benjamin. Say goodbye to every-body. Tell them where you're going. Tell them what you're gonna go do.' "

"Did you believe him when he told you this? Did you believe that he killed the doctor?" Bennett asked.

"Like I said, I didn't see it. I still don't want to believe it but —"

"What kind of feeling did you get when he told you that? Did you think he was being truthful with you?"

"I don't know. I still don't know if Virginia and Jason . . . I never know when they're telling the truth until I see it happen."

"Didn't you think it kind of strange she had you wipe down the gun and Steve coming down with cement telling you to go throw it all —"

Kris replied, "At this point I knew what was going on, but I didn't want to believe it."

"But you knew what was going on . . ." Booth encouraged.

"I knew that she had a gun. I knew that she found a gun before in the closet, and she said she didn't know where it came from."

Booth asked if Jason had participated in wiping down the guns, embedding them in cement, and dropping the cement block in a tidal pool. Kris said, "He didn't know what was going on because he was asleep. And after I thought about it awhile, I told her (Virginia) I didn't like it. I didn't like what was going on."

"Did you call Mrs. Larzelere before you came over here?" Bennett asked.

Kris said it had been a few days since she had talked with Virginia. The conversations concerned a prospective buyer of the dental practice, who didn't want Kris to work for him, and Virginia was having trouble with lawyers, cash flow, having electricity being disconnected, and being hassled by the police.

"Are you willing to cooperate with the police now and tell us everything you know?" Bennett asked.

"That's basically everything I know."

"Are you willing to cooperate with us?" Bennett persisted.

"I have ever since the beginning."

The detectives knew Kris was still holding back, and attributed it to the masterful manipulation of Virginia. They knew of Virginia's past history and the questions that still bothered law enforcement officers regarding the attempted murder of her first husband. Virginia had manipulated strong men, including a Florida Trooper, and almost a dozen employers from whom she had embezzled.

Doctor Norman Larzelere was an intelligent man, with advanced degrees, who had become a respected dentist. And Virginia had been able to isolate him from family and friends, and feed him a continuous stream of lies. She was better at disseminating disinformation than the KGB.

Was it any wonder that she could control her own son, Kris, and Heidle?

But they had elicited enough information from Kris and Heidle to arrest Virginia and Jason on probable cause.

At 7:30 P.M. on May 3, Bennett, Gamell and Booth went to the Larzelere home with warrants for the arrest of Virginia and Jason on charges of first degree murder and another warrant to search the premises. Virginia apparently knew the police were closing in; they found a purse full of jewelry and luggage in her car, along with expensive items from the house.

The detectives fought the fleas as they searched the house, but found even worse things in the cellar. There was an overpowering odor of decomposing flesh from rotting corpses of cats and rats. The cats had apparently starved to death or died of dehydration, and the rats may have been killed by the cats. There were also skeletons of cats around the cellar.

The detectives waited until 6 A.M. on May 5 in the hope that Jason would show up. When he didn't, they arrested Virginia and booked her at the Volusia County Branch Jail. Jason learned the next Sunday that his mother had been arrested while watching television in Orlando.

He called Al Stokes, a family friend, and asked what was going on. Stokes told him and said the police wanted to arrest him for the murder of his father. Jason started to cry and said, "I didn't do nothing." Stokes urged Jason to turn himself in, and said he would meet Jason at the DeLand police station.

Jason arrived at 1:30 A.M. on the Monday morning of May 6 and was placed under arrest for murder. He was taken to the same jail where his mother was interned. Both were charged with first degree murder and held without bond.

Later that day, the Edgewater police station had to call an exterminator to rid it of fleas that had come from the Larzelere house.

After the arrests of Virginia and Jason, Heidle contacted Kris and told her they should corroborate their stories. He was worried about whether or not he would be prosecuted. Although the state attorney advised him he would have immunity regarding anything he said about the Larzelere murder.

"Nothing's written in stone," he told Kris. "They could go back on their word and arrest us. If we don't stick together, we could both be in trouble for this."

Heidle said they had handed the case to the police on a silver platter, but Kris wasn't convinced.

"Steve, one way or another, they were going to find the truth," she said.

Kris was disgusted with Heidle because she thought he was on a "high horse and expected to be treated like royalty" because he went to the police. Heidle seemed to enjoy the limelight and relished his role as one of the star witnesses. He agreed to appear on "A Current Affair."

Kris was annoyed.

Twenty-four

Ordinarily, the prosecution of Virginia and Jason would have been handled by John Tanner, state attorney for the Seventh Judicial District in Florida. But Tanner asked Governor Lawton Chiles to assign the case to another prosecutor because he had been Virginia's lawyer in 1986 when she had been charged with embezzlement. Tanner's involvement in that case occurred before he was elected to the office of state attorney, but he wanted to avoid any possible claims about a conflict of interest.

On May 17, the governor appointed Lawson Lamar, state attorney for Orange and Osceola counties, to be the prosecutor. Lamar, who was Orange County Sheriff before being elected state attorney, was an unusual prosecutor. Lawyers and police officers frequently have different views on how to prosecute a case, but Lamar knew both sides from personal experience. He could offer direction from both points of view.

On May 24, Lamar represented the state, when Virginia and Jason were indicted by a Volusia County grand jury on charges of first degree murder. Following the indictments, Virginia hired John C. Wilkins III, a lawyer from Bartow, to represent her, and John R. Howes, a lawyer from Fort Lauderdale, to defend Jason. Both men were respected trial lawyers with good records. Physically, they had little in common: Howes was of medium height, pudgy, and had classic male pattern baldness. Wilkins was short, slim, wore his curly brown hair below his shoulders, and sported tinted eyeglasses. Both men virtually crackled with energy and intelligence.

Lamar assigned the case to Dorothy Sedgwick, an assistant state attorney, who was the antithesis of both defense attorneys in style, and demeanor. Sedgwick dressed in conservative suits and seemed shy and demure. Her voice was soft and melodious; even when she raised strenuous objections, the decibel level could rarely be heard beyond the third row of the gallery. She was pretty, in her thirties, and was far from being flamboyant.

Sedgwick seemed no match for either Howes's or Wilkins's dramatic style. Members of the media and even some police officers were afraid Howes and Wilkins would flatten Sedgwick like a steamroller.

Almost everyone who didn't know Sedgwick underestimated her intelligence, talent, toughness, and appeal to a jury. By June 20, Howes and Wilkins had submitted a blizzard of legal motions consisting of almost two hundred pages. More than forty motions challenged issues ranging from the Constitutionality of Florida's death penalty to the impeachment of testimony given by witnesses for the state in sworn depositions. All had to be answered by the state, read by, and ruled on by the presiding judge.

Motions made by the defense on behalf of Virginia and Jason claimed Gamell had misled witnesses, confused them intentionally and, having made up his mind that Virginia and Jason were guilty, conducted a biased investigation designed to prove his preconceived opinion.

The motions confirmed what some believed would be the defense strategy: to show their clients were innocent by showing Gamell and the Edgewater police to be incompetent bumblers. This helped explain Virginia's complaints before her arrest about how the police had ignored her broken fingernail, placed little credence on her reports of death threats, and harassed her following Doc's death.

As case detective, Gamell was on the hot seat. "I tried not to let it bother me," he said. "You know that the defense is going to do all it can to win. I knew I had been fair and impartial, but at the same time, I was worried that maybe I had inadvertently screwed something up. I was afraid that the whole case could have been thrown out because of a technicality."

Bail hearings are often routine and boring, but as with everything else in this murder case, the hearing for Virginia and Jason was explosive. The legal fireworks started on June 20, 1991. Sedgwick argued that Jason had been with Heidle after Norm's murder and "seemed excessively overjoyed." According to Sedgwick, Jason waited for a telephone call from Virginia to confirm that Doc was dead. Later, he told Heidle and Kris the murder had not gone as well as he had hoped. "If I knew my life was going to be like this, I never would have bumped off Norman for Virginia," Sedgwick quoted Jason.

Virginia wept as Sedgwick called Gamell to the stand to testify that Jason and Virginia had an incestuous relationship.

"Virginia told me she was in the same bed with Jason," Gamell said, "and Jessica told me that they live together as husband and wife." Gamell testified both mother and son used and sold cocaine; Virginia forged prescriptions for drugs, using her husband's name; and a witness had sworn Virginia had offered him $50,000 to kill Doc. In addition, Gamell testified that five days before Norman Larzelere was killed, Virginia had a fight with Doc and told Jessica, "Don't worry, I'm going to get rid of your father soon."

Sedgwick read from the transcript of Gamell's interview with Jessica following a fight with Doc. " 'I can't stand your father anymore,' " Sedgwick read from the transcript, quoting Jessica. " 'I got to get rid of him.' "

Howes and Gamell had met before and instantly disliked one another. The defense attorney often called Gamell "The Pillsbury Dough Boy" or "Slim." With the detective on the witness stand, Howes unleashed what he later referred to as "a vigorous cross-examination." He accused Gamell of intimidating Jessica so she would give the testimony he wanted. He further claimed Gamell was inept, inexperienced, and engaged in a vendetta against Virginia and Jason.

Gamell offered new information about Doc's murder and Virginia's reaction to it. Instead of trying to revive Doc, he said, Virginia had actually smothered him by placing her mouth over his. Witnesses told the detective Doc had cried "Jason" when he was shot, and Virginia was afraid he would repeat it.

"You're lying, aren't you?" Howes asked.

"Not as much as you, I hope," Gamell retorted.

Jessica wept when her recorded interview that damned her brother and mother was entered into evidence. She took the stand and recanted almost everything she had said.

"I told him (Gamell) at the time that I thought my mom had something to do with it (Doc's murder)," she testified, "but now I know she's innocent."

Judge Robert Miller delayed a ruling on whether Virginia and Jason should be allowed bail. He denied bail on July 9, after reviewing reams of witness statements and police reports. "This court finds that proof of guilt is evident," he said, "and presumption great as to the guilt of both defendants of the offense of murder."

The judge said Virginia and Jason were too dangerous to be released from custody.

The defense filed a motion on July 22 for a change of venue to move the trial to another county because the Larzeleres were well known, and "extensive, persuasive and sensational publicity" had tainted the jury pool. Howes and Wilkins claimed neither could receive a fair trial in Volusia County.

Wilkins said he hoped that the trial would be held in Fort Meyers, farther south and on the opposite coast. He also asked that Virginia be allowed to wear her own clothes during court appearances. It embarrassed her, he said, to be dressed in the jail jumpsuit because of the television cameras and newspaper photographers. People who had read about Virginia's sexuality, attractiveness, and alluring appeal were surprised at the plain woman with slightly protruding front teeth pictured on television and in the newspapers. The judge granted her request to wear her own clothes.

Howes and Wilkins filed a new motion for bail and delivered a blistering attack on the state, and Gamell in particular. If there had been doubt before as to the defense's strategy of claiming Virginia and Jason were on trial because of a bungling, inept police investigation, this motion put it to rest.

The defense attack on Gamell was withering, and few people had seen anything like it. Wilkins and Howes were fighting hard for their clients.

". . . (the) state attempted to elicit from Gamell his editorial opinion concerning the various statements made by the affiniants and Virginia Larzelere. The defendants feel it is most significant for the court to note the change in demeanor and the lack of frankness of Gamell during cross-examination."

In other words, the defense in its motion accused the detective of lying.

"Defense argues that Gamell was confused about ski mask, size of eye holes, and that no ski mask had been seized. These examples are only two of many in which it is clear that this admittedly inexperienced homicide detective involved in his first major case, saw things as he wanted them to be as opposed to objectively investigating the matter.

". . . the state failed to conduct meaningful and significant background investigations of chief accusing witnesses in the case, Steven Heidle and Kristen Palmieri. This background check and attempts to confirm these witnesses' statements is even more critical in this case due to the fact that each had previously given 'untruthful' statements and both admitted complicity in the crime and the commission of others. What Detective Gamell did was accept unquestionably admitted liars' statements because it fit within his opinion of how the events transpired.

". . . It is obvious that this court cannot rely upon Detective Gamell's theories in determining what 'proof' actually exists . . . Gamell, after a period of two months, has failed to follow-up on any background investigation of . . . Heidle or Kristen Palmieri. Detective Gamell denied undertaking the steps necessary to compile a personality profile of these witnesses. He stated that other members of the Edgewater PD were 'getting' the records from three hospitals concerning Jason Larzelere's epilepsy, but admitted that absolutely no professional medical opinion had been obtained with respect to the bonifieds of Jason Larzelere's epilepsy or whether, according to Steven Heidle, it was all part of an elaborate ruse.

"It is frightening that in a case of this type, the State would proceed to procure an indictment against Jason Larzelere without first making a valid medical determination to the best extent possible . . . Detective Gamell's lack of thoroughness and failure to follow up is demonstrated again in his failure to note the identity of Jason Larzelere's treating physician and in his failure to obtain records from that physician . . . Based upon his clear interest in the outcome of these proceedings and the demonstrated and acceptedness of his conclusions, this Court should place absolutely no weight in

Detective Gamell's assertion that Jason Larzelere began 'faking' illness when there was a meeting with Gamell outside a restaurant."

Gamell had seen Jason by accident, before his arrest, one evening outside a Quincy's Steak House. The detective waved and called out, "Hi, Jason. Feeling better?" Jason looked up in surprise, slapped his forehead, and began stumbling around, and fell against the car as if for support to keep from falling.

The motion continued to castigate the detective, the prosecution, and the Edgewater police department. It was heavy fire from a pair of highly intelligent, capable criminal defense lawyers who intended to conduct a tough, vigorous defense.

However, the second motion for bail was denied.

The state breathed easier.

Howes and Wilkins didn't flinch. They were smart, determined, and ready to go the distance. The motions they lost were long shots; there was a long, hard road the state had to travel for a conviction. And the defense would try to derail it at every opportunity.

Both Virginia and Jason entered Not Guilty pleas, and the first of several trial dates was set for August 5, 1991. The original intent was that both defendants would be tried together. Sedgwick's motion to have the trial date moved back, because the case was "complex," with witnesses scattered across the country, was granted. The trial was set for October 14.

In the meantime, the state responded to the defense's forty motions, in a single pleading "for the court's convenience." The defense motions were all denied, including, a motion for a bifurcated jury, one to render a verdict, and another for the sentencing phase if Virginia and Jason were found Guilty. The request is routine, and just as routinely denied.

Judge Miller denied the defense request for a change of venue, pending *voir dire,* the jury selection phase of a trial. When prospective jurors were questioned during *voir dire,* the judge said he might move the trial to another city if the jury pool proved to be tainted.

Virginia's trial was next set to begin January 27, 1992, following delays requested by both the prosecution and defense. Instead of being tried together, Jason and Virginia elected to have separate trials, with Jason's scheduled to start on February 24, which was overly optimistic, considering how slowly the judicial proceedings had moved. Judge Miller, who had retired from the bench, was replaced by Circuit Court Judge Jack Watson to preside at each trial.

Both Jason and Virginia appeared in court on January 27, with yet another surprise. Virginia wore a beautiful green dress with long sleeves, her face was made up, and she looked stunning in contrast to her previous court appearances. Jason was in civilian clothes, too, wearing tan pants, short sleeve shirt, and a tie.

The two defendants moved to be represented by the same lawyers, even though they were to be tried separately. Such an arrangement held inherent dangers for both Virginia and Jason. Judge Watson questioned both carefully, and told Virginia that Howes and Wilkins could try to plea bargain with Jason to get him to testify against her.

"I don't mind at all," Virginia said confidently.

Sedgwick objected to the arrangement by claiming, "There would be a chilling effect on the strategies the defense could have to choose." Among the problems Sedgwick noted was that defense attorneys could have difficulty in rigorously questioning a witness if the testimony would be detrimental to either client.

Jason rejected Judge Watson's offer of a separate lawyer and waived the right to appeal a conviction by claiming that his lawyers had a conflict of interest. "It's very beneficial for them (Howes and Wilkins) to be together," Jason said.

Virginia told the court, "I paid for them both, I want them both." Judge Watkins accepted the arrangement. Seemingly in a lighthearted mood, Virginia laughed and joked with her lawyers, and with a member of the gallery. She announced that sharing the two lawyers was her idea.

The questioning of the fifty-nine prospective jurors began, but there was another surprising interruption on the second day of *voir dire*. Gary McDaniel, a private investigator from West Palm Beach, submitted a report to the prosecution, claiming he had new information that would clear Virginia and Jason of Doc's murder and lead to other suspects. Howes and Wilkins said they didn't know McDaniel had submitted the report.

"I developed information at the last minute, and I believe she's innocent and her son's innocent," McDaniel said in an interview.

Voir dire continued, but McDaniel's information sent Gamell scurrying to West Palm Beach and Fort Lauderdale to investigate. Virginia, who wore her own clothes, initially wore a black identification band on her wrist, which she objected to. Wilkins said it branded her as a criminal as did the orange jumpsuit she had worn previously. Judge Watson allowed her to remove it during courtroom appearances.

After two days, the police and prosecution determined there was no merit to McDaniel's report. It was just another wild-goose chase in a case that had been filled with them.

After four days, a jury was selected, consisting of five women and seven men, with two alternates.

The next day, a Friday, Howes and Wilkins asked that the case against Virginia be dismissed, claiming Sedgwick had violated the Florida Bar Association code of ethics. They said the prosecutor violated Virginia's constitutional rights by ordering a holding cell bugged in an attempt to hear incriminating evidence in conversations between Jason and Virginia.

Wilkins and Howes expressed outrage in and out of the court room. Howes told the judge the bugging was an attempt to entrap his clients. Out of court, Wilkins said, "It is strictly an issue of misconduct. For this to happen of all places . . . at the Justice Center . . ." He shook his head in disbelief.

Sedgwick argued there was nothing illegal about the bugging. Anyhow, the recording was incomprehensible and could not be used.

Judge Watson denied the motion to dismiss charges. With a jury empaneled, opening arguments were scheduled to begin on Monday, February 3, 1992. Almost a year after Doc was killed.

Twenty-five

On February 3, 1992, the first row seats in the gallery of Judge Watson's courtroom were jammed with television crews' tripods and newspaper photographers carrying cameras with huge telephoto lenses. All were waiting to record Virginia Larzelere's battle against the State of Florida for her life. Reporters were in the second row, all awaiting the opening statements from the state and the defense.

Surprisingly, the courtroom was only about a third filled, composed mostly of retirees who entertain themselves by attending murder trials. There was a hush in the gallery as Virginia walked in. She was wearing an aqua sweater and a matching skirt and blouse in a red and green floral pattern. She looked and acted like an attractive socialite who might do charity work in her spare time, and attend fund-raising balls.

It became apparent early on that she was taking an active part in her defense. She whispered to her lawyers and jotted notes. Wilkins looked fast and smart, like a bantam weight boxer, while Howes gave the appearance of being a plodder. Sedgwick had been joined by Leslie

Hess, another assistant state attorney, to help with the prosecution. Most of the journalists thought the defense would outmaneuver the duo from the state, an attitude that persisted for the duration of the trial.

Sedgwick used a scale drawing of the dental offices when she began her opening statement. Her tone was friendly and conversational as she outlined how the state intended to prove Virginia was guilty of first degree murder, even though she didn't pull the trigger.

."The evidence will show that the shooter was her natural son, her eighteen-year-old son, Jason Larzelere. The evidence will show that Virginia Larzelere is guilty under the law of Florida as a principal." Sedgwick said Virginia expected to benefit from her husband's murder, and she had promised to pay Jason for his role. Virginia's plan for the murder, the prosecutor told the jury, ran into complications when Jason was late. The murder occurred at about 1:03 P.M., Sedgwick said, instead of shortly after noon when there would have been no witnesses. Instead, there were two witnesses, not counting Virginia.

Using the drawing to show how the murder unfolded, Sedgwick said, "Emma Lombardo, who was Dr. Larzelere's employee and dental assistant, . . . was standing in this exam room, and she was standing close to the doorway. This is the exam room that is the very closest to the patient waiting area." The prosecutor pointed to the chart to show where Virginia and Hilda Levezinho, the patient who was in the waiting room, were in relation to where the shooting occurred.

The evidence would show that Emma Lombardo

heard footsteps, which were those of "Dr. Larzelere as he ran for his life from the masked gunman, which was to be Jason Larzelere . . . She was to be standing by this doorway. She was to see Dr. Larzelere run through the hallway through this doorway, which separated the hall from the patient waiting area; that she was to see the gunman who is essentially only a body length away from her. She was to see the gunman standing . . . in the hallway . . . that she could see Dr. Larzelere, in his last-ditch efforts to save his own life, closed this door separating the patient waiting area . . . between him and the gunman.

"And that as she stood there, a body length away from the gunman, that the gunman pointed his shotgun — the masked dark-clothed gunman — pointed the shotgun towards the door and fired a shot through it" and killed Dr. Larzelere. Hilda Levezinho didn't see the gunman, because the door was closed, but she saw the dentist fall.

Sedgwick said the police and paramedics arrived minutes later, and at first saw "Virginia Larzelere bent over — crouched over the body of Dr. Larzelere, and she was at that point initially composed. She was immediately to present a picture of what they had every reason to expect, and what they had no reason . . . to question, the picture of the hysterical, grieving wife. Not wanting to talk, crying, appearing to be too upset to talk."

The prosecutor said Virginia was acting because she was trying to work out a scenario in her mind because the murder had not gone as planned. She did make a brief statement at the scene, Sedgwick told the jury, and another later that night at her home.

"Virginia Larzelere's presence in the dental office was a critical presence to law enforcement. She was an eye witness. She was a person who could give them a statement as to whatever it was that she saw or heard, or whatever else it was that she knew about the murder."

The police interviewed Hilda Levezinho and Emma Lombardo, who had seen the gunman. These two eye witnesses had seen and heard things that occurred during the murder, but if things had gone as planned, who would not have been in the dental office to see or hear anything.

Because of this, Virginia said the murder was "screwed up" and that she "had to fake a robbery." And although the gunman wore a mask, Emma Lombardo recognized "the height, the weight, the physique, the posture, the movements of the shooter as being the characteristics of Jason Larzelere.

"Further, Emma Lombardo heard Virginia, during the course of the murder, yell, 'Jason, is that you? Is that you, Jason?' " Sedgwick said Virginia's changing descriptions of the gunman's appearance were not the only conflicts in her statements to police. "Virginia was to weave for the police a scenario of a robbery occurring (even though) Emma said there was no robbery. Virginia was to describe . . . herself taking on the gunman, struggling with him, breaking her fingernail, while in fact nothing like that ever happened."

The assistant state attorney said Jason carried out a "charade of helplessness" just before the murder, and intensified it afterward. But, in fact, Sedgwick said, Jason was incapacitated only when Virginia kept him heavily medicated. Virginia, Sedgwick said, was ready to flee at her husband's funeral, "with her envelope of cash organized" and "someone to pose as her double in case she was going to be arrested."

Following the murder, Sedgwick told the jury, the fact that Jason's figure and movements were recognized, and his name spoken during the murder, "these matters were of great interest to the police and of great, significant anxiety to Virginia." Virginia was now faced with the problem of controlling others with guilty knowledge of the murder.

The prosecutor took a risk when she said there would be witnesses with "guilty knowledge" of the murder. In essence, Sedgwick told the jury they would hear testimony from Steve Heidle and Kristen Palmieri, who had known about the murder before it occurred. Both had perjured themselves to protect Virginia and themselves, and Sedgwick expected them to be attacked by the defense. By admitting their "guilty knowledge," she hoped to blunt the attack the defense was certain to launch against the two witnesses.

In an attempt to control events, Sedgwick continued, Virginia sent Jason out of town. Kris helped move boxes of files from one hotel to another to sort out insurance papers, and kept the fingernail Virginia claimed she broke struggling with the gunman. "And it was Kristen who was sent to pick up Jason that night (of the murder) and bring him back to Virginia's house . . . when it was very important that no one see Jason driving, at a point when he could no longer be physically capable of driving."

Sedgwick told the jury Heidle and Kris wiped prints from guns, including the murder weapon, encased them in cement, all at Virginia's instructions, and dumped them. Yet another thing went wrong, the prosecutor said, when Jason used the car belonging to Heidle's mother to commit the murder. Virginia had not counted on Heidle's resetting the odometer; damage to the car; Patricia Ann, Heidle's perceptive mother, wondering why Virginia offered to buy her a new car and, failing that, tried to change the car's appearance.

It was his mother's persistent questioning, plus Heidle's own fears, that caused him to cave in and tell the police everything he knew, which led them to the murder weapon. Heidle had testified to helping Jason clean out a warehouse the morning of the murder, and had seen two wills and numerous insurance policies on Dr. Larzelere's life. These were put in Jason's car, then sorted through later by Virginia and Kris in various hotel rooms after Doc was killed.

After Heidle told about dumping the guns, Kris admitted she had lied in her previous statements. "Kristen was to tell the police that Virginia told her that Doc was saying 'Jason' while he was on the floor of the dental office after being shot, and that Virginia, while pretending to perform CPR (coronary pulmonary resuscitation), had put her mouth over his to keep the word 'Jason' from being heard.

"Kristen was also to explain to the police that Virginia told her something that never made any sense to her; that Virginia also made [the] statement, 'And I also had to put my finger in his hole.' "

Sedgwick told the jury, the police investigation uncovered several occasions where Virginia had elicited help from people whom she first involved in a lover-type relationship, to help her kill Dr. Larzelere, "and used different ruses to explain her motivation on why she wanted Dr. Larzelere dead."

But Virginia picked the wrong men to be hired assassins. "These men declined her offer to be the killer," she told the jury, and said they would hear their testimony. Sedgwick concluded her opening statement: "Eventually, Virginia Larzelere's lack of love for her husband, and her very real invigorating lust for money, motivated her to use her son, Jason Larzelere, as the gunman. Jason was a willing participant . . . Jason, who would want his two hundred thousand dollars for taking care of business."

Sedgwick completed her statement and took her seat.

Wilkins made the opening argument for the defense. Contrary to the nervous energy he usually showed, the defense lawyer was calm, used an economy of movement, and had a calm, soothing voice. Virginia Larzelere is not guilty. This particular case arose out of perjured testimony, out of ineffective police work and presumption."

He said there were two separate parts to his argument: the alleged reason for the murder, and character of witnesses the jury had to believe beyond a reasonable doubt to return a verdict of guilty.

"The police say, the state has just told you, the reason(for the murder) is greed. Insurance money. Two point something million dollars' worth." He said that wasn't an unusually high amount of insurance. Dr. Larzelere and Virginia Larzelere made a lot of money in his dental practice. They have four children; two of them were Virginia's children by a prior marriage, but adopted by the doctor . . . They were conscientious in insuring the financial well-being not only for themselves but for their children."

Wilkins told the jury Doc periodically increased his life insurance to insure that his family would have financial security if he died unexpectedly. Wilkins showed the jury a blow-up of a life insurance policy with Kentucky Central for $150,000 that Doc obtained in May 1985, before he married Virginia.

Virginia was listed as a co-beneficiary, with Doc's parents, on that policy, which was bought "not in anticipation of any killing." Wilkins showed that the policy was increased by one hundred thousand dollars a short time after it was taken out.

There was nothing sinister about the increase in life insurance policies in late 1990, Wilkins told the jury, because Dr. Larzelere wanted to build equity for the future. At the same time, a policy with a face value of $500,000, with an accidental death benefit of $350,000 was sought on Virginia's life, naming her husband as the beneficiary.

Insurance policies with a face value of $50,000 were also obtained for each of the children, with Virginia the primary beneficiary, followed by Dr. Larzelere. "It was a family affair," Wilkins told the jury. ". . . a chance to redo all of their insurance for the whole family. Not for purposes of obtaining a million dollars so that Virginia Larzelere could kill her husband."

The policies on the children contained an additional accidental death benefit, except for Jason, "because of his condition, based on what happened to him in a car wreck."

Wilkins talked more about life insurance, and said the Larzeleres shopped for the best policies they could afford, and asked the jury "not to throw your every day experiences out the window and forget about everything you've learned in your lifetime.

"If it's the state's position that the defendant incurred and took out with the doctor over a million dollars' worth of life insurance to kill him, why does she choose, along with the doctor, the seven hundred and fifty thousand? The truth is, that's what they can afford, and it's logical."

There was a glitch in obtaining the previously mentioned life insurance policy on Virginia: It was rejected because of her medical history.

The insurance intricacies were surely daunting to the jury, with the strain showing on their faces as they followed Wilkins in his attempt to simplify complicated arrangements. As he explained the financial arrangements of remortgaging their home and analyzed Doc's will, a few of the jurors seemed dazed by the complexity of such monetary concerns.

Wilkins spent some time on Doc's will, which left everything he had to Virginia, while noting that Virginia's will named Doc as her single beneficiary. Concerning Doc's will, "The state says, 'Well, hold it. Is that will fake?'

"There is a notary seal and a notary that Dr. Larzelere signed in front of, and it was sent to the lab by the state to see whether or not Virginia Larzelere had anything underhanded to do with this will, because we know that she didn't have anything to do with the insurance. And, lo and behold, this comes back from the lab, from the state's expert at the Florida Department of Law Enforcement, stating that the will is genuine, that it bears the signature of Dr. Larzelere, and that the notary seal affixed over his signature was affixed after his signature was put on. Conclusion: The will is that of Dr. Larzelere. He signed it in front of witnesses and it's authentic.

"The motive that the state would have you believe existed for a murder in this case is nonexistent."

Wilkins told the jury Doc "made a tremendous amount of money" and Virginia could go into a bank any time she wanted and "take out ten thousand dollars. Just withdraw it. Go spend it. She had all the money she wanted. She had all the cars she wanted. She had a house. They had an airplane that she flew around the country. You've got to believe, if you believe the state's theory, that that wasn't enough."

The second part of Wilkins's statement was easier to understand because it dealt with people instead of complex financial matters. Wilkins said he wanted to talk about a couple of the witnesses and the Edgewater police department, so the jury would be prepared when witnesses took the stand.

"This particular case started on March 8 and as far as the police were concerned, ended on March 9," Wilkins said. "What the police did is decide after a one-day investigation, and learning about the insurance policy, that Virginia Larzelere probably did it, and they spent the next three months proving that she did.

"They were aided by two witnesses that I hope . . . you find to be totally preposterous liars because that's what they are. The state's two main witnesses, the ones who say that Virginia said all this, that Jason said all this, that the gun was dumped at Virginia's demand, that the insurance was the main motive—the two main witnesses are perjurers. Liars. Steven Heidle and Kristin Palmieri."

Wilkins tried to destroy the credibility of Heidle, Kris and the Edgewater police department in his statement. Kris, whom he described as Virginia's "gofer" was fired a week before the murder because she was caught stealing.

"Steve Heidle held himself out to be a nurse. Even though really all he was, was an overseer to make sure Jason took his medication, and he was paid a tremendous amount of money by Virginia to do that. He was allowed to stay at Jason's apartment, which the Doc and Virginia paid for, down in Orlando."

It was a soft easy life for Heidle, Wilkins told the jury, and one that he wanted to keep. But Jason was preparing to move back to Edgewater because that was what the entire family wanted. The move was to take place the same weekend that Doc was killed.

"Steven Heidle was going to lose his golden goose," Wilkins said. "He wasn't going to have the money coming in for doing nothing. He was going to lose his right to a car phone, his beeper, a place to live.

"And then, all of a sudden, Dr. Larzelere was killed. Steven Heidle, who barely had ever met Virginia Larzelere, now became a central figure in this case. For whatever reason, he decided to lend his lack of experience to the Larzelere family to help them get through this particularly difficult time."

So Kris and Heidle, who had not met before Doc was killed, were at the Larzelere home running errands, and doing odd jobs, while the family grieved.

Wilkins noted that Heidle did all the things he would testify about . . . if you believe him . . . "and then he's going to tell you that on at least four to five separate occasions he gave perjured statements to the police. Perjured, because he told them that Virginia Larzelere and Jason had nothing to do with it (Doc's murder), that he didn't know anything about it.

"And then, later in May, he comes up and says, 'Oh, let me tell you the truth.' And the truth is the story that the police had been wanting to hear all along. The state says, forget about the four perjured statements he gave them. Forget about the fact that he lied four times under oath," because the fifth time "he told the police what they wanted to hear: Virginia Larzelere did it.

"Kristen Palmieri is absolutely identical to him. She's a liar." Wilkins mentioned the four sworn statements Kris made, saying she knew nothing about the murder, but the police believed her the fifth time. " 'Oh, by the way, let me tell you what I know about Virginia.' " Wilkins's voice dripped with sarcasm as he offered his views on Kris and how the police reacted to her fifth statement. "Oh, we forgot about the four perjured ones. We know she's telling the truth now, because she's telling us what we've known all along: Virginia did it."

Wilkins wagged his head in disbelief. "You're going to find some preposterous responses on cross-examination by those witnesses."

For example, Kris would claim she was told to go to lunch and get an alibi. "She will tell you, 'Well, I didn't know what Virginia was talking about, but no, I didn't even ask her what she meant. I was just supposed to get an alibi.' She doesn't even know a murder was going to happen. What does she need an alibi for? It's preposterous."

Wilkins told the jury Kris made statements to the police on the day of the murder and two days later, and never mentioned Virginia telling her to get an alibi. "That came up in May when she needed to tell them (the police) a story she thought they would believe. The perjured testimony.

"She's also going to tell you that on March 10 or 11, she and Steven Heidle took the guns that Steven Heidle had encased in concrete. Now there were *two* guns. Totally unexplainable why there were two guns, because it's allegedly a shotgun that was used to kill the doc. So, lo and behold, a handgun and a shotgun were found in cement . . .

"And they both say that on March 10 or 11 . . . they drove north looking for a place to ditch the guns, because Virginia told them to.

"Well, neither of them are going to say they picked up the phone and called the police," Wilkins told the jury. "Neither of them are going to say, 'Well, hold it. I've been talking to the police twice already. Don't you think I probably ought to call them? I just ditched a murder weapon.' If it occurred.

"No, they didn't do it."

Wilkins ridiculed the notion that Emma Lombardo could have recognized the gunman as being Jason, when he was wearing a ski mask. "She can't even remember or describe the size of the gun. She says it's a big gun.

"I say, 'Is a big gun that big?' 'I don't know. I'm not good about guns.' 'How about this big?' 'I don't know. I'm not good about guns.'

"This is the same lady that can't even identify the gun, and she says, 'But he walked and he talked and he acted like Jason, but I couldn't see his face, because he had on a mask.' " The police believed her, Wilkins said, because they wanted to.

"I submit to you it's not within your human experience that when you see a person with a gun to not be looking at the gun instead of the mask."

Next, Wilkins tore into Karn and Langston. Wilkins told the jury that Langston, after having been Virginia's lover prior to Doc's death, would testify that one day Virginia said, "Would you kill him (Doc) for me?" Upon hearing that, Wilkins said, one would expect Langston to call the police, but that wasn't what they would hear him testify to during cross-examination.

The defense attorney demonstrated how the examination would proceed. "Well, I'll bet when the doctor died, you picked up the phone and called immediately and told the police that, didn't you? 'Oh, no. No, they finally called me and I said, oh, yeah, I remember that.' It didn't happen. He's a vindictive, fired, lost lover, and this is his opportunity to get back.

"Mr. Karn is even worse. (He) is going to say that he and Virginia wanted to get married. That she was supposed to divorce the doc, and he thought that she was, and she was going to buy him a mansion out in California, and they would live happily ever after — and all she had to do was get rid of the doc."

Although Karn said Virginia asked his friend, Ron Hayden, to "do" Doc for $2,000, it wasn't serious. "Mr. Hayden is going to come in here and say, 'Yeah, [we] all joked and laughed about it. Everybody thought it was a joke. [We] were talking about Mr. Karn and Virginia getting married and they had to get rid of the doc. It was all a joke.'

"Think of how many times you, or a person that you know, have said, 'If I ever get my hands on him, I'm going to kill him,' and then live in fear that person never dies in the next year, because that's what we're facing right here."

If the first part of Wilkins's argument, dealing with insurance policies and financial matters, was difficult to follow, his characterization of the witnesses was a piece of cake. The jury had no problems digesting this; it was high drama, better than any soap opera. And then Wilkins surprised everyone by saying how Virginia would be characterized.

"She has one character trait that's hard to find in a person. She can't make a friend. They describe her as cunning. They describe her as demanding. They describe her as controlling. They describe her as a master of manipulation. A nasty person.

"I think you'll find, after you've heard all the testimony in this particular case, of those witnesses and everybody else, that on first impression, they're absolutely right. She fits all of those (descriptions). For the same reason, it will force you to conclude that she didn't commit this murder. If that person with those traits was going to commit this murder, it wouldn't be done by an eighteen-year-old son in an office in the middle of the day in downtown Edgewater.

"If Virginia Larzelere was going to kill Dr. Larzelere, he would have been killed by a professional in the middle of nowhere, his body never would have been found, and if they did find it and got a time of the murder, she would have three bishops and ten hairdressers guaranteeing she was sitting right there when it occurred. And that's the truth."

Wilkins asked the jury to hear all of the testimony before they made up their minds. "One thing that's true; there was no motive. A family affair, a police-botched investigation, and perjured testimony is going to cause you to sit here for the next two and a half weeks, and I'm hoping that after hearing all of this testimony, you will find her not guilty, because in fact, Virginia Larzelere is not guilty."

The battle lines were clearly drawn between the prosecution and the defense. Virginia sat hardly moving through jury selection and the opening statements, so calm that she might have been in church. Occasionally she smiled, scribbled a note, or whispered in her lawyer's ear.

Bonnie Gilbert, a young black woman who claimed to be Virginia's jailhouse lover, sat in the gallery, as she would every day during Virginia's trial. She and Virginia exchanged a smile. Bonnie wasn't a hardened criminal, but had a penchant for writing rubber checks that routinely bounced her into jail, most recently in the same cell as Virginia.

Twenty-six

Sedgwick announced, "The state calls Norman Karn." Karn, wearing jeans, cowboy boots, a white shirt, and carrying a black cowboy hat with a silver band, walked down the aisle to the witness stand, where he was sworn. Karn was over six feet tall, looked taller because of his cowboy boots, wore a mustache, and had male pattern baldness.

Under Sedgwick's direct, Karn told about how he met Virginia, the transcontinental romance, and of her claim to be the granddaughter of a Cherokee Indian Chief who received royalties from oil wells. Karn told the court Virginia said Doc physically abused her and had tried to kill her. Virginia, he testified, said she had been run off the road, had been shot at numerous times, and had been kidnapped.

Karn surprised the gallery, after testifying that Virginia had written two checks: one for $2.5 million to buy Dover Manor, and one that was blank to buy expensive sports cars for herself and Jason. Then, he opened an envelope and pulled out the original checks he had mentioned, and three photographs of Virginia in a sexy "teddy." All were entered as evidence.

The Californian testified that Virginia wanted to have her husband killed. "She wanted him eliminated. She made mention that a shotgun would be a clean way." Karn testified that when he took Jason, Jessica, Virginia, and his daughter, Stacy, to the Dixie Bell Restaurant, Virginia first offered the star country singer, Ron Hayden, $2,000, plus a new motorcycle, to kill her husband. According to Karn's testimony, Virginia said later in the same conversation she would fly Hayden to Florida in her own airplane, and "There would be a Harley-Davidson with $20,000 in the saddlebags for him to leave the state with."

On cross-examination, Wilkins attacked Karn's credibility. He asked if he hadn't told an insurance investigator for one of the companies insuring Doc's life that he would give testimony to negate payment of the policy in return for $500,000?

"I was joking," Karn said.

Wilkins may have scored points with the jury on that question. Perhaps he had made the jury doubt Karn's credibility as a witness. "Was she (Virginia) serious about having Norm killed?" he asked.

"Yes, sir," Karn said, but noted "she didn't ask me to kill him specifically."

"You saw her as a way out of your financial problems, right?"

"Yes, sir," Karn said, and again admitted, "She never outright came out and asked me to kill him."

Under intense questioning by Wilkins, Karn admitted, "Things were moving too fast and I was having second thoughts about Virginia" and that "Jason was a nerd, a personable young man."

"Virginia dumped you, didn't she?" Wilkins asked.

"Yes, you could say that."

"Are you bitter?"

"No."

"Have you ever been dumped by a lady before?"

"Yes, sir. I've been dumped quite a few times."

This last response caused a few titters in the gallery, but the jury remained inscrutable. Virginia's fate was in their hands, and it was obvious each juror took the responsibility seriously. Many jurors, who bluff their way through *voir dire* because they care to be caught up in the drama of a murder trial, wish they had been excused, because the job is so daunting.

On redirect, Karn testified that Jason and Virginia had stayed at his house five or six days. Previous to that, he testified, "Virginia told me she didn't like guns and didn't want any in the house" in Edgewater. But in California, he testified, she told him "Norman (Doc) had stashed two shotguns. There was a .410 gauge and .10 gauge taken to the house."

Karn testified he and Virginia were celebrating the pending purchase of Dover Manor when they went to The Dixie Belle. "She said that she wanted Norman killed," Karn said.

Doc had heard about his affair with Virginia from A.J., Karn said, and testified, "I didn't lie. I just beat around the bush and didn't give him any answer at all."

The next witness for the prosecution was Ron Hayden, the country singer Karn said had been offered a contract by Virginia to kill her husband. Hayden was dressed in a Western motif, with cowboy shirt, boots, and carried a black cowboy hat with a plain band. Like

Karn, Hayden was also tall, standing 6 feet, 3 inches.

When the country singer was sworn, he was asked if he recognized Virginia Larzelere in the courtroom. He did not, even though he was sitting no more than twenty feet away from her. Hayden testified that the woman named Virginia at The Dixie Belle was waving a stack of one hundred dollar bills around, and asking everyone what they wanted. Virginia asked the singer, Hayden testified, and he wondered, "Why did they ask me about what I could have?"

Under Sedgwick's direct, Hayden said, "Norm (Karn) told me she wanted someone to murder her husband." They talked about it further. "Virginia asked me if I knew anyone who could do it. I said, 'Probably.' I knew people around the Miami area who would do it."

"How much would it cost?" Sedgwick asked.

"About three hundred dollars."

There was a collective gasp from the gallery, which was stunned at how cheaply human life was held by certain members of society. It was a sobering, frightful revelation.

Hayden remembered that the woman he talked with was named Virginia, even though he didn't recognize Virginia Larzelere in the courtroom.

"Virginia said he (her husband) was very routine and she could write down the things he did and when he did it." Hayden testified that Virginia said she was rich but, "She said the only way she could get the money was if he (her husband) was dead."

Sedgwick asked Hayden to state his height and weight, as she did all of the state's witnesses, to establish that they didn't fit Emma's description of the masked gunman who killed Doc.

Howes's cross-examination was brief. Hayden said he was on is first break of the night, but that he had been drinking "stingers," a potent alcoholic drink composed of brandy and *creme de menthe*. The singer said he polished off several before, and after, he joined the table, where Virginia was waving money and asking people what they wanted. It was just barroom fun to him, including his agreement to find someone to kill Virginia's husband.

"You were joking, weren't you?" Howes asked.

"Yes."

"You thought Norm (Karn) and Virginia were joking, right?"

"Yes."

It was Karn who first brought up Doc's murder, Hayden testified, and who discussed Doc's weekend routine. After the night, killing Doc was discussed, Hayden testified he never saw or heard from Virginia again.

"It was never agreed that you were going to kill anybody, was it?" Howes asked.

"No, sir," Hayden replied. He passed off the entire incident as "bar talk."

On redirect, Sedgwick attempted to dispel any damage Howes had done by making light of the talk about killing Dr. Norman Larzelere. She didn't want the jury to think planning a murder was a joke, or that Karn was the instigator rather than Virginia. Hayden said when the discussion occurred, "Virginia was sitting right there" and "She never contradicted the fact that she wanted her husband killed."

"Did she deny it?" Sedgwick asked.

"No."

"Did she laugh?"
"No."

The next witness called by the state was Phil Langston, who stood 6-feet, 5 1/2-inches, had wide shoulders, and a trim waist. He wore a short-sleeved shirt with epaulets, open at the throat. For a man his size, he had an incongruously soft, tenor voice.

Sedgwick had him tell the jury how he had met Virginia, his taking care of a supposedly incapacitated Jason, and how Jason had run from the car to a store, and Virginia's reaction when he told her about it. "She said I had miraculously cured him," he testified.

Langston testified Virginia told him her husband beat her and was a homosexual. He described an incident that occurred after Virginia had a fight with her husband. "She called my house and said they had a fight. She pulled up and blew the horn, and was in a rage, cursing. 'I've got to get rid of Norm.' I told her, 'Don't look at me. I'm not capable of that.' 'Do you know anybody?' I told her, 'You need to cool off.' She was furious. She said, 'I have to get rid of him.' She offered me fifty thousand dollars, and I said, 'Believe me, I wouldn't do that.' "

On another occasion, Langston testified, Virginia wanted to buy into his business for $200,000, which would make her half owner. Even though Langston refused the offer, Virginia had contracts drawn, he said. He also admitted, "She was giving me money all the time."

In previous depositions, estimates were that Virginia had spent $70,000 on Langston during the time he cared for Jason and knew her. Langston never tried to hide it.

"Did she lie to you?" Sedgwick asked.

"Continuously."

She asked about his first contact with the police to blunt Wilkins's statement in his argument that Langston waited until the police contacted him. That wasn't true, he testified. "I called Leo Booth at the Edgewater from Nicaragua. It was about six weeks after it (the murder)."

Langston also testified, "She (Virginia) called me and said her attorney had advised her to fly to Las Vegas and marry me for seventy-two hours to protect her millions from her husband."

"What was your answer?"

"I said there was no way."

Wilkins cross-examined Langston, and tried to impugn his character, and show that Virginia's actions couldn't be taken seriously because of her personality and addictions.

When Virginia spoke to him about killing Doc in her Mercedes, Langston testified, "She was furious."

"You didn't think she was serious?"

"No, I didn't."

"Was she a liar?"

"Yes."

"An addict?"

"Yes."

"You didn't report it (Virginia's request to have her husband killed) because you didn't think she was serious, right?"

"Right."

Langston testified he didn't have a message in Nicaragua to call the Edgewater police, but did it on his own. Doc had telephoned him once, he testified, and asked him not to see Virginia anymore. The witness was excused. He told the author later he had paid his own air fare, and other expenses, to return from Nicaragua to testify.

"I'm glad that I'm here in the present tense," he said. "She paid me a lot of money, but it wasn't worth it. At a thousand dollars a day, it wasn't worth it."

The next witness called by the state was Hilda Levezinho, the patient who had been in the waiting room and had witnessed Doc's death. She had gone for a routine dental visit only to have a first row seat to murder.

Hilda arrived at 1 P.M. for her appointment and had only been in the waiting room for a minute when she said she heard "quick, heavy footsteps. The door just flew open and Dr. Larzelere came out and as he came out, he faced me and said, 'Oh, no.' His face was in fear.

"In a split second, I heard this explosion like a shotgun. He went down, facedown. As he was going down, he said 'Where are you, Jason?' He said that a couple of times. Then he looked at me and said, 'Help me.' "

The memory was difficult for Hilda, a woman who appeared to be in her sixties, whose expression was anguished as she testified. Virginia listened with tears streaming from her eyes to Hilda's account of Doc's murder.

When she was cross-examined, Hilda wavered, and said she wasn't absolutely certain Dr. Larzelere had said "Jason."

Court was adjourned. The testimony had been dramatic, but the state seemed to have won the day by a comfortable margin.

Newspaper headlines and television stories roused public attention and Judge Watson's gallery was jammed with people as Emma Lombardo, Doc's dental assistant, testified. Emma said Virginia didn't act the same as usual when she came to work on the day of the murder.

"She was shaky and nervous that morning," she testified in a voice softened by a slight Filipino accent. A slight, bespectacled woman, Emma seemed nervous as she sat on the witness stand, and described what she saw and heard.

The dental assistant testified that she had just returned from lunch, and was disinfecting a room, when Doc ran past her. "I thought he was having another fight with his wife," she testified. "They fought all the time in the office."

Doc ran into an adjacent waiting room and slammed the door, so that Emma couldn't see him. But she saw the man who immediately fired the shotgun through the door. Although the gunman wore a dark ski mask, gloves, and dark, form-fitting clothes, Emma recognized him.

"It looked like Jason," she testified. "His body was built just like that. He was tall and skinny. His left shoulder is higher than the other one. All I can say is that the body build is just like him."

Virginia had described the gunman to police as being short, stocky, and with a short ponytail held in place by a blue rubber band. The dental assistant contradicted another one of Virginia's stories: There was no gold in the safe and there had been no robbery.

The gunman was no more than six feet away from her when he fired, Emma testified. She heard Doc say, " 'Oh, no.' Then he looked up and said, 'Help me.' "

Virginia didn't chase after the gunman, Emma testified, nor did she try to grab him. She said there was no scuffle. Instead, Virginia rose from her chair and yelled, " 'Jason? Is that you, Jason?' She said it three times."

Howes, in a sarcastic tone that marked all of his cross-examinations, picked at every detail of the dental assistant's story. Emma admitted she couldn't remember a lot of details, including the exact description of the gunman's clothing, or whether he was right or left handed.

"The most you can say is that the person had a build like Jason, correct?" Howes asked.

"That's correct."

During the two and a half hours Emma testified, Howes chipped away at things the witness couldn't remember. Emma admitted she didn't know what kind of a gun was used in the slaying. Howes elicited testimony that the gunman's posture, with the left shoulder higher than the right, could have been because of the way he was holding the shotgun.

When Emma left the witness stand, she was obviously exhausted, and somewhat shaken. The jury was also tired from the tedious, but thorough cross-examination by Howes, who had raised questions about Emma's testimony.

* * *

Sedgwick called five other witnesses to prove that Jason was not disabled, as he and Virginia had claimed. Witnesses testified that he drove his car, went to night clubs, and partied. Christie Butler, a longtime friend and confidant of Jason, testified that he wasn't the least disabled, and in late 1990, he intended to buy a Nissan 300 ZX, an expensive car. "He said he was used to being seen in sports cars," Butler testified.

The gallery was amused when the state called Kenneth McCain as a witness. They saw a rather heavyset platinum blond in a black leather shirt outfit take the stand. McCain testified he had seen Jason walk and drive, undermining the defense contention that Jason was an invalid.

The state continued to build its case by calling Claude Murrah, a car salesman. Murrah was tall, balding, had a full mustache and wore eyeglasses with metal frames. He testified that he met Virginia when she came to the dealership where he worked, and said she wanted to buy a car for her son.

"She said he was in a hospital in a coma," Murrah said, "and thought it would be a nice surprise for him when he woke up."

Murrah soon became one of Virginia's lovers, and heard her stories about being a multimillionaire, a Cherokee Indian princess, the daughter of a robotics engineer, and that she was going to buy the DeLand Airport.

The car salesman testified that Virginia visited the dealership several times with a young man named Dale, who Virginia said was her nephew. Later, Murrah testified, Virginia said that "Dale" was actually her son, Jason.

The night before Doc's murder, Murrah testified, Virginia stayed with him, and went outside on three occasions to make calls on her car telephone. He had no idea what the calls concerned.

"Virginia told me that Jason was the product of her and her father," Murrah testified. "The father impregnated her when she was about thirteen years old."

Inexplicably, Virginia gave Murrah a loving smile when he stepped down from the witness stand, after having brought up the subject of incest. It was the only time incest would be mentioned in her trial, although it had been a central theme in depositions given during the investigation.

Perhaps Virginia believed the story would defuse the allegations of incest between her and Jason, because Murrah's account was not credible. Had Virginia been made pregnant by her father when she was thirteen, given birth at fourteen, Jason would have to be around twenty-six years old. Instead he had just turned nineteen.

Although it had caused a sensation in pretrial publicity, incest played no role in the state's attempt to prove Virginia had been the mastermind behind the murder of her husband.

Twenty-seven

A cold rain drizzled from a gloomy sky as the jury waited to board a bus that would take them, under heavy police escort, from the Daytona Beach Justice Center to Edgewater, about twenty miles away. Cars passing by on Ridgewood Avenue kicked up rooster's tails of water, and the yellow rain jackets the police wore added a splash of color to a world that had turned the color of lead.

The rain still fell when the jury arrived at the stucco building on Knapp Avenue where Dr. Norman Larzelere had worked and met a shocking, brutal death. Virginia was brought to the scene in a patrol car. Police secured the area and kept watchful eyes on a curious crowd that had gathered in spite of the cold rain. A fire truck with a medical rescue team stood by.

The building showed signs of neglect, with blotches of greenish-brown mildew near the roof line, and fingers of the growth clawing its way down the sides. A dark wooden sign had white letters that read: "N.B. Larzelere D.D.S."

Sedgwick wanted the jury to see the actual room and

outside stair design of the building to help them understand points she had elicited, and which she would attempt to elicit, in future testimony. But first, Judge Watson, his clerk, a court reporter, Virginia, a bailiff, and lawyers for the state and prosecution entered the building while the jury waited in the bus. Virginia wore a blue dress, accented with small designs in pale pink.

Virginia was in the building just a short time, then emerged, obviously in distress. A bailiff held an umbrella to protect her from the rain. Suddenly she broke into tears, seemed to collapse, and grabbed a deputy's arm to keep from falling. She was escorted back to the patrol car in which she had arrived.

"She was fine until she hit the front door of the office," Howes said. Wilkins added, "Having to go back into the room where her husband was killed, it had to be hard. Emotionally, I don't think she could handle it."

The jury and two alternates filed into the building, saw the office layout, and the rooms where Virginia, Doc, Emma, the gunman, and Hilda Levezinho were when the murder occurred. They walked down the hall where Doc had been chased by the gunman, and into the waiting room where he had been killed after slamming a wooden door. The jury saw the side door from which the gunman made his escape, and the four-foot railing Virginia said he jumped over, dropping another two feet to the ground, before he fled in a car with two motorcycle escorts.

There was no testimony during the tour, and after viewing it once, the jury walked through it a second time before returning to Judge Watson's courtroom in Daytona Beach. The trial reached a long, tedious stage, dealing with life insurance policies and forensic evidence. Some newspapers didn't send reporters. One television camera recorded the events, which would be shared by all the crews, many of whom didn't send correspondents for days at a time.

For a while, the trial moved off the front page, the local page, and even to inside pages. Testimony regarding Doc's insurance was presented in the business section of *The Orlando Sentinel*. The gallery groaned during breaks at how dull the trial had become, and some wondered aloud when incest would become a major part of the live theater in the courtroom.

While much of the testimony was dry, it was important. Leslie Hess, another assistant state attorney from Orange-Osceola counties, helped Sedgwick in the prosecution. The state had to establish a motive, and to do that, Hess had witnesses testify about the $2.1 million worth of insurance on Doc's life, for which Virginia was the only beneficiary. The prosecutor had witnesses talk about credit cards, remortgaging, and wills; all of which, he said, would lead to Virginia's financial gain after her husband's death.

There were seven different life insurance policies, with the most recent purchased from Allstate Insurance Co. for $203,000 just two months before Doc was killed. James Armstrong, a claims adjustor for Allstate, said Virginia purchased that policy and another one on Doc's life, but did not tell him that there were other policies in force on Doc's life.

All seven policies were in effect when Doc was killed, but none had paid, pending the outcome of the trial.

According to the testimony of Nancy Swiney, a State Farm agent in Edgewater, Virginia wrote to her to collect on a policy for $500,000 three weeks after Doc's death, Swiney testified that Virginia wrote in the letter, "My life ended at the same moment his did." Swiney testified that in 1989 Virginia asked her about insuring Doc for $2.5 million.

In cross-examination, Wilkins had witnesses testify that Doc had signed each insurance policy. Virginia laughed and joked with her lawyers, ate mints, and scribbled on a legal pad. Apparently she believed testimony that Doc signed the insurance policies raised a reasonable doubt against the murder charge against her.

Testimony from Steven Heidle was expected to begin the next day. It was expected to be long and crucial to the state's case. Howes had already demonstrated a style of cross-examination that was sarcastic and exceptionally thorough. Steven Heidle was in for at least one rough day. "I'm going to wear my comfortable shoes," Howes told reporters when court adjourned.

Steven Heidle strode confidently to the witness stand. He wore a white shirt and tie, dark trousers, and no jacket. He seemed remarkably composed for a young man who was under considerable pressure. He was a key witness for the state who had, by Sedgwick's admission, "guilty knowledge" before Doc's murder occurred.

The twenty-year-old witness, a homosexual who had a one-time sexual encounter with Jason, testified how he had met Jason in Orlando, run errands for him, and was paid well for his work by both Jason and Virginia. Under detailed direct examination, Heidle testified that Jason drove, partied at home, and went to nightclubs.

The day of the murder, Heidle testified, he and Jason went to a storage unit in Edgewater to transfer files containing insurance policies to Virginia's home in DeLand. Both returned to Orlando, Heidle testified, and Jason took his mother's car to be cleaned and refueled. Heidle outlined the instructions Jason had given him, concerning picking up dry cleaning, and keeping receipts for two from a fast food franchise, which Jason used as an alibi to prove he was in Orlando when Doc's murder occurred.

Jason didn't return from having the car washed until after 3 P.M., Heidle testified, and appeared "very excited." Heidle testified he wanted to leave, but Jason said, "Just wait here until my mom calls and tells me that Norman's dead."

The young, blond witness testified he had driven to the Larzelere house the night after Doc's murder. In the intervening days, Heidle testified, he lied to police three times because Virginia had threatened him.

Heidle recounted Virginia's orders for him to change the appearance of his mother's car, and said tension in the household caused arguments between Virginia and Jason. One argument occurred when Jason complained that he wanted his money, Heidle testified, and Virginia answered that he "would get his $200,000 for taking care of business."

The day after Doc was killed, Heidle testified, Virginia, Jason, Kris and himself sat at a table as Virginia spread insurance policies and commented on them.

331

Virginia, Heidle testified, was upset about a policy from Allstate.

"(Virginia) was complaining that one of the policies for$750,000, she might not be paid on," Heidle testified. Jason was also worried that the payoff might not be quick, Heidle testified, because he wanted his $200,000 fast.

Heidle testified Virginia said, "I'll find a way around that. No one is going to be getting in the way of me collecting the insurance money. Not you, not Kris, not Jason, or they'll end up like Norman."

The admitted co-conspirator in the murder scheme recounted the time he went to Doc's office to get papers. Heidle testified Jason showed him where pellets from the shotgun had hit and how close they came to where Virginia sat. "He said he was glad he didn't hit her," Heidle testified.

Virginia blamed Jason for botching the murder plan, by showing up late, Heidle testified. If he had arrived on time, Heidle said, there would have been no witnesses in the dental office. Because Jason was late, Heidle said, Virginia invented a cover story about a robbery.

"There was some discussion about the time frame at which the murder took place. Virginia had got through a discussion with Jason—actually yelling at him—about him being late on March 8."

Heidle recounted how he and Kris had disposed of the murder weapon, a sawed-off shotgun, and a .45 caliber pistol, under Virginia's orders. The witness testified that Virginia and Jason tried to keep him in their house after Doc was killed. But he left and stayed at his mother's house and with a friend. Virginia and Jason telephoned him, but he didn't answer the telephone. The state played an edited version of a tape left by Jason on Heidle's telephone answering machine.

"Damn you," Jason said on the tape. "If you're there, pick up. *You know what the consequences are for screwing up.* Steven, you better not be with Scott."

Heidle testified Virginia insisted that Jason pretend to be an invalid who couldn't drive, and kept him in the house, doped up on barbiturates.

"She said, 'You're not leaving the house. You're going to stay drugged up and in that room so you better get used to it,' " Heidle testified.

During the time Heidle testified, Jason, in his orange jumpsuit, was brought in so the jury could see the difference between their heights and builds. Jason was led away to his jail cell, after a few minutes, while Heidle resumed his seat on the witness stand. Virginia brightened considerably on seeing her son, and flashed a warm smile.

Heidle had been on the stand for six hours when court adjourned for the day. But he was far from being finished. Howes had no need that day for the comfortable shoes he promised to wear during what he said would be a vigorous cross-examination.

When Howes put his comfortable shoes on, he was like a master chef, cooking a meal for six hours, and Heidle was the main course. Heidle was touted as an important witness for the state, but there were weaknesses in his credibility Howes intended to exploit. The defense attorney attacked Heidle's homosexuality, and said the so-called "threatening message" left on his answering machine was really just the result of a lover's spat.

On the tape, Jason had said, "You better not be with Scott."

"Was Scott your lover?" Howes asked.

"Yes."

Howes failed in an attempt to have Heidle admit he was jealous of Scott and Jason, but he scored points with the jury. The defense lawyer examined almost every aspect of Heidle's testimony and the discrepancies in his statements to the police. He even had Heidle admit he used a fake identification card, showing him to be of age to get into nightclubs.

Heidle admitted he had lied to the police on three separate occasions when questioned about Doc's murder. During those times, Heidle was a conspirator, willing or not, in covering up Doc's murder, and said he lied to police to give Jason an alibi for the time of the murder.

The witness admitted he had lied several times to the police.

"You've committed perjury before, have you not?" Howes asked.

"In my first statement to the police, yes I did."

"Does it bother you that you're a liar?" Howes asked in a sarcastic tone.

"It bothers me."

Heidle testified that he finally cooperated with the police because he was afraid Virginia had ties to organized crime, and that his life was in danger.

"Virginia and Jason had told me for three or four months before that they had Mafia ties," Heidle said.

"That's all Jason would talk about. I was scared to death."

Howes's questioning was relentless. He had a stack of depositions on the defense table, which he referred to. He sipped sparkling water and mopped his face with a handkerchief as he kept Heidle on the hot seat. The defense attorney asked what time Heidle's mother's car was returned to DeBary the day Doc was killed.

"What time did your wife come home on March 8, 1991?" Howes asked.

The gallery tittered, knowing from press reports that both Jason and Heidle were gay, and had at least one sexual encounter. Heidle, who had kept his composure fairly well, answered in an unemotional monotone, "What time did *your* wife come home on March 8, 1991?"

Howes was able to get Heidle to testify that Jason was jealous of his other homosexual lovers. Having elicited that admission, Howes started using a bright pink marker to note highlights on a chart he used to denote the times and sequences of events. The pink marker, of course, was a ploy to discredit Heidle with the jury as a spurned lover seeking revenge, and perhaps appeal to any homophobic prejudices on the part of jurors.

The defense lawyer made additional points, eliciting testimony that Heidle spent several nights a week with Jason in Orlando, and was paid handsomely to be sort of a valet.

"Jason was kind of the goose laying the golden egg for you, wasn't he?" Howes asked.

"You could say that."

Heidle testified that he finally volunteered to be

truthful to the police because he was afraid of Virginia's alleged ties to organized crime. The shotgun, alleged to be the murder weapon, had been removed from the concrete but Heidle could not positively identify it as the gun he had disposed of.

"Was your reason for going to the police to tell them what you know, or to stay out of trouble?" Howes asked.

"It was to tell the truth."

Under further questioning, Heidle admitted he had received limited immunity from the state attorney: He would not be prosecuted in return for his testimony.

"You hate Virginia now, don't you?" Howes asked.

"Yes, I do."

Heidle had been cross-examined for six hours and had only cracked once when his homosexuality was ridiculed. He was obviously getting tired. But when court adjourned, he was to be on the witness stand the next day.

Howes continued to pummel Heidle on the second day of cross-examination. The defense attorney picked at inconsistencies in Heidle's memory regarding insurance policies, when the witness couldn't remember the amount of the policy. Asked to examine the gun found in the concrete which was said to be the murder weapon, Heidle seemed flustered and said he couldn't be sure.

The cross-examination raked across Heidle's statements to the police and his testimony like a machine gun. Heidle ducked but found nowhere to hide. Although the rapid-fire questions caused him to stumble several times, Heidle never lost his composure.

"Are you starting to get a little confused?" Howes asked, capitalizing on his advantage.

"I can't remember exact times."

"You intend to be more specific in the book you're going to write about this?" Howes asked sarcastically. He referred to Heidle's appearance on a national television show, where he said he intended to write a book about the case. Heidle's appearance on the show not only angered the defense but the prosecution, too.

"I'm not going to write a book," Heidle responded.

Howes's cross-examination wrung Heidle like a washcloth, extracting every bit of information from the witness: exact times, what clothes he wore, when he ordered pizza, why he lied to the police. The questioning demanded such precise answers that Heidle couldn't always remember and sometimes contradicted himself.

The defense attorney asked sarcastically why he didn't go to the police when he knew Virginia and Jason were going to kill Doc and after the murder was done. Why didn't he say anything after he dumped the murder weapon?

"I was scared to death of Virginia Larzelere and her family," Heidle said.

On redirect, Heidle told Sedgwick he didn't know about the murder until after Doc was killed.

Before Heidle's cross-examination was finished, a juror almost caused a mistrial. At a mid-morning break, the juror told Judge Watson he wanted to see Jason again, because the first time, he thought Jason was slumping over to conceal his height.

Judge Watson thanked the juror, and sent the jury out of the courtroom. Although the judge gave no hint to the jury, the question could have resulted in a mistrial. With the jury out of court, Judge Watson expressed fear that the jury was discussing the case before deliberation. He offered to quiz each juror to see if that was the case, to dismiss the jury, or declare a mistrial.

Sedgwick agreed that the inquiry could lead to a mistrial, but Wilson and Howes were feeling confident, as was Virginia. They wanted no mistrial. The judge asked Virginia if she wanted a mistrial or to continue. She smiled. "I agree with my attorneys."

Heidle's cross-examination continued and, after two days of being battered by the defense, he was dismissed.

By this time, veteran courtroom observers were leaning toward the defense. They thought Heidle had been thoroughly discredited by Howes's vigorous cross-examination.

Twenty-eight

Kristen Palmieri was impatient as she waited to testify. It was obvious she didn't like being in court. When she was called to the witness stand, she seemed anxious to get it over with. That didn't happen. She testified for the better part of two days.

Virginia's former Girl Friday described her activities up to Doc's death, and how she was drawn further into the intrigue by Virginia, who was able to get her to lie to the police, and help dispose of the gun that killed Doc.

Kris testified Jason had confessed to killing Doc, but her statement was made outside the presence of the jury. In one of many confrontations between opposing counsel, Howes and Wilkins argued that the testimony was hearsay. Judge Watson later ruled that the jury could not hear that part of Kris's testimony, because it could influence the outcome of the trail.

The temporary victory did little to brighten Virginia, who seemed drawn and tired, although she had enough energy to give Kris several dark looks.

Kris testified that Virginia and Jason argued frequently after Doc was killed, and Jason rebelled against his mother for forcing him to stay in the house and pretend to be an invalid.

"He said he was tired of his life like this," Kris testified. "He wanted to turn himself in, and said his money better be in the bank when he got out."

This prompted Virginia to reply, "Okay, but before you do, just go tell your brother Ben what you did."

Kris said the words stopped Jason in his tracks. "He didn't do nothing," she said. "He just started to cry."

On another occasion, Kris testified, Jason was sorry about the murder, not because of Doc, but because it had made his own life difficult.

"We were in the car, and he said if he had known that his life was going to be like that, he wouldn't have bumped off Norm for Virginia," Kris testified. As the strain increased on Jason, Kris said he told her he was a homosexual, and was disgusted and depressed with his life. Weeping, he said "all he was good for was doing drugs, pushing drugs, or hurting or shooting or killing.

"I asked if he killed Norm. He said, 'Yes, I did kill Norm.' "

The prosecution wanted to edit Kris's testimony by having the words "for Virginia" omitted, so the jury could hear the rest. In case Virginia was convicted, the state said, those words could be grounds for an appeal. The defense wanted the jury to hear none of it.

When the jury returned, Kris's testimony echoed much of what Heidle had said on the witness stand. But she had additional testimony to present to the jury.

Kris testified that Virginia was nervous and shaky on the morning of the murder. Virginia wanted her to get out of the office. "Her words were to 'have an alibi and be seen,' " Kris said. "And then she handed me a coffee cup with Valium and tissue in it. And she told me she would need it later."

Virginia sent her to the bank and the post office, but when she returned, Kris testified, Virginia sent her out for a long lunch. "I told her I would take a half-hour." When Kris returned shortly after 1 P.M., Virginia came out of the building in tears. Kris said she embraced Virginia: "I asked her what had happened and she said somebody shot Doc."

At the hospital, Kris said Virginia faked grief, "crying, rocking back and forth, and saying she wanted to see Doc." But when they were alone, Kris said Virginia stopped weeping. "Virginia could cry at the drop of a dime," Kris testified, "and when it was convenient for her not to cry, she would stop."

The witness testified, as Heidle had previously, that Virginia coached her on what to tell the police, and to tell them the family was happy.

Even at this late date, Kris seemed to resent being a witness. She sometimes gave hostile answers to Sedgwick and tossed her head defiantly. Although her testimony was riveting, the expressions of the jurors seemed cast in stone: It seemed clear she was not a popular witness.

When court adjourned for the day, Kris was far from being finished. She was to resume testimony the following day. A detective who worked on the case didn't understand Kris's attitude.

"Considering what she knew, and the extent of her participation, she got off easy," he said. "She was given immunity by the state attorney for what she told us and her testimony."

When court convened, Sedgwick elicited testimony from Kris that pounded the defense with one shocking revelation after another. The witness said Virginia and Jason made fun of the murder in the DeLand house while she watched from the top of the stairs.

Kris said Virginia and Jason reenacted Doc's murder because Virginia didn't understand the coroner's report showing how Doc fell. The witness said Virginia played the part of Doc, while Jason portrayed the masked gunman. Kris held her hands as if pointing a shotgun as she described the scene.

"Jason was holding his arms like this, as if he was holding a gun, and Virginia was acting out as if she was Doc," Kris testified. "Jason pretended to shoot her and Virginia would spin around and fall down on her face. They were laughing. She would make a couple of jokes, and they did another reenactment."

Kris said Virginia talked openly with her about Doc's murder. "She had said to me she had to fake a robbery because Jason was late," she testified. "He was supposed to be there between twelve and twelve-thirty." There would have been no witnesses if things had gone as planned, Kris testified, but two witnesses were there because of Jason's tardiness.

The witness said Virginia explained why she had kissed her husband after he had been shot: "She said when he fell to the floor, that he was calling Jason's name, and she covered his mouth with hers to make it look like she was giving him mouth-to-mouth." Kris said Virginia told her she put her fingers into Doc's shredded windpipe to smother him to death.

Wilkins cross-examined Kris in much the same way Howes had questioned Heidle. Kris admitted she had lied to the police several times, and noted inconsistencies in her depositions and court testimony.

"You've admitted then, you've committed perjury?" Wilkins asked.

"Yes, I lied in that statement."

Kris also admitted she didn't tell police Virginia wanted to keep her out of the office during the time the murder was supposed to take place, and telling her to get an alibi "and be seen."

"You didn't think that was significant?" Wilkins asked.

"No."

Under further cross-examination, Kris said she had a reason for not telling the police about her part in getting rid of the murder weapon . . . until they had it.

Her testimony: "I wasn't sticking my neck out."

Kris was on the witness stand about five hours that day. Judge Watson ruled that her testimony concerning Jason's "confession," heard outside the presence of the jury the previous day was inadmissible. He agreed with the defense that the statements were hearsay.

Heidle and Jason were brought in once more to stand side by side in front of the jury so their height could be compared. Virginia, who had been gloomy throughout the day, smiled brightly at Jason when he entered the courtroom. Judge Watson asked him if he would testify in his mother's trial, but Jason declined, invoking his rights under the Fifth Amendment.

He smiled and waved to his mother as he was escorted to the holding cell, then back to jail.

The prosecution, having heard two of its witnesses degraded as liars, tried to present Virginia as a liar the next morning. One witness was Caroline Stokes, a family friend Virginia tried to portray as Doc's mistress, and whose husband had a motive to kill him.

Somehow Virginia had resolved differences with the Stokes family following Doc's murder. She would have reason to regret it. Caroline said Virginia changed her description of the man who had killed Doc.

"He went from being medium to tall," she told the jury. "He went from average size to bigger."

Virginia told her the gunman was masked, Caroline said, and later told her he was unmasked. The gunman in the next version, Caroline said, had greasy hair slicked back into a ponytail and had dirty fingernails.

A special agent with the Florida Department of Law Enforcement testified that Virginia told him over a two week period the killer "did not look anything like Jason." Bob Darnell, the agent, also testified Virginia's description of the gunman changed. Her descriptions to him were compatible with what she had told Caroline Stokes.

According to Darnell's testimony, Virginia told him the gunman was unmasked, had an olive complexion, short hair turning gray and thinning, and made into a short ponytail. The man had sideburns and wore a hat, the agent said Virginia told him. Darnell testified Virginia said the man vaulted over a railing, ran to a car, and drove off with a motorcycle escort. The FDLE agent testified that Virginia told him the getaway car had a red and white bumper sticker reading: Plant a Garden — Grow Marijuana.

The last description Virginia gave of the gunman, Darnell said, was that he was about 5 feet, 10 inches tall and weighed between 195 and 200 pounds. The description given by Emma Lombardo, who was only a body length away from the shooter, was of a skinny man, 6 feet tall, weighing about 135 pounds.

Charles Sylvester, a private investigator Virginia had hired a short time after her husband's murder, testified that Virginia had one of her sisters pretend to be her at Doc's funeral. Virginia was afraid she would be arrested, Sylvester said, and the decoy would allow her time to escape.

Judge Watson adjourned the trial after half a day of testimony to preside over sentencing in an unrelated case.

Detective Gamell walked to the witness stand on

February 17 and Howes eyed him like a tasty morsel he was eager to devour. The two men disliked one another, and Howes never let a chance go by without trying to insult Gamell.

Courtrooms are forums where facts are presented, and a jury's decision is ideally made on the facts alone. But juries are human and are sometimes influenced by how they respond emotionally to defendants, witnesses, prosecutors, defense attorneys, and even the judge. Reporters wondered how the animosity between Howes and Gamell would play in the courtroom theater to the only audience that mattered: the jury.

Gamell testified Virginia had changed her story about a number of things, excluding previous witness testimony about her changing the appearance of the gunman. The detective told the jury Virginia gave him several reasons why she had called the name of her son, Jason, when Doc was killed.

On one occasion, Gamell said, Virginia told him she and Doc had been talking about Jason just before the shooting occurred. During a second interview with Virginia, the detective said she told him Doc had called out the names of all their children before he died. At yet another time, he testified, Virginia denied mentioning any names.

The detective told the jury Virginia had denied having affairs, but told him that Doc did. Several witnesses had already testified to having affairs with Virginia, but not one witness stepped forward to say she had an affair with Doc.

Gamell testified that Virginia lied to him when she

said there were no guns in the house, then told him later where a shotgun was kept.

The detective played taped recordings of conversations Virginia had with Steven Heidle and Kris Palmieri after they had finally come clean with the police concerning their involvement with Doc's murder.

Virginia laughed during a telephone conversation with Kris, and said, "God, they've got you paranoid." When Virginia talked with Heidle, she said, "They can take anything in the hell they want and piece it together, but they can't prove anything."

Just two days after the murder, Gamell testified, Virginia described a man who looked like a member of a motorcycle club who was in the office just before the murder. Oddly, Virginia laughed as she tried to remember the name of the man's motorcycle gang.

"He's a Warlord . . . Warlock, I'm sorry. I like Warlords."

Gamell testified Virginia was angry when told people suspected her of killing her husband for $1 million in insurance. "I'd like to know who in the hell knew we had exactly $1 million worth of insurance," Gamell said Virginia told him.

The amount of insurance was just under the actual amount, but it was double indemnity for accidental death, which included murder if the beneficiary wasn't the killer. Payoff due on Doc's life insurance policies was $2.1 million.

The detective offered testimony reinforcing that of other witnesses who said Virginia changed her version of the shootings. Virginia called him on several occasions, Gamell said, to say her life was in danger, and once claimed an intruder had entered the house and left the shotgun.

At first Virginia said she didn't touch the gun, Gamell told the jury, then claimed she was cradling it in her arms, rocking it, back and forth, and weeping "thinking it was Norm." This brought a titter of disbelief from the gallery, and even a few jurors smiled.

Gamell testified for several hours, then Howes got his chance to cross-examine. He tried to show Gamell had decided at the very first that Virginia was guilty, then set about gathering information to prove it. Gamell denied it.

Howes made light of testimony that Virginia changed stories, saying it was perfectly natural for a person who witnessed such a tragedy to remember additional details as the shock wore off. As usual, Howes questioned every aspect of the testimony. Once he dwelled on a point so long, Judge Watson told him to move on.

Virginia had told police the gunman had jumped over a four-foot railing, while still holding the shotgun he had used to kill Doc. Gamell testified he didn't think such an athletic move was physically possible.

"Aren't you looking at that from the point of view of your own stature?" Howes asked Gamell, who didn't quite top 5 feet, 6 inches.

"No," Gamell answered.

"What about me? What about a man of my height and build?"

Gamell jumped at the opening he got from the portly defense lawyer. He pointed to the railing, about two feet high, that separates the court arena from the gallery. "Mr. Howes, I don't believe you'd be able to vault over *that* rail."

The gallery and the jury laughed.

The prosecution wound up its case with other police witnesses: a dry cleaning store operator in Orlando, and Patricia Ann Heidle, Steven Heidle's mother. Detective Sergeant Bill Bennett testified Virginia told him what her last words were to her husband: "She tried to initiate some sort of CPR and she tried to plug the pellet wounds with her fingers. I think she said, 'Remember to love me.' " Mary Jenkins testified that Heidle was at her dry cleaning shop in Orlando at noon, the day of the murder, and he was alone. Further, Heidle called her the next day to remind her "because someone was trying to pin a murder" on him.

Patricia Ann Heidle testified Virginia wanted to buy her a new car. "She kept saying that she had to get out of town. I was under the impression that time was of the essence." Patricia Ann, who was in Massachusetts when Doc was killed, found her son at home with the blinds pulled and the garage locked. "It was like a fortress," she testified.

With the jury out of the room, Howes told Judge Watson the police investigation was "incompetent and negligent, and that they had gone into this case with blinders on. What Edgewater did was reach a conclusion and then do everything they could to prove that conclusion and nothing else."

The prosecution rested its case after presenting testimony for thirteen days and entering seventeen pieces of evidence. Now it was time for the defense to show that the state had not proved Virginia guilty beyond a reasonable doubt.

Chipping away at the state's case by vigorous and extensive cross-examination, to discredit witnesses and prove a bungled police investigation to show reasonable doubt, apparently was the primary strategy developed by Howes and Wilkins.

Continuing their attempt to discredit the state's case, the defense called three witnesses to show Steven Heidle was a liar and a drunk. Jeff Sansbury, who had been an object of desire for both Jason and Heidle, testified he had seen Heidle with the .45 pistol that had been embedded in concrete with the shotgun police recovered. Sansbury testified he saw Heidle with such a gun in early March, before Doc's murder.

Glenn Pace, one of Heidle's former friends, had nothing good to say about him, but most of what he said was outside the presence of the jury. Judge Watson ruled that Pace, who met Heidle in late 1990, didn't know enough about Heidle's reputation in the gay community to allow the jury to hear his testimony.

Outside the jury's presence, Pace testified Heidle was "a liar who drank too much" in Orlando's gay bars. "He didn't have a good reputation," Pace said, and said Heidle had driven to a friend's house once in a rage. "He was angry and saying that somebody was going to die that night," Pace said. That scared Pace, but he said Heidle reassured him, "Don't worry about it. I don't kill anybody. But I know somebody who will."

The last defense for Virginia was not a person, but a tape recording of the call to EVAC after Doc had been killed. Virginia wept quietly as her hysterical voice begged help for her husband.

When the tape was played, the defense rested its case. The strategy had apparently been to discredit the Edgewater Police Department and prosecution witnesses. The main defense strategy had been to show prejudice and self-interest on the part of state witnesses, and to show the state had not proved its case beyond a reasonable doubt. Still the brief defense seemed anticlimactic.

In her closing argument, Sedgwick used charts to simplify the complications surrounding insurance policies, the will, and other financial aspects of the case. "Virginia Larzelere meant to kill Dr. Larzelere over money, money plain and simple," she said. "When she looked on Dr. Larzelere's face that morning, she looked with the expectation of murder, the anticipation of murder."

After reviewing testimony from witnesses in the trial, Sedgwick, speaking in a conversational voice, said the only appropriate verdict would be "guilty."

The closing argument for the defense was made by Wilkins, who said the state had not proved its case. In a surprising accusation, Wilkins blamed Heidle and Kris for Doc's murder, claiming they planned to stage a robbery in which he would be killed. They were going to be fired, Wilkins said, and didn't want to get off the "gravy train."

He neglected to mention that Kris and Heidle had not met until *after* Doc was killed.

The defense attorney said there was no reason for Virginia to kill Dr. Larzelere because he was a forgiving, generous husband, and she could write a check for any amount of money whenever she wanted. "She had everything that Virginia Larzelere wanted," Wilkins said. "She could even have affairs and the doctor would say, 'Please come home.' "

The jury began deliberations at 2:34 P.M. on February 24, 1992 and returned to the courtroom at 8:55 P.M. Virginia stood to hear the court clerk read the verdict:

Guilty of First Degree Murder.

As she heard the verdict, Virginia closed her eyes briefly but appeared calm.

Judge Watson set the sentencing portion of the trial to begin March 9, a year and a day after Doc was killed. The attorneys for both sides had little to say after the trial. Sedgwick simply commented that the jury had done its job. Howes and Wilkins slipped out a side door but reporters caught up with Wilkins.

He was so shocked by the verdict that you could see

it in his eyes, even behind his tinted glasses. "I felt extremely disappointed," the lawyer said. "I felt it was going to be the other verdict, obviously."

Another drama was occurring as Wilkins spoke. Bonnie Gilbert, Virginia's alleged jailhouse lover, had rushed out of the courthouse in a rage. In the court's parking lot, she yelled at several jurors who were walking to their cars, "I'm going to blow your car up!"

The Larzelere family was too civilized to volunteer to "pull the switch" as do many relatives of murder victims. Members of the press asked Lucille Larzelere, Doc's mother, if she wanted Virginia to get the death penalty. "We feel Virginia should be where she can never be able to hurt anybody again," Mrs. Larzelere said sadly. "She's hurt so many people."

Doc's cousin, Rory O'Connor said simply, "It won't bring Norm back."

They wanted others protected from Virginia, but Doc was still dead.

Twenty-nine

Bonnie Gilbert's bomb threat created havoc with the jury. Judge Watson reconvened court on March 13 to hear a defense motion that Virginia receive a psychological examination before sentencing, David Day, the jury foreman, reported Gilbert's outburst two days before. Gilbert was arrested on charges of threatening to detonate an explosive device, and obstruction of justice. Judge Watson feared the threat might intimidate the jury's sentence recommendation.

So when the jury arrived at 9 A.M., they were not taken to the courtroom; instead they were isolated from one another, in separate rooms, questioned individually. Robert Nolin, court reporter for *The News-Journal,* wrote that the jurors "must have felt like political prisoners of the legal system."

The March 13 session was one the judge held in secret so that jurors could be individually questioned by lawyers on both sides and himself, to determine if the threat had affected their ability to recommend what they considered a just sentence. Questioning went on for hours behind locked courtroom doors, and even an appeal by a lawyer representing *The News-Journal* failed to get them open.

Virginia's defense attorneys pounced on the situation and asked for a mistrial, claiming the jury could no longer render a just verdict. The motion was denied, and the defense asked for a new jury to be seated for the sentence hearing. That motion was also denied. Howes and Wilkins then asked that jurors who had been threatened be removed; Judge Watson denied that motion, as well.

By the time the jury was called to hear arguments concerning aggravating and mitigating factors, it was almost 6 P.M. The jurors had been at the Justice Center for nine hours, and didn't get lunch until 2 P.M. They didn't look happy when they took their seats.

A sentence hearing in Florida is a procedure to help the jury recommend punishment. A mitigating factor favors the defendant, while an aggravating factor weighs against him. The jury makes a sentence recommendation, based on these factors which, in Virginia's case, could only be life in prison or death. Judge Watson was not bound by the jury's recommendation, but only rarely does a judge overrule a jury on its sentence recommendation.

Sedgwick spoke to the jury in her friendly, conversational way. She asked for the ultimate penalty in her second sentence: "The reason why Dr. Norman Larzelere was shot to death in his office at the age of thirty-nine, and the circumstances leading up to his death . . . are reasons that justify a sentence of death rather than a sentence of life for Virginia Larzelere."

The prosecutor told the jury Florida law considers murder for financial gain an aggravating factor, deserving of the death penalty. Sedgwick mentioned evidence from different witnesses, who testified that Doc had been killed for insurance money and other financial gain.

"In this case, beyond and to the exclusion of every reasonable doubt . . . Dr. Norman Larzelere died for money. He died that day, shot to death in his dental office, so that Virginia Larzelere would have the opportunity to carry through this fantasy of lots and lots of money. His life was measurable in terms of dollars and in terms of material items. That is the significant factor to which you may attach weight."

A second aggravating factor which should result in a death sentence, the prosecutor said, was, "This murder was committed in a cold, calculated, and premeditated manner . . ." Doc's murder, Sedgwick said, had been planned for years, with Virginia trying to find someone to kill her husband.

"This coldness, premeditation and calculation continues over a period of years, even to July 1990 when she (Virginia) has her conversation with Phil Langston," Sedgwick said. "She's still determined, she was still willing to pay fifty thousand dollars for a human being who would kill her husband." The prosecutor said Virginia was cold and calculating from beginning to end.

"It is even present at the last day at the office," she said. "Virginia Larzelere was willing to be there, willing to smile and greet patients, willing to be there during the last hours of Dr. Larzelere's death — anticipating his violent death — she was willing to participate in the manner that she was and, further than that, she was so cold that she was willing to use her own son to carry out the murder . . . to use her own flesh and blood, and for that murder to have whatever impact it might have upon him, just as long as it would carry out her purpose. And that is a factor to which you can attach weight and significance."

It was up to them to decide how much weight the jury should give those factors, Sedgwick said, but added that her points had been proven beyond a reasonable doubt. The prosecutor told the jury mitigating evidence doesn't have to be proven beyond reasonable doubt, but must be supported by a preponderance of evidence. If they are not, she said, the jury should attach no weight to them.

"You can look to see if the murder was committed while Virginia Larzelere was under the influence of extreme mental or emotional disturbance," Sedgwick said. "I would argue to you there is no evidence presented during the trial to support that as a mitigating factor.

"The evidence shows a very cold, execution-style murder of Dr. Norman Larzelere for money," Sedgwick said. "This is not the type of murder that society has any obligation to tolerate or minimize. It is a murder that, under the law, is aggravated. There is absolutely no reason not to support death for this cold, calculating, execution-style murder."

Sedgwick thanked the jury and took her seat.

Wilkins had the difficult task of arguing for Virginia's life. The defense had already said it would not use psychiatric evidence to show diminished mental or emotional stability to plead for Virginia's life. Wilkins had said it would be ridiculous to claim that, when the defense had a simple premise: Virginia did not have anything to do with Doc's death.

The defense attorney was a small, wiry man with long hair, tinted glasses and a stubble of a beard. But even the most conservative jury would have liked him; he had a soft, friendly southern drawl, and his words seemed to be spoken from the heart. He was not trying to prove Virginia innocent of murder as he stood before the jury, but pleading to save her life.

"My presentation to you is much more simple" than what Sedgwick had offered, he told the jury. He noted other states had said the death sentence was inappropriate, but Florida had disagreed. "But we're in the state of Florida, and they (the legislature) decided that under certain circumstances the death penalty is the appropriate thing."

Wilkins pointed out that Florida law gave the jury great influence in recommending a sentence. ". . . They (the legislature) also decided that twelve citizens like you would have great influence in helping His Honor make a determination as to what sentence is appropriate on the facts that you just heard.

"You can listen to the state talk about aggravating circumstances, and you can talk about lack of mitigation," he said. ". . . The judge is going to tell you that even if you find aggravating circumstances, that if you don't feel the death penalty is justified, you can recommend life. Our legislature says we want twelve people to sit on that jury to lend great weight."

Wilkins told the jury its recommendation "was not an exercise in futility" but had a great deal of influence on the judge who would pass sentence.

Secondly, Wilkins told the jury they could review the evidence to see if there are mitigating or aggravating circumstances. He said they could say the sentence for this crime should be life in prison, which would mean a mandatory sentence of twenty-five years with no possibility of parole.

"There are only two alternatives," Wilkins said. "Death or life without parole for twenty-five years."

Wilkins reminded the jury that a majority vote was needed for the recommendation of a death sentence. The jury should not consider only that Virginia had been found guilty, Wilkins said, but whether the state had proven that death was the appropriate sentence.

Although he said our judicial system is the best in the world, Wilkins expressed doubts that a civilized society should sentence people to death. A civilized group of individuals, such as those on the jury, he said, should ask themselves if a civilized society should seek "an eye for an eye."

"We are a civilized country," he said, "still going down the road, saying we may still believe in an eye for an eye, and the fact is that, if that is the case, Dr. Larzelere's death requires a death sentence. But I don't believe that's the case.

"Even though I believe in my own conscience in my client, I realize that . . . this case is in your hands. I do hope that even though you thought the evidence sufficient to return a verdict of guilty . . . if it does not establish (aggravating factors) for imposing the ultimate sanction, I urge you to return a recommendation for life imprisonment without the chance of parole for twenty-five years."

Concerning the death penalty, Wilkins reminded the jury, "You can say no."

Following the final arguments, the defense asked that the jury be released for the night so they could review the evidence with "fresh minds" after having endured a difficult ten-hour day. The jury was surprised when Judge Watson, because of Bonnie Gilbert's bomb threat, unexpectedly ordered them to be sequestered for the night. More appropriately, most seemed to be disgusted. Police patrol cars went to the jurors' homes to get personal items they needed, and the jury was escorted under heavy guard to an undisclosed hotel.

The next morning, the jury retired to study the mitigating and aggravating circumstances to decide if Virginia should live or die. A majority vote of seven to five was necessary for recommending the death sentence: a tie of six to six would automatically result in a recommendation for life in prison.

The strain was evident on the expressions of the jurors, who came into the courtroom, looking grim after almost three hours of deliberation. Some appeared to have been weeping. One juror dabbed at her eyes with a rumpled handkerchief. Judge Watson asked Virginia to stand as the recommendation was read.

The jury's recommendation was that Virginia should be executed.

Virginia closed her eyes for a moment, but showed no emotion.

The death sentence was recommended by the smallest possible margin: Seven jurors voted for death while five voted for life in prison.

Judge Watson thanked the jury for its patience and conscientious duty and dismissed it. The judge set April 12 to hear final arguments before setting a date for sentencing.

Some of the jurors answered questions after the trial indicating testimony by Heidle and Kris was not as crucial as the state thought. A number of jurors didn't believe either witness. The evidence that held the most weight with the jury was testimony by the police, the insurance on Doc's life, testimony by former lovers Virginia had asked to help kill her husband, and Emma Lombardo's recognition of the gunman as being Jason.

Detective David Gamell, the lead detective on the case, believed the conviction and sentence recommendation were just. "I feel we've proven Virginia to be a greedy, manipulative, evil woman. Now she won't be able to harm anybody else."

Epilogue

When court reconvened on April 12 to hear final arguments and set a date for Virginia's sentencing, the defense succeeded again in slowing adjudication of the case. Howes and Wilkins requested that Virginia be examined by a psychiatrist to determine her state of mind during the time she planned to kill her husband. They argued that Judge Watson was obligated to grant their motion.

Sedgwick disagreed, noting the defense had specifically waived the right to use psychological experts during the trial. The prosecutor argued that Howes and Wilkins had changed their minds only because the jury had recommended the death sentence.

After listening to both sides, Judge Watson told them he would hear additional arguments on April 20 before making his decision. During the April 12 hearing, Virginia was declared insolvent, forcing the taxpayers to pick up the tab for her future legal expenses. Virginia glared at the prosecutors as Judge Watson granted the defense motion: The woman who for years had carried thousands of dollars in cash was not only broke, her account was overdrawn by $45.

At the hearing on April 20, Judge Watson ruled for the defense motion to have Virginia psychologically evaluated. Results of the examination were not available to the press five months later, and were not expected to be released for at least two months. The results were not available at the end of August—and Virginia still had not been sentenced.

Virginia's case dragged on, pending Jason's trial for first degree murder. Judge Watson was not expected to sentence Virginia until after Jason's trial, and although he offered no reason for the unusual delay, a high official in the state attorney's office said the judge wanted to avoid the possibility of influencing a jury against Jason.

Because of the publicity generated by Virginia's trial, Judge Watson granted a change of venue and moved Jason's trial to Palatka, a town in Flagler County. Initially, Jason was to be tried in February but that date was pushed back to April 13 when Virginia's trial ran longer than expected.

Another delay came about in an unexpected way. Despite the fact that Howes and Wilkins had worked on Jason's defense for months, he fired them on March 30. "It has come to my knowledge that there are too many conflicts of interest for you to remain on my case," Jason's letter of dismissal said. "As of this date 3-30-92 you are fired." In a separate letter to Judge Watson, Jason called the defense lawyers an obscene name and said they followed their own course without listening to his wishes.

At their request, Howes and Wilkins were released from the case at a hearing on April 10. Judge Watson was churlish about continuing delays in the judicial process.

Surprisingly, Jason's action had been prompted by Harry Mathis, his natural father, who had divorced Virginia twelve years previously. Since the divorce, Mathis had seen Jason only once.

Now he wanted to help his son. He mortgaged his home to pay for Jason's defense and hired Bill Lasley, a lawyer from West Palm Beach to represent Jason. "He (Mathis) felt like he lost Jason twelve years ago in a custody battle," Lasley said. "It was something he always felt bad about."

Lasley was inaugurated as Jason's attorney, forcing Judge Watson to push the trial date back again, this time to June 22, so Lasley could prepare a defense. When the trial date arrived, the prosecution asked for another delay so expert witnesses Lasley intended to use in Jason's defense could be questioned. Clearly frustrated by the sand thrown in the gears of the legal system, Judge Watson ordered the trial to start on August 18.

And it finally did.

Fifty-two prospective jurors streamed into the Flagler County Courthouse on the appointed date and jury selection began. In an attempt to speed up the *voir dire* process, each was given a fourteen page questionnaire to complete so prospective jurors could be screened and dismissed before questioning by the attorneys.

During a break in jury selection, Lasley revealed his defense strategy to the press: He would try to prove that Heidle killed Doc instead of Jason, and Virginia and Kristen conspired with him. Lasley said Doc and Virginia were drug dealers who sold Valium and cocaine from the dentist's office. Lasley said he would prove Heidle killed Doc at Virginia's request and was paid $3,000 by her the following day.

A integral part of Lasley's strategy was to question the practice of "use immunity"—the granting of immunity by the state to persons involved in a crime in return for their testimony against the defendants. It doesn't protect them from being prosecuted if evidence against them is found in an independent investigation. Regarding use immunity, Lasley was speaking of Steven Heidle and Kristen Palmieri, who were granted immunity from prosecution for testimony against Virginia and Jason. Use immunity is frequently used by prosecutors to catch the big fish instead of the small fry, even though they don't particularly like the arrangement.

Heidle was the state's key witness in Virginia's trial and testified for three days. Palmieri was also an important witness. Lasley claimed he could convince a jury that Heidle was the real murderer after three hours of cross-examination. "The state has its hand on the switch when Heidle sits on the witness stand," he said. According to Lasley, Jason was nothing more than a "mule," who delivered drugs for his parents. But because he talked about the operation, Lasley contended, he was kept heavily medicated to keep him quiet.

A jury was empaneled on Thursday, August 21, and testimony began August 24. The prosecution's opening argument was much the same as it had been during Virginia's trial. True to his word, Lasley told the jury he would show that Heidle and Kris killed Doc instead of Jason. He clarified "use immunity" for the jury and told them both Heidle and Kris were protected under that umbrella.

The state called its first witness on August 25, followed by a parade of others over the next two and a half weeks, most of whom gave testimony essentially the same as it had been during Virginia's trial. During vigorous cross examination, Lasley chipped away at their credibility, particularly that of Kris and Heidle, and their testimony about the roles they played in the murder scheme.

When Kris testified that Virginia tried to have Ted Goodman find someone to murder her husband, and acknowledged she spent two days with him in West Palm Beach, Lasley pounced.

"You didn't tell Dr. Larzelere that Ted Goodman and you were planning to murder him?" Lasley asked.

"Ted Goodman and I were not planning to murder him," Kris said. "He discussed it once, but I didn't think he was going to do it."

Lasley asked Kris why she didn't tell Doc that Virginia planned to have him killed: "Don't you feel a little guilty?"

"I feel like I could have said or done something," she answered.

The defense attorney also attacked Steven Heidle's

credibility, and hinted that the state's key witness had stepped forward only to save his own skin.

"From day one you knew that they (the police) wanted the shooter," Lasley said while questioning Heidle, "and if you gave them a shooter you would not face any criminal penalties, right?"

"Right," Heidle replied.

During the two days he cross examined the witness, Lasley attempted to show that Heidle, along with Virginia and Kris, had planned Doc's murder, and that Jason wasn't involved. To support his theory, Lasley noted the numerous calls to the dental office from telephones in Kris's and Jason's cars the morning of the murder. He accused Heidle of being the driver of Jason's car, not Jason. That made the witness smile.

"Do you think it's funny I'm accusing you of this, Mr. Heidle?" Lasley asked.

"Yes, I do."

Lasley grilled Heidle for an explanation as to why he stayed in touch with Jason and Virginia when he knew the shotgun that killed Doc was in his own home, and that his mother's car had been used during the murder.

"They used me well and planned it well," Heidle replied.

When the prosecution rested, Lasley introduced another murder plot into the trial. He called four witnesses who testified outside the jury's presence that Virginia, Goodman, a hit man known as Tony, and what the lawyer termed "the Lake Worth Mafia," were behind Doc's murder.

Rose Myers, Ted Goodman's sister, said her

brother talked openly about being hired by Virginia to find someone to kill Doc. She testified that Goodman told her about the plot about three months before the murder occurred.

"He told me that Virginia wanted him to kill her husband, and I told him to please don't do it," Rose testified.

Instead of dropping it, Rose said Goodman called her later to say he had found someone to kill Doc, and told her the hit man was a member of the Lake Worth Mafia.

Goodman's niece, Shannon Goodman, testified that she had met a man her uncle said was the contract killer. But, according to her, Goodman, a diagnosed manic-depressive, often exaggerated things.

"My uncle Ted was a very sick man and basically everything he told us we didn't believe," she said. "He just talked a lot of bull to make himself seem a lot more than he really was."

Goodman's brother-in-law, Darrell Myers, and sister-in-law, Rebecca Goodman, also testified that Goodman told them Virginia had hired him to find someone to kill her husband.

Sedgwick argued that the plot outlined by the defense witnesses was hearsay, based only on Goodman's word. Goodman couldn't be called to testify because he died of natural causes three weeks before Doc's murder. In spite of the prosecutor's arguments against it, Judge Watson ruled that the jury could hear the testimony.

Later in the trial, Harry Mathis testified about being shot several years ago. When he was married to Virginia, he testified, she told him a cousin's car had broken down in a remote area, and sent him to help. But instead of finding a relative, Mathis said, he found a gunman who shot him four times.

The shooting occurred when both he and Virginia were twenty-two, Mathis said. "I believe she tried to have me killed," he testified. The jury and gallery gasped at this testimony. Until this revelation, Mathis had never accused her of being involved with the shooting.

"You hate Virginia Larzelere, don't you?" Lasley asked.

"That's putting it mildly," Mathis replied.

In private, Sedgwick expressed doubt that the state would get a conviction of first degree murder, but hoped Jason would be found guilty of a lesser charge. Lasley had introduced two other murder schemes through witnesses, each independent of involvement by Jason. It appeared that the defense attorney was creating reasonable doubt, which would obligate the jury to acquit Jason, if the testimony was believed.

Missing from the state's list of witnesses were Phil Langston, Norman Karn and Ron Hayden, all of whom had testified during Virginia's trial about her schemes to have her husband killed. They had been key witnesses in Virginia's trial, where she was found guilty. The state's case against Jason was also weakened because witnesses to Doc's murder had not seen the masked gunman's face.

Lasley struck at the prosecution's case in his closing argument to the jury.

"The evidence against Jason Larzelere is weak and insubstantial," he said, and insisted that Norman

Larzelere was killed by a contract killer, an unknown gunman, or perhaps even Heidle. But Jason was not involved, he argued. Instead, Lasley said, Jason had been set up by Kris and Heidle, who feared being prosecuted for murder. To save themselves, he said, they contrived a story that framed Jason.

"They can see themselves sitting where Jason is," Lasley said. "They were thinking, 'Who's the sap? Who's the patsy that buys his friends? Jason Larzelere.'"

The attorney said Kris could have driven the killer to the dental office. And that killer, he said, may have been Heidle, who had time to commit the murder and prepare an alibi. Lasley said the police should have pursued other leads, particularly that of Goodman, rather than focusing on Jason.

Pointing out that Virginia had conceived several plots to kill her husband, Lasley argued that the killer could be anybody. Perhaps, he said, the real murderer was still free. There was strong evidence for reasonable doubt as to Jason's guilt, he told the jury, and asked for a verdict of Not Guilty.

The jury of nine women and three men began deliberating after receiving instructions from the Judge at 9 A.M. on Saturday, September 19. They were sequestered at 8 P.M. and resumed deliberations the next morning. At 7:10 P.M., Lasley got what he wanted: the jury returned a verdict of Not Guilty.

Jason walked out of the courthouse with his sister, Jessica, who brought him a bouquet of red and white carnations, and Harry Mathis, their natural father, who said he hopes to rebuild the family he lost several years ago when Virginia won custody of

Jason and Jessica in their divorce.

David Gamell, the chief detective in the murder case, was still convinced of Jason's guilt. "I think he had a real good attorney," Gamell said. "We tried. It's our system, we've got to go with it."

Doc's mother, Lucille Larzelere, was bitter about the verdict. "He'll get some insurance money, blood money," she said. "He should not benefit."

But the reality is that with his acquittal, Jason stands to inherit a fourth of Doc's $2.1 million in life insurance and other assets of the estate, sharing it with Jessica and his brothers, David and Benjamin, who have been adopted by Doc's parents.

WALK ALONG THE BRINK OF FURY:

THE EDGE SERIES

Westerns By GEORGE G. GILMAN

DEATH, DESTRUCTION, DEVASTATION, AND DOOM
EXPERIENCE THE ADVENTURE OF

THE DESTROYER SERIES

By WARREN MURPHY and RICHARD SAPIR